Outback Spirit

Sue Williams is the author of eleven books, including the best-selling *Women of the Outback*; *Peter Ryan: The Inside Story*; *Mean Streets, Kind Heart: The Father Chris Riley Story* and *And Then The Darkness*, about the disappearance of the British backpacker Peter Falconio, which was shortlisted for the prestigious Golden Dagger Award, the True Crime Book of the Year and the Ned Kelly Awards for Crime Writing.

An award-winning journalist, Sue was born in England and worked in print and television in the United Kingdom and New Zealand. She spent many years travelling the world and wrote about her experiences in *Getting There – Journeys of an Accidental Adventurer*. In 1989 Sue fell in love with Australia and its Outback. Since settling here she has since written for many of Australia's leading newspapers and magazines.

Unlike those in the Outback, Sue lives in the most densely populated part of Australia, Sydney's Kings Cross. She lives with her partner, writer Jimmy Thomson.

For more information, please visit suewilliams.com.au.

Outback Spirit

SUE WILLIAMS

PENGUIN BOOKS

PENGUIN BOOKS

Published by the Penguin Group
Penguin Group (Australia)
250 Camberwell Road, Camberwell, Victoria 3124, Australia
(a division of Pearson Australia Group Pty Ltd)
Penguin Group (USA) Inc.
375 Hudson Street, New York, New York 10014, USA
Penguin Group (Canada)
90 Eglinton Avenue East, Suite 700, Toronto, Canada ON M4P 2Y3
(a division of Pearson Penguin Canada Inc.)
Penguin Books Ltd
80 Strand, London WC2R 0RL England
Penguin Ireland
25 St Stephen's Green, Dublin 2, Ireland
(a division of Penguin Books Ltd)
Penguin Books India Pvt Ltd
11 Community Centre, Panchsheel Park, New Delhi – 110 017, India
Penguin Group (NZ)
67 Apollo Drive, Rosedale, North Shore 0632, New Zealand
(a division of Pearson New Zealand Ltd)
Penguin Books (South Africa) (Pty) Ltd
24 Sturdee Avenue, Rosebank, Johannesburg 2196, South Africa

Penguin Books Ltd, Registered Offices: 80 Strand, London WC2R 0RL, England

First published by Penguin Books Australia Ltd, 2010
This paperback edition published by Penguin Group (Australia), 2011

1 3 5 7 9 10 8 6 4 2

Cover design by Cathy Larsen © Penguin Group (Australia)
Text design by Karen Scott © Penguin Group (Australia)
Map by Pamela Horsnell, Juno Creative Services
Cover photograph: St John Ambulance volunteer Mick Lanagan
courtesy of the Royal Flying Doctor Service
Typeset in Fairfield by Post Pre-Press Group, Brisbane, Queensland
Printed and bound in Australia by McPherson's Printing Group, Maryborough, Victoria

National Library of Australia
Cataloguing-in-Publication data:

Williams, Sue, 1959–
Outback spirit : inspiring true stories of Australia's unsung heroes / Sue Williams.
2nd ed.
9780143205340 (pbk.)
Frontier and pioneer life – Australia.
Rural men – Australia – Biography.
Rural women – Australia – Biography.

994.0099

penguin.com.au

In memory of Mandy,
spirited daughter of Outback legend Maree Stockman

CONTENTS

Foreword   *xii*
Her Excellency Ms Quentin Bryce AC,
Governor-General of the Commonwealth of Australia

Introduction   *1*

CHAPTER 1
In Giving, You Receive   5
Marian Gauci, Gulgong, New South Wales

CHAPTER 2
Do You Want This Job or Not?   23
Alistair Miller, Port Augusta, South Australia

CHAPTER 3
The Loudest Laugh in the Outback   41
Marguerite Baptiste-Rooke, Alice Springs, Northern Territory

CHAPTER 4
Guesswork and God 59
Anne Kidd, Windorah, Queensland

CHAPTER 5
Amazing Grace 75
Ricky Grace, Kalgoorlie and Perth, Western Australia

CHAPTER 6
Stopping the Poison 93
Eileen Kampakuta Brown, Western Desert Region,
South Australia

CHAPTER 7
A Chance to Shine 115
Mitchell Litchfield, Griffith, New South Wales

CHAPTER 8
Cheeky Dogs and Lost Boys 131
Joie Boulter, Tennant Creek, Northern Territory

CHAPTER 9
Angels Really Do Have Wings 149
Cheryl Arentz, Brisbane, Queensland

CHAPTER 10
Broken Wings and Fading Frills 165
Stephen Cutter, Palmerston, Northern Territory

CHAPTER 11
Taps, But No Water 181
Paul Pholeros, Sydney, New South Wales

CHAPTER 12
Secret Men's Business 201
Yvonne Evans, Mount Beauty, Victoria

CHAPTER 13
Ready for Anything 221
Mick Lanagan, Sandfire, Western Australia

CHAPTER 14
A God-given Desire to Fly 237
Elaine Crowder, from Bourke to Broken Hill,
Oodnadatta to Alice Springs

CHAPTER 15
The Power of Humanity 251
Olga Havnen, Darwin, Northern Territory

CHAPTER 16
A True Rose of the Desert 269
Sue Le Lievre, Looma, the Kimberley, Western Australia

Acknowledgements 288

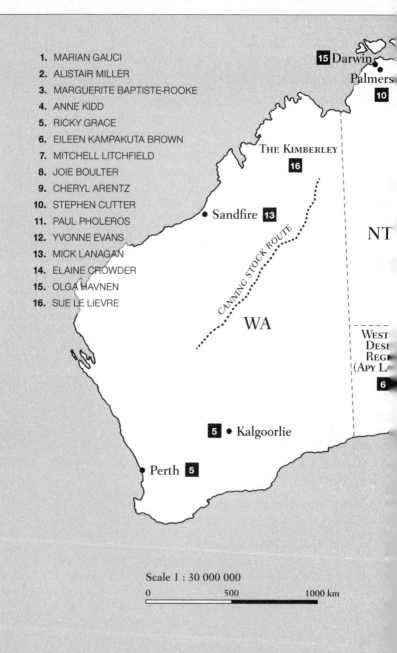

1. MARIAN GAUCI
2. ALISTAIR MILLER
3. MARGUERITE BAPTISTE-ROOKE
4. ANNE KIDD
5. RICKY GRACE
6. EILEEN KAMPAKUTA BROWN
7. MITCHELL LITCHFIELD
8. JOIE BOULTER
9. CHERYL ARENTZ
10. STEPHEN CUTTER
11. PAUL PHOLEROS
12. YVONNE EVANS
13. MICK LANAGAN
14. ELAINE CROWDER
15. OLGA HAVNEN
16. SUE LE LIEVRE

15 Darwin
Palmers
10

The Kimberley
16

Sandfire 13

NT

WA

CANNING STOCK ROUTE

West
Dese
Reg
(Apy L
6

5 • Kalgoorlie

Perth 5

Scale 1 : 30 000 000
0   500   1000 km

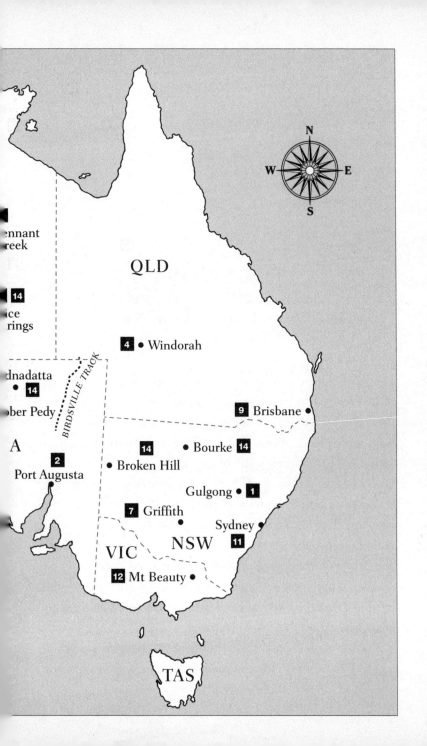

FOREWORD

Her Excellency Ms Quentin Bryce AC,
Governor-General of the Commonwealth of Australia

I grew up in the tiny town of Ilfracombe, deep in the central west of Queensland, not far from that quintessential icon of Outback Australia, Longreach. My home was in the midst of dusty, dry, wide brown land: sheep- and cattle-grazing country that in the 1940s and 1950s grew some of the best wool in the world. The goats chewed out the scrub and the bore water scoured the wool but killed almost every form of plant life. Until the early 1950s, we didn't have electricity, sewerage or reticulated water.

Yet for me, it was a marvellous childhood. My family was part of a close-knit community. People respected and looked after one another. They were as tough and resilient as the country they inhabited, but they were also considerate and well-mannered and made friendships that lasted lifetimes.

It's been a real pleasure to introduce this new book celebrating the spirit of the Outback I came to love; and the commitment, generosity and courage of those who are today helping improve the quality of people's lives in rural and remote Australia.

As Patron of the Royal Flying Doctor Service, it's been with great pride that I've read of the dedication shown by our nurse volunteer Mick Lanagan, who has pledged his life to helping Western Australians living far from any regular medical services. I was thrilled, too, to follow the adventures through South Australia and the Northern Territory of Dr Alistair Miller as he crisscrosses our nation's centre to treat the sick and injured, and preserve the health of so much of our remote population.

And, in a similar role as president of the Australian Red Cross, I have learnt of Olga Havnen's fine work continuing the organisation's great tradition of being there for people in need, providing relief in times of crisis, and caring for our most vulnerable in Australia and around the world. I also loved reading about Olga's time with The Fred Hollows Foundation, having known the legendary eye surgeon in his later years, and having worked with his wife Gabi on human rights issues.

Indigenous Australians have been honoured too, particularly in the story of Eileen Kampakuta Brown, a proud Aboriginal elder and survivor of Maralinga who won the international Goldman Prize – the environmental equivalent of a Nobel Peace Prize – for her remarkable stand against nuclear dumping in her cherished Outback lands.

Despite the great advances of the twenty-first century, the Outback is perhaps now suffering its hardest times. Drought has desiccated huge tracts of our beloved land, and floods have turned other parts to swamp. We've had horrendous bushfires, acid rain, swarms of locusts, slumping commodity prices and rising costs of feed, fuel and water. And, in all this, there is the constancy of isolation.

In my experience, however, Outback people just get on with the job, with plenty of humour and little fuss.

Although most Australians today live close to the coast and in the big cities, I like to think that we stay connected in some sense, real or spiritual, with the great red deserts, the bare brown lands dusted with mulga and Mitchell grass, and the people who've made the Outback their home.

This book, *Outback Spirit: Inspiring true stories of Australia's unsung heroes*, is a wonderful inspiration for us all to make new connections and refresh the old. Through its moving and heart-warming stories, I offer my gratitude and praise to all who have served the great cause of our Outback and its people.

Her Excellency Ms Quentin Bryce AC

INTRODUCTION

What the hell was I doing? Sitting in the tiny cockpit of a Royal Flying Doctor Service plane with the temperature soaring above 50 degrees Celsius, sweat trickling down my face and stinging my eyes, lurching wildly in the air over some of the most empty, barren terrain in the world. I realised I'd never been so uncomfortable and scared at the same time in my life.

The week before, I'd asked myself the same question as I sat stranded in the tiny eighty-person Outback Queensland town of Windorah, with the floodwaters rising from rains further north, an insect plague on the attack and the solitary hotel having run out of all food . . . even peanuts. And the previous month I'd asked it too, lying in a cold bath for an hour in country New South Wales, recovering from agonising burns I'd received after standing for hours on a bare patch of land in the glaring afternoon sun.

1

But these are the relatively minor sacrifices you have to make if you want to meet some of the Australian Outback's most remarkable people.

I'd spent chunks of the previous month in a Greyhound bus, trundling thousands of kilometres across the continent from south to north, being tipped out at various points in South Australia and the Northern Territory at all hours of the day and night – including a memorable arrival in Tennant Creek at the God-awful time of 2.15 a.m.

Along the way, I'd been commandeered to drive a Troopy packed with people into the desolate Outback beyond Coober Pedy, in a vehicle whose ignition had failed even to fire without the intervention of a mechanic. 'But what if it doesn't start again when I'm out there and want to get back?' I asked. He looked at my anxious face and grinned. 'Oh, we'll come to find you,' he said. And then he laughed. 'Eventually.'

And I couldn't even say I didn't know what I was in for. Two years before, I'd crisscrossed Australia's vast empty spaces to write *Women of the Outback*, a collection of profiles about incredible women who'd overcome enormous challenges to build adventurous and fulfilling lives there. As a born-and-bred city girl, happily living in the most densely populated part of Australia – Sydney's Kings Cross – I'd found the courage and resilience of these women simply mindblowing, as too was the vast Outback that was their home. I was thrilled when the book went on to be bought by the ute-load.

It was everything I had wanted and more but . . . as they say, be careful what you wish for. Almost before I knew it, I was being bundled back out to write the sequel. This time, the premise was

2

a little different: to tell the stories of a bunch of women *and* men who'd dedicated their own lives to helping others in the Outback. I set out to find ordinary people doing quite extraordinary things – true heroes in those great Outback traditions of mateship, resilience and generosity.

As soon as I'd got in touch with some of the people whose lives seemed to fit the bill, I couldn't help but feel the excitement mounting about the idea of a new book. These characters had often endured tough times themselves, but still they pressed on to help others make their lives in some of the most harsh, unforgiving and isolated spots in Australia. Their stories were heroic, stirring and touching by turn.

There were all sorts, too. From salt-of-the-earth Aussie battlers to migrants who had settled in the Outback, all were achieving incredible things and sometimes against the most challenging of odds. They'd endured setbacks along the way, sure enough, but they'd just gritted their teeth, put their heads down, summoned extra reserves of strength from God knows where, and kept on keeping on.

And so it was that I found myself once again travelling all around Australia, and to some of the most truly remote spots on the planet, to meet these people, to chart their lives and to tell their stories.

So how on earth could I complain about a little discomfort in the great scheme of bringing their colourful tales, and the Outback people and communities they were helping, to others? What price over a hundred insect bites in a single night, several hours of anxiety in the wilds off the Oodnadatta Track, terror in the air over the Simpson Desert or the misery of being lost in the wilds of the Kimberley, in Western Australia?

This book is a tribute to all those Australians who have over-come hardships a million times greater than my minor complaints just so they can help others doing it even tougher in the world beyond our cities. These previously unsung heroes truly do embody the daring, the courage and the big heart of the Outback. In short, they're the real Outback spirit, and we all salute them.

Sue Williams

1

In Giving, You Receive

MARIAN GAUCI, *Gulgong, New South Wales*

The life-changing phone call came at 9 a.m. one Monday morning, just as Marian Gauci was on her way to work at her local fruit warehouse.

'There's been a tragedy,' came the breathless voice of her mother-in-law. 'You've got to go home! I'll call you there.' Marian pulled her car over to the verge, a feeling of dread in her stomach. Her first thought was for her two adult sons, Shane and Mark, and their children. Something must have happened to one of them. But *what*? How bad did something have to be to be called a tragedy?

With trembling fingers, she pressed her husband Dominic's number on her mobile phone. His cheerful voice answered immediately. But with a sinking heart, she heard him tell her to leave a message. 'Ring me as soon as you get this!' she implored. 'Ring me!'

Marian then drove home in record time, terrified of what might be waiting. When she arrived, however, no-one was there, and everything was just as she'd left it. She snatched up the phone and called her mother-in-law back. 'What is it?' she asked. 'What's happened?' At the other end of the line, she heard Michelle Gauci take a deep breath. 'It's Chris,' she said, naming Dominic's younger brother. 'He's dead. We think . . . we think . . .' her voice cracked with emotion. 'We think he shot himself.' Marian's hands flew to her face. 'Oh my God,' she said. 'Oh my God! I'll try Dom again.'

He still wasn't answering his mobile, so this time she called the store where she knew he'd been planning to buy food for the animals they kept on their acreage in western Sydney. She described her husband and the manager eventually spotted him and passed him the phone. 'You've got to come home,' she told him. 'Something bad has happened.' Then, knowing how panicked she'd been, she added, 'But it's nothing to do with our kids.'

Dominic was just walking in through the front door when the phone rang. It was Michelle again, and this time her voice was dead of all emotion. 'It's about Julia,' she said flatly. 'She's gone too. They're both gone.'

Marian turned to greet her husband, her face ashen. Gently, she broke the news that his beloved brother, and his brother's wife, had both been found dead on their isolated property outside the town of Gulgong, in New South Wales's dusty central west. Their five children were unharmed. Marian and Dominic sat down on the sofa, silently, numbly, holding each other's hands as they each allowed the news to sink in.

Suddenly, Marian broke free and stood up. 'But what about the children?' she cried, thinking of the couple's children orphaned so abruptly and cruelly. 'What about them? Where are they? How are they going to cope?' Dominic looked back at her, alarmed. He glanced around their own small house. 'There's room for them here,' he started saying. 'We can reorganise the space at the back of the house . . .' Marian interrupted him, midstream. 'We've got to get up there,' she said, a note of urgency in her voice.

Immediately, they both walked into their bedroom, pulled out a suitcase and started throwing a few things into it. They'd each made a split-second decision and, after thirty-four years of marriage, they'd both come to exactly the same conclusion at precisely the same moment. As they locked their house up and called one of their sons to arrange for him to look after their animals, Marian glanced at her watch. It was a few minutes before 11 a.m.; it was just under two hours since that phone call had changed their lives forever.

The next few weeks were a whirlwind. The younger children – Tamara, fourteen, Alexandra, eleven, Josh, eight, and Bethany, five – appeared stunned and confused about what had happened that fateful day, 9 June 2008. But their older sister, Cassandra, sixteen, seemed to have moved from childhood to adulthood almost overnight.

Haltingly, she told the police how her parents had been out the evening before, at the Gulgong Gold Cup race meeting. They were cheerful and ebullient, their natural loving selves, when they returned to their ramshackle home on the parched dirt beyond town. There was absolutely no sign of anything wrong at all. In the morning, however, her dad woke her up. He was pale and his voice was low and grave. 'Cass,' he said urgently. 'Mum's passed away. Promise me you'll look after the kids.' And then he kissed her lightly on the brow.

Half asleep, and thinking her dad must have been having a joke with her, Cassandra didn't really understand. But there was something about the note of deep sadness in his voice and the despair in his eyes that made her feel uneasy and, when she saw him walk into the big machinery shed close to the house, carrying a shotgun, something froze inside her. In her nightdress, she ran to the shed and watched, horrified, as he put a rope around his neck and began to climb a ladder, the gun in his hand. She shouted to him, but he didn't seem to hear. She then raced back to the house and called triple 0.

When the police and ambulance arrived, they found the body of Chris Gauci, forty-five, in the shed. In the house, in the bedroom, they found his wife of seventeen years, Julia Gauci, thirty-six, also dead, and dressed in Cassandra's white debutante gown, with a little figurine of the Virgin Mary placed on the bedside table beside her.

The tragedy shocked everyone. The couple had always been a popular pair, absolutely devoted to each other and their kids. Chris was funny, friendly and outgoing, a happy-go-lucky man with a big personality who charmed all he met. He always had a smile, knew everybody in town, and was generous to a fault. 'In giving, you receive' was his mantra. His wife was the most important person in his life, his princess, and he idolised her. He'd always introduce her to others: 'This is my beautiful wife, Julia.' Indeed, Julia was a beautiful woman, with a smile that seemed to glow and warm everyone, and a fabulous mum. Quieter than Chris, she was much more gentle and serious. Somehow, they balanced each other out perfectly.

'Dad was such a character; he was very lively and funny and would talk to everyone, and knew everyone,' says Cassandra. 'He was loud and told a lot of jokes but was very caring and generous and giving. Mum was much more quiet and really pretty. She was a dancer, which we do now too.'

The family had moved to Gulgong, the old gold-rush town 30 kilometres north of Mudgee and 300 kilometres north-west of Sydney, eight years before, looking for a quieter, healthier life in the country. In that short time, they'd managed to win the hearts of many of the locals in the close-knit community. Chris would often invite people back to their place after the Sunday service at the local St John the Baptist Catholic Church. He'd enjoy chatting to the blokes, while Julia would glide happily between them all, offering food and drink.

No-one could make any sense of what had happened. Locals were only just recovering from the shock of another violent death in the usually quiet town. The month before, real-estate agent Tony Riley had been jailed for two years after shooting dead his wife's lover, David Nichols, on Valentine's Day 2007 and then turning the gun on himself, causing massive brain injuries.

But these latest deaths seemed absolutely incomprehensible. Rumours began racing around town: maybe Julia, known to suffer from epilepsy, had died in her sleep and Chris, her carer, was too devastated to continue living without her; or perhaps it was a murder–suicide.

*

The children went to stay with Julia's parents, John and Pam Delaney, and after spending time with them all, Marian and Dominic went home to Horsley Park for a couple of days before the funeral. They planned to bring the children home with them afterwards to give them a new life far away from the horror of what had happened. A family member phoned, however, and said he'd been talking to the children's counsellor, who thought it might be best for them to go back to live at their home in Gulgong. That would be the ideal way of helping them to cope with the loss of their parents, and face whatever life had left to offer them.

Marian phoned the counsellor herself to talk things over. The counsellor confirmed that home would be the best bet, and felt the grandparents might struggle to look after five boisterous children, especially as Pam had been battling cancer. The invitation was clear: would Marian and Dominic consider moving to Gulgong to care for the children? When Marian finally put the phone down, she was thoughtful. She relayed the counsellor's thoughts to Dominic. He didn't hesitate for a moment. 'Let's go now!' he said.

It took a couple of days to organise the house and animals, and to put their eldest son Shane in charge of it all, and then they drove to Gulgong. They'd expected to visit the kids at their grandparents', then go straight to the house to organise it ready for everyone's return. But it didn't quite happen the way they planned. As soon as they arrived, the kids all piled into the car, and off they went. 'It wasn't what we'd thought would happen at all but I think, that day, they were all very keen to get back to their home,' laughs Marian. 'We just followed their lead. They make a lot of the decisions, then we help them to put those decisions into effect!'

Back at the house in Gulgong, Cassandra called a family conference. Everyone had their say, then Cassandra announced that they'd decided they wanted to stay together – and at home. 'We love it here,' she explained, looking around the narrow, cramped house that looks on to open paddocks. 'It's so quiet and nice and peaceful. And even though our parents aren't here, we feel they want us to be here.'

The news quickly spread around the community that the kids were back, and big-hearted neighbours did everything they could to give the family a break, from delivering food to the house – including a total of 14 litres of pumpkin soup – to donating toys and clothes. The neighbours also packed the parents' funeral; the church was overflowing, with as many people outside as in, both to pay their respects to the 'lifelong companions' whose lives 'were characterised by devotion and affection for their children, and for each other', and as a show of support to the grieving Gauci children. The coffins, piled with flowers, were brought to the church on a horse-drawn wagon, and then taken to the Gulgong cemetery.

Afterwards, everyone gathered at the Gulgong RSL, where the children were amazed to win meat trays in all the raffles. 'Everyone kept buying us tickets,' smiles Cassandra. 'It was incredible.'

As Marian, nicknamed Mazza by the doting kids, tried to bring some sense of normality back to the children's lives, locals continued to rally round them, bringing still more food, with companies in the area providing other donations and holding fundraisers. Cassandra, who runs dancing classes for younger children, performed at one variety concert to raise money for the family, together with her star pupil, her sister Alexandra. They received a standing ovation.

'Seeing Ally up on stage, dancing for the first time in a concert, I was so glad the lights were down because I just became over-whelmed,' says Marian. 'I cried and cried. I was so proud of her, and I felt her parents would have been as well. It was wonderful.'

Cassandra quickly proved a good, strong spokesperson for the entire family, and the perfect loving older sister for the younger ones. 'We have to stay together,' Cassandra explains. 'Your broth-ers and sisters are your own blood, from the same parents. We want to stay together and you just have to keep going on and be strong. There's nothing else you can do. I'm the oldest, so they're my responsibility. We're very close.'

Dominic set to work on the property immediately, checking fences, looking after the animals and trying to save the crops, while Marian cared for the kids. She was meticulous about always involving them in every decision that affected them. 'We're happy to stay here as long as the kids want us to stay,' she says. 'It could be months, a year, ten years. We'll be there for them all the time. No decision is made in the house without seven people contribut-ing. There's been enough tragedy in their lives already.'

A few weeks after the funeral, on a regular trip back to the cemetery to remember their mum and dad, five-year-old Bethany surprised everyone by suddenly starting to dance. They watched, silently, as she concentrated fiercely on her ballet steps and turns. As she finished, she turned to face her parents' gravestone. 'Did you like it, Mum and Dad?' she asked. 'I learnt that today, and I wanted to show you.'

Marian's eyes fill with tears at the memory. 'They're very easy children to love,' she says, huskily. 'They've touched us right where it hurts, deep, deep inside. We want to try to help them have the kind of lives their parents would have wanted for them. They deserve nothing less.'

Marian Gauci is no stranger to life's tough setbacks. In 1967, aged ten, she came to Australia from Dorset, England, with her older sister Dawn and younger brother Wayne, after her parents Brian and Joyce Hardy decided to emigrate as ten pound poms. Her mum, a part-time worker in a nursing home, had always wanted to visit Australia and she and her labourer husband hoped it might provide a fresh start for their troubled marriage.

The family spent the first year in their new country in an army hut hostel in Sydney's south-western suburb of Cabramatta, having to march to the kitchen mess hut for their meals. The kids thought it great fun. But tensions between their parents steadily grew. Eight weeks after their arrival, Brian bought a car without consulting his wife. In an attempt to mollify her, he took the family out for a drive to show them what a wonderful purchase he'd made. On the way down the Hume Highway, a wheel fell off. The family took shelter in a fish and chip shop while Brian tried to fix the wheel, and Dawn threw up everywhere.

After a year, Marian's parents bought an old fibro and weatherboard house in nearby Fairfield and Brian found a job on the railways, then worked for a landscaping and trucking business. Later, they moved to Horsley Park, further west. For Marian, it was an extremely happy time. Her mother hid her husband's drinking and occasional drunken domestic violence from the children, who were free to enjoy their new life in the sunshine. At school, Marian met a boy called Dominic, the brother of one of her schoolmates.

One of fourteen children, his family was from Malta and he'd arrived in Australia the year after Marian's family in 1968. 'He's always been a lovely man,' says Marian. 'I went to the wedding of one of his sisters and when a friend got drunk, I asked Dominic to take us home. Two weeks later, we were going out together. I was just thirteen.'

Her parents both liked her boyfriend, but they were at odds on nearly everything else. In 1973, on the October day the Sydney Opera House opened to the public, they finally split up. It was a big year for the whole family. That February, Dawn was diagnosed with diabetes, and later lost her leg to the illness. And that April, Marian found out she was pregnant to Dominic – four months shy of her sixteenth birthday.

Her mum, however, was understanding. After all, she'd become pregnant to Marian's dad out of wedlock, too. At that time, her father had sat her and Brian down and insisted they get married. She didn't want her daughter to have to go through the same thing. 'She told us she'd never pressure us to get married,' says Marian. 'She spoke to us and said she understood that these things happen. But we decided we wanted to get married. All I'd ever wanted was to be a mother. At school, people would ask me what I wanted to do when I grew up, and I'd say I wanted to be the mother of eight kids.'

Marian and Dominic married in July 1973, and had their first son, Shane, six weeks later. The trio lived for the first eight months in a caravan at the back of Marian's mum's place at Horsley Park, before renting a house nearby in the same suburb. Dominic got work as a butcher, then at Austral Brickworks, and Marian worked in a factory that crushed rock for talcum powder, then at Amco Jeans. A year later, they had their second son, Mark.

Although they had so much on their plates, Marian was always keen to help others. When the wife of one of Dominic's friends had a nervous breakdown, Marian was happy to take their three young children to give the couple a break. She took having five children under the age of four in the house, one of them autistic, completely in her stride. Later, in 1980, when her younger brother Wayne was killed at the age of eighteen in a car accident, she proved to be a tower of strength for everyone around her.

But Marion and Dominic's own *annus horribilis* came in 1982. They'd just bought their first home, on six hectares, again in Horsley Park, when Dominic had an accident at work. His leg was crushed in a machine, severing his flesh and muscle right to the bone. He had to take the next two and a half years off work to recover. A month later, Amco Jeans closed down. With two children, now aged eight and nine, no jobs and a $1200-a-month mortgage, the future looked bleak.

But they rallied and Marian found a job gutting chickens: 'The worst job I've ever had,' she says with a laugh. 'One minute you'd be talking; the next you'd have a mouthful of chicken poo!' They tried to live off their land and cows. Any money the youngsters made from little after-school chores for neighbours, they gave to their mum to help pay the bills. They swapped milk for eggs from Marian's mum's hens. They traded beef from their cows for vegetables from her sister Dawn's vegie farm. 'We all worked on the barter system,' says Marian. 'We did that for eight years and mostly paid the interest off on the house. Everyone pulled together. We couldn't have done it without the boys, either. Any money they got, they'd come to me and say, "Here, Mum, take this, it's for the electricity bill." They were fantastic. Eventually,

Dominic recovered enough to get another job, and we paid the house off in fifteen years.'

Such setbacks still didn't stop them from being generous to others. Kim Harvey was the young daughter of a single parent, and called around regularly to Marian and Dominic's place, to ride horses, play on the farm and swim in the dam. 'Dad would be busy working and me and my sister would go over to Marian's,' Kim says today. 'She helped bring me up, in a way. If you were in trouble, you knew you could always go to her, and she'd always have time to listen and help you out. She was so caring and a great person to know – and you can see in what she's doing for those children now, she still is!'

For Marian's own sons, Shane and Mark, it was a good child-hood. With Dominic's parents living on a farm nearby at Lethbridge Park, Shane was put on a horse for the first time when he was just a week old. The two boys roamed free across the land and enjoyed helping with the cows and, later, the sheep and ducks, too. After a period working as a concreter, Shane, now thirty-six, loved it so much that he ended up working on the property, and eventually brought his partner Andrea there to live. They had two children, Sarah, five and Dominic junior, three. Mark, thirty-five, is an electrician and has a three-year-old daughter, Shontel, with his partner Sharon.

After all the traumas of their early years, including the death of her father Brian in 1999, everything was turning out wonderfully for Marian and Dominic. They'd even started working out a five-year plan for their retirement, when they hoped to leave Sydney to set up home by the ocean. 'Dom always wanted acreage – having land and animals was always his dream, and I was adamant that

I wanted to be by the sea,' says Marian. They'd even started looking at land and property near Taree, on the mid-north coast of New South Wales. 'The one proviso was that it had to be by the water,' Marian smiles, sitting on the verandah of the house, overlooking kilometres of drought-stricken plains outside Gulgong, about four hours' drive from the coast. 'But you never know what life's going to bring you . . .'

Gradually, Gulgong, which means 'place of the deep waterhole' in the local Aboriginal language, has won a place in Marian's heart. Although it's been badly affected by drought – and there was a one-year period from October 2008 when she didn't see a single drop of rain – she's now extremely fond of the place. Much of the small town itself is an historic relic from the gold boom, with many of the old hotels and shops still looking just as they did when they were built in its heyday of the 1870s. There are those who continue to refer to Gulgong as the 'town of the ten-dollar note' since a picture of the town used to feature on the old note, before it was replaced by the current version. The poet Henry Lawson also once made his home there.

Around the 32-hectare property where the family lives, however, it looks more as if everyone's farming dirt. 'It's been all heat and no rain for a long time now,' says Marian. 'It's terrible when the dust storms come through, too. The heat out here has hit 54 degrees. But I really don't mind. I do think of it as God's country. I just love it. If only there was a river nearby, it'd be absolutely perfect!'

Two months after Marian and Dominic arrived to care for

the children, to help them realise their dream of staying together in the family home, the Nine Network's *60 Minutes* TV crew arrived to film a story. They were entranced by the idea of a group of children battling to stay together in the face of such adversity, and presented a story about a brother and sisters united by tragedy and their sixteen-year-old sister, in Year 11 and about to start her HSC, vowing to keep holding everything together. The hardest thing, Cassandra told them, was accepting it. 'I think I am still in shock. I don't think I have accepted it at all. That's really the hardest thing because our lives were turned upside down and I just think they still are.'

She also took the opportunity to thank the local community, who'd taken it in turns to feed the family. As well as the food, they'd taken the children shopping and held auctions and fundraisers, collecting around $130 000 for their future. Cassandra had been busy too, studying at school, running dance lessons, helping Josh at his first communion, and supporting Bethany when she performed in her first local eisteddfod. After the program aired, more money poured into the fund set up for the family.

Afterwards, life calmed down and became increasingly set-tled. Marian and Dominic were awarded legal guardianship of the children and, in March 2009, the TV show *Backyard Blitz* visited to carry out a secret makeover of the house, giving the children each their own bedroom. A few months later came more sadness: the death of their grandmother, Pam, Julia's mum. But then, in September, they were all finally given the greatest gift of all: the New South Wales coroner ruled that the children were orphaned by their parents' 'act of love gone terribly wrong', with a finding of misadventure.

Coroner Hugh Dillon said Julia's death by asphyxia had been a terrible mishap: '. . . something that went terribly wrong in their bedroom, not because of anger . . . but paradoxically, because of their love for one another'. Of Chris's subsequent suicide, he said, 'His remorse was so deep, so profound, he felt that he could not go on living himself.'

The younger children didn't really understand, but Marian explained that their mum had died in an accident. 'It doesn't change anything,' she told them. 'Your mum and dad really loved each other, and you. Maybe one day later, you'll understand more. But it really doesn't make any difference.'

As for Marian, she welcomed the verdict and says that with some of the mystery cleared up life can just continue now. 'You just get on with your life and make the best of it,' she says. 'Life always does throw you a few curve balls from time to time, but you go ahead, catch them, and do the best you can. The way ahead for us has always been very, very clear.'

Her latest project is teaching all the children to cook. She never learnt when she was young and, going into married life at sixteen, found it a huge problem. 'I couldn't cook for sugar and these kids are going to learn!' she pledges. Dominic is very busy with all the cows, sheep, horses, goats, ducks, chickens, peacocks and a piglet called Ziggy that are now part of the property. He's also breeding dogs, training them with sheep and then selling them to bring in extra income. At the moment, he has fourteen dogs. Josh, now ten, has become his right-hand man, proudly displaying his own miniature six-pack every time Dominic strips off his shirt.

Cassandra, who's just turned eighteen, is hoping to go to university to study journalism. 'But I'm always there for them all,' she says. 'I can never replace Mum and Dad, but I do as much as I can. I'll always be looking out for them.'

On their dining-room table are two candles sitting in elegant glass holders. These were carried up the aisle of the church during Chris and Julia's funeral. 'Sometimes we light them during meals but while they're not always lit, they're always there,' explains Cassandra. 'It's a way of remembering our parents. We talk about them all the time. We don't want to forget them. Bethany tells funny stories about them, and we always laugh.

'It has been hard at times, but we've had a lot of support. Everyone in the community has been so good to us, I thank them from the bottom of my heart. It's so nice to know that so many people are looking out for Bethany and all of us. We've also had so many letters from people wishing us well. I just don't know how to thank them . . .'

For Marian and Dominic, the decision to uproot themselves from their home at Sydney's Horsley Park is one they've never regretted. 'We just dropped everything to come here as soon as we heard,' says Dominic. 'We felt for the children. It's all about them, it *has* to be. You can't really make sense of what happened, but you can't dwell on that. You just have to think of their future, and move on and make sure everything is all right for them.'

Marian nods in agreement. 'I made a promise to the children, right from the beginning, that the only way Dom and I will leave this house is when the children say, "Thanks, but no thanks",' she says. 'I told them that we're going to make some mistakes, and we'll probably fight and argue sometimes, but we'll all be doing the best we can. And so far, we're going good. Chris and Julia did a wonderful job. The children are respectful and have good manners, although they can be a bit cheeky!'

Marian's mum Joyce, now seventy-four, is filled with admiration for her daughter and what she is doing. She says she doubts if she could possibly have done such an amazing thing. 'She has a heart of gold, and always has. She'll give anything away to help anyone, and do anything she can to help them afterwards. What you see, with her, is what you get. And those kids are beautiful. She's doing a wonderful job.'

A friend of the family and trustee of the children's trust fund, Nick Wake, agrees. 'She's doing a good job with those kids and she's so down to earth – I think that's what the kids need after everything that happened. She's super-generous with her time, and she's always happy and cheerful, and I think she's giving them the best start. They're getting looked after very well.'

Marian might make it look easy, but it's often not. At night, Tamara likes to play practical jokes, sometimes performing a midnight jump on the bed in which Marian is sleeping – 'But hopefully she'll grow out of that!' Marian laughs indulgently. Josh often ends up in bed with Dominic while Alexandra will usually go to Marian for a five-minute cuddle before going to sleep. 'For that, I have all the patience in the world,' she smiles.

Bethany, at seven the baby of the family, has recently become a bit unsettled, waking up in the middle of the night crying, and pleading with her dad, 'Don't, don't, don't!' Marian will lay down next to her to comfort her, or sometimes take her back to her own bed. 'It's a slow process,' says Marian. 'The counsellor warned us it could be up to five years for the grief to come to the surface. Each one has their difficult times.'

The other day, Alexandra, now thirteen, was pushing the boundaries about bedtime, saying it was too early to go to bed. 'My mum and dad let me stay up much later!' she complained. Marian frowned. 'The last time we looked, our names are Marian and Dom,' she told the little girl. 'We're not your mum and dad. And we want you to go to bed now!'

It's hard at times, but Marian is determined to do the very best she can for the children. 'And I do love being here with them,' she says. 'I think, in the process, I've become ten years younger. I still have aches and pains, but I get up in the morning now and I have a purpose. I've got a new lease on life. It's fun.

'Yes, I never got my place near the water, but this is a kind of sea change . . . except that it's a tree change, I suppose. These kids had a pretty tough upbringing, and their parents were struggling. I know just a little bit of what they went through. But we had one night out recently, leaving them with their grandad, and I felt like I had a finger missing. They're part of me now. What their dad Chris said was right: in giving, you receive. And I'll carry on giving for as long as they need me.'

2

Do You Want This Job or Not?

ALISTAIR MILLER, *Port Augusta, South Australia*

The nose of the plane tilts downwards towards the vast ruby-red plains, speckled with the dark green scatter of spinifex. Below, there's absolutely no sign of life: no buildings, no cattle and definitely no people. But still the pilot steers his aircraft down, and the dials in the cockpit show 500 feet above the earth, 400 feet, 300 feet . . .

'All secure at the back?' he asks softly through his headset mike. 'All secure,' comes the reply, as everyone on board strains their eyes to see what he must have already spotted. And as the plane drops lower and lower still, in the distance, there it finally appears: the slightest smudge of paler earth, a dry creek bed lined with gum trees and just a split-second flash of burning sunlight on metal.

The dials continue the steady descent: 200 feet . . . 100 feet . . . and suddenly a corrugated-iron roof comes into view, a house,

23

a rickety shed and an old outbuilding. Just as quickly, they're gone again, out of sight in the dust of a lonely dirt airstrip that feels like it's in the middle of absolutely nowhere. The plane touches down and trembles to a halt, the whine of the engine slowly fades, and the world gradually shudders into a deafening silence.

Dr Alistair Miller puts his newspaper crossword to one side, unsnaps his seatbelt and heaves himself to his feet, his back bent under the low ceiling. As he opens the door, a cloud of flies bursts in to sample fresh pickings. He waves one hand in front of his face, then climbs down to the ground, just as a weather-beaten old ute jolts into view.

'Hullo there!' he calls in a soft Scottish brogue. The driver, Theresa Gilby, smiles back as she pulls up beside the plane. 'Alistair! Good to see you, and thanks for coming.'

As a 21-year veteran of the Royal Flying Doctor Service (RFDS), Alistair's journey has been epic, and not just this flight to this remote cattle station in the far north-eastern corner of South Australia. Originally from the bitterly cold Shetland Isles, a place that has only one spot from which it's impossible to see the sea, he's now perfectly at home in Australia's searing hot Outback, in one of the furthest points on earth from the ocean.

'I love it here!' he shrugs, gazing out at the wide sunburnt land before him. 'It's so full of challenge. I can't imagine a better life.'

One of the very best things about being a doctor with the legendary RFDS is that everyone is always exceedingly pleased to see you. It's rare for many who live in the deepest, most isolated recesses of the country's Outback to get any visitors at all, and locals, particularly those with young children, might often need a helping hand. For Alistair, that's the enormous reward of this kind of work, and the real reason he's here, so far from his own homeland.

Today, he piles all his bags and boxes of medical equipment into the back of the ute, with the help of the two nurses who are accompanying him and the pilot, then he too clambers into the open tray, ready for the 750-metre drive to the homestead.

Inside the house, Theresa's husband, Travis, also greets him. Together they are station managers of the remote 7000 square kilometre cattle station Clifton Hills, off the Birdsville Track at the meeting point of the Tirari and Sturts Stony deserts, with the Simpson Desert starting just 50 kilometres to the west.

'There'll always be a need for us as long as people live in the Outback,' says Alistair, forty-eight, a craggily handsome, silver-haired man, quietly spoken but with a solid, reassuring presence. 'People will always get sick and injured and, while we've seen a lot of changes to health care, that's the one thing that will never change. It's taken us an hour and a half to get here today, but when you fly, sometimes you forget really how far that is on the ground from anywhere else. You have to do the odd road trip every now and again to remind yourself of the true distances involved.'

Theresa, Travis and their three children, Wayne, sixteen, Kai-lee, thirteen, and Trevor, five, don't have too many people drop by at their property. Kailee and Trevor look at us curiously when we arrive and are eager to talk. Studying through the School of the Air, the only chance they have to see any other kids is when they go on their annual holiday, attend functions or visit town. 'But it's good here,' says Kailee, whom Alistair is calling on for an immuni-sation jab. 'And we have two foals, Baby and Four-Ex.'

Theresa, who's now been working at Clifton Hills for fifteen years, says it's a great place to bring up children. 'There's plenty of freedom and room to move,' she says. 'When we do go to town, they always want to get back home. They don't like it much.'

Alistair delivered her two youngest, so she feels the family knows him well. 'He's really good,' she says. 'He's thorough and takes his work seriously, but he's a friend as well. We only ask him to come when we really need him, but it's always good to see him.'

Kailee drives us back to the plane – she's been driving since she was very young – and the engine soon roars into life and sets off south down the track. The next stop is Cowarie Station, 120 kilometres away as the crow flies, the property of Sharon Old-field, a Scottish nurse who fell in love with her husband first, and the Outback second. After that, it's a flight further south, over the bleached, pale sands of the Tirari, down past the blind-ing white crust of Lake Eyre, empty once again after the rains of a few months before, and crossing over the vast line of the dog fence built in the 1880s to keep dingoes out of the more fertile south of the country. 'It's easy to see,' advises pilot Neil Tucker. 'Engineers love straight lines, and it's the only straight thing you'll ever see down there.' He's right; against the curves of the landscape, the ridges of dunes and the soft mounds of hills, the 5614 kilometre fence couldn't stand out more starkly. At two and a half times the length of the Great Wall of China, it's the longest man-made structure in the world.

Finally, a neat settlement of tin roofs comes into view, and the descent starts once again. Marree, the 120-person town 685 kilo-metres north of Adelaide, at the start of both the Birdsville Track to the north-east and the Oodnadatta Track to the north-west, is a regular fortnightly routine, and a number of regulars have already booked in to see Alistair. This town was once a major destination, with Afghan cameleers using it as a base to transport goods further north, and it became home to Australia's first official mosque, made of mud bricks. Later, when the railway arrived in 1883, it developed into a railhead for the cattle industry; it was also the home of the legendary Tom Kruse, the mailman who drove trucks the 700 kilometre route across some of the most treacherous desert in the country to Birdsville. The new Ghan line, however, completely bypassed the town, and from when it was built in 1980 Marree lost much of its traffic and reason for being. Today, a lone railway carriage sits in a clearing in the middle of a row of homes as a reminder of its proud past, while the world-famous Marree Man, the mysterious 4.6 kilometre-long etching of a hunter from the Pitjantjatjara tribe discovered in 1998, lies unheralded in the red soil 60 kilometres west of town.

'We see people here on a needs basis,' says Alistair, dressed casually in a pale blue shirt that matches his eyes, grey shorts, white socks rolled down to his ankles, and sturdy boots. 'It's a really mixed population. Probably 50 per cent are Aboriginal, and there are quite a few people related to the Afghan cameleers. The RFDS has a little hospital run by a community nurse, which is a very handy place to take people who've had accidents, or to observe people if they're having trouble breathing. It's great to have this as a health-care base.'

As Alistair installs himself in the doctor's surgery of the small rickety building – the only room with airconditioning in the 42 degree heat – the waiting room gradually fills. One of the first in is road worker Greg Cooper. His story is a surprise: he's driven

240 kilometres from Port Augusta just so he can see Alistair. 'I went to him once in Port Augusta, and liked him so much I decided to make him my doctor,' he says, sweating in the blistering heat in the queue.

'Now, the only way I can get to see him is by coming up here. But I'm happy to do it. He's an exceptional doctor, and it's only a four- to five-hour drive . . .'

It was at the age of fourteen that Alistair Miller decided he wanted to be a doctor. He had been flown to hospital from his home in the Shetland Isles, 213 kilometres off the north coast of Scotland, by a worried GP who'd looked at lumps that had suddenly appeared on the boy's neck and feared they might be the first signs of lymphoma. It was the first time he'd been in a hospital, and he spent over a month there in the Scottish city of Aberdeen before finally being discharged, with the diagnosis of an infection that simply aped the symptoms of cancer. But that experience of being examined by doctors, watching them go about their daily business from his hospital bed, and seeing them nobly curing, hopefully, the sickest of patients, stayed with him.

'At the time, that's what inspired me,' he says today. 'That made me consider becoming a doctor when I grew up. Seeing the doctors there, the nurses and their medical skills, I thought it would be a good profession to be in.'

Up until that point, Alistair hadn't had much experience of life. Born in the East African country of Tanganyika – encompassing the modern-day countries of Tanzania, Rwanda and Burundi – he left at the age of two, the year it became independent from Britain, when his parents, originally from Scotland's Ayrshire, decided to settle in remote Shetland. His father Andrew, a teacher, had been working to help develop the African country's fledgling civil service, while his mum Martha was a full-time mother to their three children, Alistair and his sister Alison, four years old, and brother Andrew, three years his senior. Why their father chose to relocate to the chilly, tiny Shetland Isles after the hot, vast plains of East Africa was anyone's guess. As kids, they used to make believe he was a wanted criminal in hiding.

Back then, in the early 1960s, the isles would have been the perfect place to hide out in, too, sitting on the spot where the North Sea and Atlantic Ocean meet, 377 kilometres away from the nearest Scottish city, Inverness, and 365 kilometres from the closest Norwegian city, Bergen. Notable mainly for its stark lack of trees and the richness of its bird life, Shetland's major industries were fishing, keeping sheep and crofting – farming on small plots of land. 'And knitting!' says Alistair. 'It was a very quiet place, and very isolated. It took a twelve-hour overnight boat journey to get to the mainland. People didn't fly so much then, either. That was a bit dicey because of the weather and the sea fogs.'

In the early 1970s, everything changed with the discovery of oil and gas off Shetland, in one of the largest petroleum sedimentary basins in Europe. Suddenly, workers were brought in from all over the world, more housing was built, and money flowed through to develop the islands' infrastructure. 'The place took off, and it became a much more exciting place,' says Alistair. Nevertheless, at eighteen he left to go to university in the Scottish capital Edinburgh, to study medicine.

He loved the city from the moment he arrived, and even took

an extra year to finish his degree, his father joking that he'd obviously make an *excellent* doctor, since he'd taken every exam twice. He did his internship, one year pre-registration and one year post-registration, at a time when interns actually lived at the hospital, working every day, every second night and every second weekend. It was a punishing schedule, but it did leave him with a good grounding in every aspect of medicine and its practice. 'I find now a lot of medical students, or more junior doctors, don't get that breadth of experience,' says Alistair. 'It was pretty harrowing at the time, but it left you prepared for anything, and everything.'

Everything, that is, except for true love. When he met a beautiful young trainee midwife, Mary, at his graduation party, he was taken aback to learn she was from Australia. As the couple became closer, he wondered if they could ever have a future together.

Mary liked Alistair from the first moment they met. 'He was very friendly, and seemed a really nice guy,' she says. 'We started going out together immediately.' After a year, they married, and then started talking about where they would settle. With her working visa running out, Mary was keen to return home to Sydney, and the more Alistair thought about it, the more he liked the idea of striking out in a new country. He'd graduated as part of a glut of new doctors in Britain and there were at least a hundred applicants for every job. The work appeared unrelenting, too: many positions offered nothing but twenty-four-hour shifts. In addition, the mood in Britain was gloomy. Prime Minister Margaret Thatcher had just begun her third term in office; the northern economy was depressed after the long-running miners' strike and the continued closure of the pits; there'd been the Libyan bomb-ing of the small Scottish town of Lockerbie; and there was much talk of a regressive new personal tax, the poll tax, which was to be introduced in Scotland first as an experiment for the whole of the United Kingdom. Australia began to look more and more attractive.

In 1987, the couple flew over to see how it might work out. They never looked back. The country was gearing up to celebrate its bicentennial, and it appeared to them a hip, happening place in the world, full of excitement and optimism. In addition, it turned out to be incredibly easy to find work, with a marked shortage of junior doctors, and – even more welcome – a new system had just been introduced where they only ever seemed to work eight- or twelve-hour shifts. Alistair began work immediately in a variety of hospitals in Sydney – in Accident and Emergency, Obstetrics and Orthopae-dics – gaining new skills in every field, and working shifts as a GP.

Then, in 1989, his eye caught an advertisement in a news-paper for a doctor to work with the RFDS, based in Port Augusta in the Spencer Gulf, 322 kilometres north of Adelaide. 'When you're growing up in Scotland, the RFDS sounds so exciting,' says Alistair. 'You think that's what all Australians would love to work for. I'd always had a bit of an interest in aviation, and the idea of it really appealed. I was looking for something that was completely different from anything I'd done before. I'd hated the sessions I'd done as a GP, sitting in one place, the same place, all day, every day. I'd go in to work in the morning but, after lunch, the thought of going back to the same place in the afternoon would fill me with dread. I thought with the RFDS you'd have a job that would be different every day. So I went for the interview.'

At that interview, the panel asked him about his medical quali-fications, about his background, and about why he wanted to join the RFDS. At the end of it, Alistair asked when he might find out whether he'd been successful or not. The chair of the panel fixed him with a hard stare. 'Do you want this job or not?' he asked. The next minute, they were all drinking cold beer to celebrate.

The job was everything Alistair hoped it might be. His RFDS Central Operations section takes in all of South Australia and the southern half of the Northern Territory, with bases at Port Augusta, Adelaide and Alice Springs and clinics at Marree and Tennant Creek. The section was formed in 1936, eight years after founder the Reverend John Flynn first launched the service as part of his plan to provide a 'mantle of safety' for Outback pioneers. When Alistair joined, the work was done mostly from Piper Chieftains and Beechcraft King Airs. 'And they can land very hard,' he smiles. He still remembers vividly his first day, when he turned up in a white shirt and tie. The first stop was in Nepabunna in the upper Flinders Ranges and a ute turned up to meet him from the plane. After travelling in the back for twenty minutes, through the thick, soft bulldust of the region, he was covered head to toe in dirt. 'By the time I got to my first consultation, the tie had come off, never to come back,' he says.

'In those days, it was extremely busy and much more arduous than it is today. There were only two doctors and we each did one week of clinics and then one week on call, having to cover twenty-four hours a day, whereas now there are four of us to share the shifts. Back then, we'd work long and hard, and the aircraft were slower and didn't have the same range, so it would take you, for instance, three hours to fly to Marla, and you'd have to stop for fuel in Coober Pedy on the way, and then it would be another three hours back. The aircraft also flew lower, were more cramped and were unpressurised so conditions were more turbulent. Now, if there's a patient with chest injuries, you can use pressurisation to help you keep their chest pressurised. But then, as you got up to altitude, some conditions would worsen without it. Night flying was also more precarious.'

One of Port Augusta paediatrician Dr Nigel Stewart's first memories of Alistair is when he returned from one of those early flights. He looked pale, shaky and horribly sunburnt, and was also suffering terrible dehydration, after spending a day in 40-plus temperatures in a cramped, uncomfortable plane that had been continually buffeted by thermals. 'He'd had a young medical student with him at the time, but I don't think Alistair looked much better than her,' he says. 'But he adapted really well to the change in lifestyle. He's got such a fantastic personality, he's larger than life, outgoing and so positive, as well as being an excellent, thoughtful, genuinely concerned doctor.'

The health of people in the Outback has changed, too. Immunisation campaigns have eradicated many illnesses, such as tuberculosis and some skin, throat and ear infections – except in a number of Aboriginal communities plagued by ill health – but other conditions have emerged to pose serious threats, such as type 2 diabetes, heart disease and problems related to smoking and drinking. 'A lot of people in the Outback have pretty hard lives, and it's a tough existence,' says Alistair. 'They work hard, but they play hard as well.'

In his time in the job, he's also seen huge shifts in remote areas. Once, station life involved a number of families, staff and a full social life – morning teas, tennis parties, balls – between neighbours. Now, with the increasing ownership of properties by commercial operations, there is often only one family around to manage the business, with a couple of station hands to help. After years of drought, cattle numbers have plummeted, too, and falling wool prices have caused sheep numbers to dwindle. 'So there's been a gradual reduction in the number of people in these places,' he says, 'although that's been offset, to some extent, by the huge numbers now working mines, like the Challenger Gold Mine near Coober Pedy and the Olympic Dam mine at Roxby Downs. But they tend to be fly-in, fly-out workers, so they're very different.

'There's been all the technological changes, too, with phones and the internet. Before, communications were by radio, and everyone had their radios on all the time, with everyone else's conversations chattering away in the background. Now you have phone calls, which are a lot more private, but much more isolating in a way. Often, people might want to invite us for tea but unfortunately we have a lot of ground to cover so can't stop for long. In the Outback today, I think the isolation is as bad as ever it was.'

At the Marree clinic, there's now a fresh group of people standing chatting, waiting for Alistair to finish with his last patient. They're here for a variety of reasons: antenatal services, diabetes tests and medication, hypertension, ear and eye checks, follow-ups on test results, treatment for kidney and bladder problems.

'You know, without the flying doctor and Alistair, we'd be buggered,' says local power-station manager and station worker Robert Khan. His grandfather came to Australia from Baluchistan, by the

Pakistan–Iran border, and his father used to drive camel teams along the Birdsville Track, so he's no stranger to hardship. 'We wouldn't survive out here. For us, Alistair is the main man in the world. We know him and he's a good bloke with it. He's one of us. He's more than a doctor; he can sit down and he'll talk to us like anyone. You sit down and talk to a fella, and know what he's like. He tells us like it is, too. He'll tell you if your foot's going to fall off.'

Cath Morgan, who used to live at Cowarie Station, is also patiently waiting with her eight-month-old son Toby. 'We had a few emergencies up there over the years, and it was always good to know he was on the end of the phone, or ready to come if he was needed,' she says. 'You really couldn't live in these places without people like him. He's very caring, very genuine and empathetic, and an amazing doctor. He has a great rapport with the community.'

The Central section of the RFDS has eleven planes, which carry out patient transfers between hospitals as well as ferrying doctors, community nurses and mental health nurses to conduct clinics and individual consultations in remote areas, and taking them to emergencies when they're needed. The new fleet are Pilatus PC-12 single-engine turboprops, which are smooth, fast, fuel-efficient, have the latest in navigation technology and are fitted out like flying intensive care units, thanks largely to fund-raising and donations from the community, which supplement government grants for the not-for-profit organisation. People receive treatment via an extensive primary health program, including tele-health consultations, remote primary health clinics where doctors travel either by air or road to patients, and its two health clinics, where patients travel to see the doctor. Nationally, the 146 pilots together fly the equivalent of twenty-five round trips to the moon each year and are responsible for more than 36 000 medical evacuation flights and 234 000 consultations annually – that's one every two minutes – over an area of 7.1 million square kilometres.

'And it's a pretty amazing journey to work!' Alistair laughs, taking a quick break during a lull in patients. 'It beats driving and traffic jams. I just love the challenges of the work, and being part of a team. People know they can phone us at any time of the day or night, and there will always be a doctor available. You never know what each day is going to bring.'

Sometimes, that can prove problematic, especially if there's an emergency like a car accident and the doctor has to fly off at a moment's notice with only the sketchiest idea of what will confront him at the scene. It's for this reason that Alistair travels with so many different medications, types of equipment and manuals. 'You might only ever need 10 per cent of it, but you can never be sure which 10 per cent you'll need,' he explains. He might also be called out of his bed at 3 a.m. to make the journey. 'You always need to come up with Plan A, B and C, too. Plan A might be your ideal course of action, but it might not be possible, so you always have to have backups, and be ready to think on your feet.'

A pregnant woman's baby might have to be delivered mid-flight on the plane, or a delicate operation performed on someone's kitchen table, by the roadside, in a shed or, again, in the plane, without running water, and with flies, dust and little space to spare. Improvisation becomes the order of the day. The thermos flask, for instance, is never drained completely of hot water for coffee – its contents have regularly come in useful when there's no other source at hand. The worst times are when children have to be treated then flown back to town after an accident in which their parents may have perished, their bodies waiting to be picked up by the police. It can also be terribly sad when a consult over the phone fails to save a life. It's heartbreaking telling a parent to stop CPR on a cot-death baby when you know the child was discovered too late. In those situations, the doctor is faced with not only trying to console a grief-stricken mum or dad, but also trying to assuage any guilt they might be feeling.

'There have been times when he's returned quite traumatised by something that's happened,' says Mary, now fifty, who has three children with Alistair: Siobhan, now twenty-one and studying English at Adelaide University, Robbie, seventeen, and Patrick, fourteen, both still at school. 'It can be a very difficult job at times. Something horrendous happens and he'll be called off and you never know when he's going to be back. It can be hard for family life, and for him too. But he's always loved the job, has developed an affection for the Outback and its people, and has a real passion for what he does.'

Yet there are plenty of lighter moments. Once Alistair was picked up from the plane by an ambulance. Sitting inside, he noticed the walls were smeared with blood. Tentatively, he inquired what the previous emergency might have been. It turned out to have been nothing of the sort: an Aboriginal passenger had spotted a massive 1.8 metre-long goanna on the road and had insisted on bringing it on board for a feast later. 'Whatever's happened, Alistair has managed to slot in very well,' says the RFDS Community Clinical Health Nurse at Marree, Sister June Andrew. 'He's very friendly and approachable and people react to that.' She also remembers fondly the early days, when Alistair would play his guitar in a band for the local races and balls. 'He wasn't too bad at that either – and he got to know people in a different way as a result,' she says.

RFDS Community Health Nurse Christine Freeman also likes working with him. 'He's very easygoing, down to earth and great at improvising, which you really have to in this job!' she says. 'He's also extremely popular with his patients, which can be rare for a doctor . . .'

Indeed, Alistair is routinely approached around Port Augusta by people who ask how they could become patients of his. His answer never changes. 'Go and live in Marree,' he tells them. Over the years, he's grown very fond of his new home, too, finding it a great place to bring up children, while in his spare time he plays golf and his guitar and watches cricket.

But those in Marree, its environs and further into the Outback all feel pretty fortunate to have someone who's dedicated his life to helping them. Marree's Caroline Dadleh, for instance, says Alistair delivered her cherished twins, Donald and Danielle, now sixteen, after she'd spent a long period of trying to conceive with IVF. He is currently helping her get through the shock death of her partner of twenty-two years, Clive, from a heart attack, as she looks after her five-year-old step-granddaughter. 'As well as him being a doctor, you can talk to him about how you feel, and he'll listen,' says Caroline. 'He's always been there for me. You can ask him questions, and tell him how you're coping, and he'll always be very supportive. He's very, very good.'

Pilot Neil says it's not only his compassionate manner and obvious professional skill that endears him to people. 'I think any-one who comes out here and decides to do anything like this with their lives is, by their nature, courageous and daring, willing to give it a go,' he says. 'He's always interesting, and good to talk to.'

All in all, Alistair's service to both the RFDS and the people of the South Australian Outback has been simply outstanding, the CEO of the RFDS, John Lynch, believes. 'He's engaged so strongly with our traditional area of rural and remote South Australia and also with Port Augusta itself,' says John. 'He's become an integral part of the health service and the community. He made such a strong commitment and is a very, very involved person. We are very proud.'

As for Alistair, there's simply nothing else he'd prefer to be doing with his life. 'I love my job, working for such an iconic organisation,' he says. 'It's nice to have been here so long, too, as you get to know people, their health and their families, and they come to respect you and, hopefully, like you too.' He pauses to wave more flies away from his face – they're the only things out here he's never been able to get used to, he later admits. 'But it's good to be able to offer continuity of care,' he continues. 'Many of the people I see, I've delivered their children and then looked after their health as they've grown up. I guess soon I'll be looking after their children's children too. Now, that's a scary thought!'

3

The Loudest Laugh
in the Outback

MARGUERITE BAPTISTE-ROOKE, *Alice Springs,*
Northern Territory

The tiny Vietnamese woman stands in an office, smiling beatifi-
cally. Marguerite Baptiste-Rooke wonders if she's heard right. 'You
want to buy a farm?' she repeats. 'You . . . *you* . . . want to buy
a *farm?*' The woman nods, and Marguerite shakes her head in
disbelief.

The woman had only been in Australia a year after fleeing Vietnam as a refugee with her husband and their two sons in a tiny
wooden boat, spending eleven days at sea – most of those without food or water – and then being imprisoned in a Hong Kong
refugee camp for three years. Now living in Alice Springs, in the
red heart of the country where the culture could hardly be more

41

foreign, she can barely speak English, brings along a dictionary to every meeting, has no money and faces huge challenges adjusting to life in a tough Outback town. But she's delivered her bombshell in Marguerite's office: she'd like to talk to someone, please, about borrowing enough money to buy a farm that might one day come up for sale. Could Marguerite point her in the right direction?

Marguerite, a long-time volunteer with the town's Migrant Resource Centre, set up to help new migrants settle and integrate into life in Alice Springs, couldn't help but admire the woman's pluck. As soon as the couple had entered Alice Springs, by bus from Darwin, her husband had found a job cleaning at the airport. She, however, had been adamant she didn't want to start work straightaway. She wanted to learn English, because eventually she wanted to run her own business.

Every day, Marguerite had taken her by the arm and shown her a little more of her new home town. This is where you can shop. This is where your children can go to school. This is how we do things around here. The woman, Dung Le, had observed it all with wide eyes, trying to repeat the words Marguerite used. Her English dictionary was always either in her hand or in her bag, and she referred to it constantly. Every night, she fell asleep with it open beside her on her bed.

And now she'd obviously seen an opportunity: a farm 10 kilometres out of town, where she'd cycle each day to help out the old owner, might be put on the market. Marguerite smiles back, hoping it shows the kind of encouragement she's not sure she really feels. 'Well, I've got a friend who's an accountant,' she says, slowly, as Dung Le scrabbles once more for her dictionary. 'I'll talk to him. He can help you.'

True to her word, Marguerite introduced the pair, then helped Dung Le with all the necessary paperwork, came along to meetings to explain what she needed to do, and made sure she was with her every step of the way. Marguerite had herself only been in Alice Springs for five years, and she knew how difficult it could be even for someone who speaks perfect English. And this is exactly why she'd volunteered to help new migrants to the town; everyone deserved a chance to make the best of their new lives.

Besides, she couldn't help admiring Dung Le's drive, vision and, yes, *nerve*. 'I knew how hard it was for her here,' says Marguerite, sitting in her airless little office. 'She'd have to use a telephone interpreter to make herself understood at first, and then every meeting we'd have, out would come that dictionary. She'd show me a word in English and in Vietnamese, so we'd communicate through that dictionary. Hers were always long appointments!'

Dung Le refused to be put off by any of the obstacles and, soon after, with Marguerite's help, she and her husband were the proud owners of a new market garden in the red soil outside town. A few years later, with their business blossoming, they built a stunning indoor–outdoor restaurant there too, an oasis in the dirt. Today, to be sure of a table, you often have to book at least four weeks in advance. The other night, Marguerite had her birthday party there.

'It's incredible what they've achieved,' says Marguerite. 'They started out with so little, but they were determined. It's been wonderful to play a part, however small, in such a fabulous success story.'

But in the restaurant, already beginning to fill with diners at just 6 p.m., Dung Le has no doubts at all about the true secret of her success. 'Without Marguerite we just couldn't have done it,' she says in her halting – but much improved – English, and with no longer any sign of the dictionary by her side. 'She was so kind to us. She gave up so much of her own time to help, as she has over the years for so many other newcomers, too.' Her eyes suddenly fill with tears. 'She's been amazing. She is a very, very kind woman.'

The first time Marguerite ever heard of Alice Springs was the day her husband Eric announced he was being transferred there from his job in Brisbane. They'd been in Australia less than a year and so her response was understandable. 'Where on earth is that?' she asked.

Originally from the Seychelles – the islands in the Indian Ocean, north-east of Madagascar – in 1989 Marguerite moved from Queensland to Alice Springs with her husband and their three children, aged ten, four and thirteen months. They found it a bit of a culture shock. Marguerite quickly discovered she was one of only three non-Aboriginal black people in the town. It simply wasn't possible for her to blend in seamlessly, but then her larger-than-life personality, her big laugh and her outgoing manner mitigated that anyway.

'I remember the first time I saw her, looking statuesque and absolutely splendid, moving majestically into the room like a black Queen Mary,' says Meredith Campbell, a local marriage celebrant who was later to become one of her closest friends. 'She sails along like an ocean liner, and has a tall, proud, regal stance. She really stood out in those early days in Alice Springs. She'd wear colourful dresses and she'd always be changing her hairstyle, using braids and hair accoutrements and extensions and wigs. Everyone got to know her very quickly. She's not a quiet person, either. When she laughs, you can really hear it!'

For Marguerite's kids, growing up in a small town – just as in their home town back in the Seychelles – that could sometimes be excruciating. 'She's a strong personality with a lot of charisma – very, very upfront, and happy to express that,' says her middle son, Fabien. 'She'd talk to anyone, anywhere, and always be making friends with strangers even in the middle of the supermarket. As a kid, that used to be embarrassing. *And* she could never talk at a normal volume. People always noticed her. People in the Seychelles tend to be loud and very dramatic and laugh a lot and express their emotions. But even in the Seychelles, she's extreme!'

Determined to make new friends in those early days, Marguerite went along to the multicultural children's playgroup to meet people, and there she heard talk of a Migrant Resource Centre in town. A branch of the main centre in Darwin, it was only open for twenty hours a week and run by a single part-time staff member. Immediately, she turned up at the front door and offered to volunteer her services. 'I decided that, with all the migrants we had here, we needed to do something about the centre,' she says. 'So I applied for funding to do a survey of how many migrants there were in the area, to show the government there were enough of us to justify funding.' It was a long, slow process, but Marguerite wasn't deterred. She ended up working as a volunteer for the centre for the next eight years, bringing along her youngest in a stroller as she worked, and serving seven of those years as president of the centre, helping new migrants settle.

It involved long hours, hard work and oceans of patience. But she found Alice Springs to be very welcoming to its new migrants, with the resident population often keen to know about their cultures and very happy to give them a go. 'Migrants and refugees have been arriving in Alice Springs since its earliest days,' she says. 'The first migrants came from the UK and, from 1886, the "Afghans" came from India, Pakistan, Lebanon, Afghanistan and many other Middle Eastern countries, building the town's first mosque in the early 1900s. Other very early arrivals came from Germany, China, Denmark, Switzerland, Russia and Italy, and later refugees arrived from Vietnam, Cambodia, Bosnia, Chile, El Salvador, Sudan, Liberia and Sierra Leone.

'People have always come from everywhere else to live here. They might even come from Victoria or South Australia for a holiday, and end up staying thirty-five or forty years. People come here and love how easygoing the place is; they like the atmosphere and they love the landscapes. And the people here are very accepting. They're very willing to give others a chance.'

Studies show that, in a population of about 26 500, around 6500 are from a different cultural and linguistic background than the local Aboriginal people and whitefellas. Residents now come from more than sixty different countries. For the newcomers, the advantages of living in a town like Alice, right in the middle of the Outback, seem clear. A small, remote town encourages integration, it's already very multicultural with many migrants achieving visible success, there's better access to local MPs and dignitaries and there's always been a high level of acceptance and interest.

Marguerite leapt into her new role with both feet – literally – organising multicultural dance groups so newcomers could showcase and promote their own cultures by performing an array of dances including German, Filipino and Seychellois dances; running workshops to educate people on what services were available in town; and encouraging and creating opportunities for community involvement. There was a multicultural dinner and plenty of opportunities for everyone to take part in regular events on the Alice Springs calendar, with cultural performances at a variety of community events, and participation in the Bangtail Muster Parade and Harmony Day.

Some experiments worked better than others. A cultural exchange program with a group of Aboriginal women proved a little out of the comfort zones of many. 'They'd take us out bush and show us about bush tucker,' says Marguerite. 'The first time, I told the ladies from my class to wear gym shoes or walking shoes, but they didn't understand. Some of the Thai and Vietnamese ladies came in stilettos and beautiful silk dresses. I thought, oh my God! The bus dropped us off, we had to walk on the red dirt and their shoes were getting completely bogged.

'When we were there, an Aboriginal lady pulled a big lizard from a hole, and we all thought, how lovely! But then she killed it and cooked it and we had to eat it, along with some witchetty grubs. This is where cultures meet – and it can occasionally be difficult!'

Marguerite Baptiste was born in the Seychelles in the 1950s, and lived in its capital, Victoria. Originally a trading post between Africa and Asia, the nation came under French control, and then British, before finally winning independence in 1976. Its population has always been made up completely of migrants, from Africa, India, France, China and the UK, with its official languages being French, English and Seychellois Creole. Today, its main industries are tourism, tuna fishing, farming and small-scale manufacturing.

'It was a very multiracial society and I grew up assuming the rest of the world was exactly the same,' says Marguerite. 'I didn't realise there was anywhere in the world where people *weren't* mixed. The first time I ever travelled overseas, to Kenya and then to Europe, I was really shocked. In Africa, they were mostly black, and in Europe mostly white. I found it very strange.'

She was the third of four children to her father, Eugene, who was conscripted to World War II to fight for the Allies, since back then Seychelles was still a British colony. Before the war, he'd met Marguerite's mother Elisabeth, a nurse, and they became engaged. It was a long wait for their wedding. He was dispatched immediately to fight in Egypt, Libya, Palestine, the Suez and Italy and, even when the war was over, he was sent to Uganda and Kenya to guard prisoners of war. It was six long years before he was finally able to return home and marry his fiancée. Their children Erica, Jean-Claude, Marguerite and Philomena grew up listening to his stories of the war, and of far-flung places. The spot in front of the local shops where he recounted many of his adventures was later dubbed 'The Golan Heights' by all the locals – after the highly contested mountains on the border of what became Israel and Syria, and the subject of one of his most riveting reminiscences.

Marguerite went to a good Catholic private school run by nuns along highly disciplined lines. One Friday, on a visit to a French Navy ship, the sailors gave all the children salami baguettes to eat. When the nuns discovered they'd eaten meat on a Friday, they immediately rang the hospital to find out how best to make everyone throw it back up again. The doctor in charge advised it was too late; they would already have been digested. That Sunday, the confession boxes were full.

The nuns gave her a completely bilingual education – although neither language was her own. In the morning, all the lessons would be in English; in the afternoon, they'd all be repeated in French. At home, however, her first language was Creole, the local patois, but that was strictly banned everywhere else. In the classroom, if she was caught speaking it, she'd have to do lines and an announcement that she was being punished was pinned on her back with safety pins.

She finished her education in Switzerland and England and grew into a young woman who always wanted to do something to help other people. 'I wanted to fight for the rights of people who couldn't fight for themselves,' she says. 'And, as a woman, I decided to do something different.' Back in the Seychelles she began working in the nation's fledgling trade union movement, and became the first woman to achieve high positions in the food and beverage industry unions, the fishermen's union and, finally, the building construction union. 'I think in those days the guys gave me the real hard jobs so I would leave. They thought, this skinny little lady, she won't last. But I did!' In her various roles, she studied trade unionism in both the United States and Russia, amazed at the vast gulf between their styles, with the shop steward in the United States spending most of his time behind a bar, and his equivalent in Russia preaching for hours about Marx and Lenin until 'my ears were sore'.

Afterwards, she worked with a political party during the

struggle for independence. 'If we were still a colony, I felt that our country would stay in the dark ages, especially with housing, health and education,' she says. 'Independence was the best thing my country has achieved.'

A few years later, Marguerite met and married Englishman Eric Rooke, who'd come to work in the Seychelles for eight years. She took a job in human resources for one of the hotels on the islands, then moved to an insurance company. Eric was offered overseas postings and, in 1984, they left the Seychelles for Port Moresby, the capital of Papua New Guinea. Marguerite soon found work there, managing an import–export business, had their first two sons, Vincent and Fabien, and became pregnant with their third, Adrian. But more and more they felt PNG, with its rising levels of violence, wasn't the ideal place to bring up children. They'd had holidays in Cairns and had liked it, so they decided to return and settle in Queensland. Then in 1989, after a year in Brisbane, Eric's job was moved to Alice Springs. For Marguerite, it was to be the start of a whole new life.

Marguerite's work as a volunteer in migrant services seemed to be expanding exponentially. She appeared on community radio every Tuesday evening and organised a number of multicultural dinners.

'The idea was always to help new migrants integrate and participate but, at the same time, allow them to preserve the best of their cultures,' says Marguerite. 'We wanted them to continue living their culture, speaking their language and teaching it to their kids, but also to be able to participate fully in Australian society. There were already a number of strong social and cultural groups, and the Migrant Resource Centre helped others to start too. I was active in the Alliance Française.'

Offering personal help to newcomers was some of the most valuable work Marguerite did. One young man, who'd been born in a refugee camp and had never known any other life, naturally had little idea of how to look after himself. Marguerite took him shopping on one of his first days in Alice Springs, and found she had to start right from scratch. He was overwhelmed by the range of food for sale, and was confused about how to shop – since he'd never actually been shopping before in his life. 'You have to start from showing him how to push a trolley in a supermarket,' says Marguerite. 'Then you start getting things – meat, vegies, fruit, bread or rice – explaining how you have to have a balanced diet. Then you go home with them and teach them how to cook it all, and how to use the appliances in their kitchens. It can be just the simple things that me and you take for granted because we were brought up in countries where we could lead normal lives, and we know the language. For others, starting out can be so hard.'

Another time, a new arrival from Bosnia asked Marguerite shyly if she'd accompany her to a chemist. She wanted to buy some sanitary protection but had no idea what to buy. In her country, nothing was packaged like it was in Australia. 'She was an educated lady, but she didn't have a clue what to do,' says Marguerite. 'It was a difficult experience as she didn't speak much English and we didn't have an interpreter with us . . . Just imagine the explanation in the middle of a chemist shop with so many people all around . . .'

One of her friends, former school principal Mary Blaiklock,

always admired how far Marguerite would go to help others. 'She'll help people, no matter what,' she says. 'If there's a wedding, she'll be there helping with the catering; if there's a birthday, she'll be organising the party; if there's a dinner for everyone, she'll be cooking. She's so energetic and always so involved, it's wonderful to see. She's also a great organiser and she's so inclusive, she just draws people to her.'

In 1997, a full-time paid position was created at the centre, and Marguerite applied. With so much hard work and experience, and so many unpaid hours behind her, it was little surprise that she was given the job. It gave her the room to start up more of the programs she thought would be of most use to new migrants, and also to keep the Alice Springs community aware of and informed about migrant and refugee issues. Many of her clients were skilled migrants getting themselves established in an unfamiliar environment; others were refugees who relied on the support provided by what was renamed the Multicultural Community Services of Central Australia.

Some of the refugees' stories were truly heartbreaking. They tended not to open up straightaway but, little by little, as Marguerite gained their trust, more and more would be revealed. Sometimes a half-hour appointment with her would last an hour and a half, as they relived the agonies of their lives before arriving in Australia. Some had seen their mothers raped then killed, family members beaten, children raped or taken away to become child soldiers; others were themselves victims of unthinkable brutalities. Some who left by sea in leaky boats ended up in the water when their vessels sank or they were thrown overboard. From war-torn Sudan, one man talked of himself and other villagers fleeing from rebel soldiers and, by the time they arrived at the relative safety of a refugee camp after weeks of stumbling through the bush, their shoes were completely worn through. But while physically they were better off in Australia, many still woke at night in a terrible cold sweat, wreathed in nightmares about the times they were tortured or were forced to torture others, and about all the atrocities they'd seen being committed on their families, friends and community.

But Marguerite never failed to be taken aback by their determination to make a go of the second chance they'd been offered in Australia. One young Sudanese man phoned Marguerite one afternoon and asked her for help. He wanted to hold a birthday party, and wanted to make it extra special. After all, he said, it was his first birthday party to celebrate his rebirth – the start of his new life in a new land. Marguerite gently suggested he tell all his guests to bring along a plate of food special to their own culture. He shook his head. 'I don't want anyone to bring anything to my party,' he said. 'You tell me how much it costs and I'll give you the money. I want proper party invitations and we'll have a drink and a barbecue like the Aussies do, and I'll have the words "Born New" on my birthday cake, and a picture of a rainbow.' Despite Marguerite's attempts to dissuade him, he was adamant, and the party turned out to be a huge success. 'Since then, he's never looked back,' she says. 'He says he's too busy living forward, not looking behind. He tries so hard to be an Aussie.'

The rewards of her work seemed many. One day, she was out shopping when she was stopped by a smart young Latin American man, dressed in a suit and holding a briefcase. She didn't recognise him at first. 'Surely you remember me?' he smiled, amused.

'You settled me eight years ago. You can't have forgotten!' Marguerite peered at him more closely and slowly it dawned on her who he was. 'But he'd changed so much!' she laughs. 'When I knew him, he was so gaunt, this skinny little thing. Now he's got a degree in legal services and a great job with a law firm. It's stories like those that make me feel so good. You don't want rewards for this kind of work; you get the reward when you see that someone has really blossomed and is building a good life for themselves. That's all the reward you could ever need.'

Yet while Marguerite was always on call to help the new Australians every step of the way, there was the occasional misstep. One new arrival in her twenties had few possessions with which to start her new life, and Marguerite gave her a present of a pair of gorgeous silk pyjamas that she could wear on Alice's cool winter nights. A few days later, she caught sight of her at the local school fete – in the pyjamas. Marguerite felt terrible. But the woman herself was quite happy and, within four years, could speak English perfectly, had melded in beautifully and had the best wardrobe – and shoes – in town.

A few years later, that woman's life improved a hundredfold, too, when she received news that the son who'd vanished from her village at the age of three had finally been located in a refugee camp. After they were finally reunited, Marguerite was the guest of honour at his eighteenth birthday party in Alice, and contentedly surveyed the happy family scene – the son cooking sausages and lamb chops on the barbecue. 'But now I want to say a few words,' the woman announced in the middle of the party. 'I want to say a prayer and a special thank-you to Marguerite for everything.' She fixed Marguerite with a smile and raised her glass.

'Thank you,' she said. 'Thank you.' Marguerite couldn't stop the tears that suddenly began to flow down her cheeks.

In a garden full of flowers, there's an open-air raised platform filled with tables and chairs and baskets of even more brightly coloured blossoms. In the centre, a crowd of people are milling, drinking champagne, the night lit by both a brilliant chandelier and a glorious sky beyond, full of dazzling stars. Marguerite stands and lifts a glass. She's celebrating the twentieth anniversary of her arrival in Alice Springs and she's surrounded by all the friends she's made over the years – a large swathe of them refugees to whose lives she's made an enormous difference.

Looking on, Dung Le, the owner of the Vietnamese restaurant where the lively party is gathered, can't stop smiling. 'I am very happy she comes here to celebrate,' she says. 'I could never forget Marguerite. She's a very, very kind lady. When I first came here, she taught me ABC, every day she took me somewhere to show me and she took me to English class to help study English with my dictionary. I have very much to thank her for.'

For today, Dung Le and her husband Tinh Nguyen, together with their sons Tuan and Zung, have a spectacularly successful business along the red earth of the Stuart Highway out of Alice Springs. There are queues at the gates of their market garden when it opens to the public on Saturdays, supplies at their market stall invariably run out long before their customers do, and it's hard to even get a booking at their restaurant, its dishes made from the fresh ingredients plucked from their gardens that very day. Eager diners without bookings have been known to wait two hours at reception in the hope of a table. In many ways, Dung Le would have been happy to simply run the market garden, but so many locals asked her if she might consider opening a Vietnamese restaurant that she eventually relented and built it in 2006. 'I feel I want to do something for Alice Springs as Australia has been so good to us,' she says. 'I wanted to say thank you, everyone! But most of all, thank you, Marguerite!'

It's a sentiment shared by many around Alice Springs. Abdul, a refugee who arrived by boat from Afghanistan, says she's a marvellous woman. 'She helped me a lot,' he says, 'especially with filling in forms! She's a very, very good person.' Christine Keji, from Sudan, is another big fan. 'From the start, when we were newcomers, she was always there for us,' she says. 'She helped us get a house, if we'd have to go to hospital, she would come with us, and she'd talk to us if ever we had problems. She's wonderful – and she even makes us be on time, since we Africans are always late. And now I'm a real Australian. I support the soccer team, the rugby team, whatever's Australian, I'm there for them.'

There have been changes in Marguerite's life along the way, too. Her husband's work later took him to Adelaide and, although the couple bought a house there, with Marguerite intending to move south when she could, the right time never came. She was always too busy with her job, and with the people of Alice Springs, and eventually the marriage broke down. 'I loved it here too much and felt I couldn't leave,' she says now. 'My love of the Outback ended up costing me my marriage.' Her husband now lives and works in Melbourne. Her three sons are no longer in Alice Springs, either, with Vincent working in geoscience in Canberra, Fabien also in Canberra, with the Australian Federal Police, and Adrian in electronics in Melbourne. Now fifty-four, Marguerite's also had to battle a few health problems; the eye disease glaucoma has left her blind in her right eye, with only 45 per cent sight in the left. That hasn't slowed her down much, though; she's just extra careful whenever she has to cross a road. She's recently found love again, too, with Egyptian Kamile Georgious, whom she met at a multicultural gathering she'd organised.

Likewise, she continues to help new Australians make the most of their lives in the red heart of the country, and to help the locals understand and accept them. For Marguerite, it's always been easy to shrug off any hint of resentment towards her, as a newcomer, which was especially evident when she spent four years as an alderman with the town council. 'I don't think it was racism, I think it was more to do with me coming from somewhere else and getting into government,' says Marguerite, now the head of the settlement branch of Multicultural Community Services of Central Australia. 'But listen: I don't give a stuff. I'm twenty years in this town and I've contributed as much as anyone has contributed, my kids were educated in this town, and I'm a citizen of this country. If anyone doesn't like that, they can lump it!'

But generally, she's always found the vast majority of people to be extremely welcoming. She says that even perhaps the most hostile of the tiny group of racially prejudiced locals in town have generally been won over by how hard the new migrants are prepared to work, and how much effort they make to become part of the community. She couldn't believe how, when the first group of Sudanese refugees arrived in Alice Springs, one man was offered a job to start the very next Monday. 'I think some people are curious to see where they come from, and they can be so hardworking,' says Marguerite. 'Many of them lost years of their lives in refugee camps and are now determined to get their lives back, and make the most of them. They are very dedicated.'

Her own dedication was rewarded in 2005 when she became the inaugural winner of the Northern Territory Multicultural Affairs Award, in recognition of the work she's done assisting migrants to the Territory, and promoting multicultural diversity and harmony. 'She's done so much for the town,' says Meredith, who served on the council with her. 'And she's always fun to be around. She can talk about absolutely anything, and she likes to share. She loves to get together with friends in the evening and her laughter gets louder and louder. Outside her little house, you can probably hear her laughter a couple of blocks away.'

Yet at the end of the day, Marguerite is just thrilled she's managed to make a difference to so many. And Alice Springs, she believes, was the perfect place to do it. 'It's been generally so warm and welcoming to all these new Australians,' she says. 'In a little Outback town, there's nowhere people can melt away into little conclaves; they have to mix and mingle. As a result, we've ended up with a very rich and diverse community that's all the stronger for being so mixed.

'And I believe most people, like me, have come to love the landscapes here. There's a vastness and a timelessness about it that's just stunning, and it has a real spirituality. You can always get away from it all out there for a few hours, and be peaceful in your own world – which is something many of these people just love.'

4

Guesswork and God

ANNE KIDD, *Windorah, Queensland*

The temperature's a sizzling 42 degrees in Windorah, right in the heart of the Queensland Outback, and the town's been cut off from the outside world by rising floodwaters from rain further north. The local hotel has run out of food, its fresh supplies marooned on the far side of the swollen river, while the sudden wet has spawned a veritable plague of insects laying siege to the locals – thick clouds of mosquitoes, sandflies, moths, flying beetles and grasshoppers – and forecasts of even more rain to add to the 6.8-metre floods on the way. But Anne Kidd isn't perturbed. She's standing in her kitchen, making cream puffs.

All around her, it's absolute bedlam. Windorah's getting ready for one of the biggest events it's ever seen: the seventieth birthday party Anne's organising for her husband, Sandy. For days, family and friends from all over Australia have been drifting into the

Channel Country ready for the bash, piloting their own planes, flying in on the tiny airline that services the area or driving, then abandoning, their cars and having to be ferried the last part of the trip by boat. All the accommodation in town has been booked up for months, and dozens of party-goers will be forced to battle the bugs sleeping out in swags.

'But it'll be all right on the day.' Anne smiles evenly. 'It always is.'

It's precisely this calm under pressure that has made Anne Kidd such a treasured figure throughout the state's west, and beyond. After all, many people's lives have depended on it over the years . . . and they're still around to tell the tale.

At twenty-one, as a newly qualified nurse, she first arrived in Windorah, 1060 kilometres west of Brisbane and 319 kilometres south-west of Longreach, for a few weeks' work. Forty-seven years later – the first twenty-nine of those spent working as a nurse for the local community on a completely voluntary basis – she's recognised as a true pioneer in Outback health and is still treating patient after patient in the town's health centre, and anywhere else she's needed.

Today, the cream puffs are a labour of love, but she knows that at any moment she could be called away to a medical emergency. And that's the role always dearest to her heart.

When Anne arrived in Windorah in April 1963 to take the short posting as a private nurse, she was met by her new employers and their handsome, albeit a touch dishevelled, son. Obsessed by planes, 23-year-old Sandy had actually driven out to the aerodrome to check out the DC3 and help refuel it, but the fresh-faced young woman from Brisbane also caught his eye.

She'd come to help care for his elderly grandmother, Frances Kidd, who suffered from fits and high blood pressure, and was the widow of the great rural empire founder James Kidd. But soon Anne was spending more and more time with their grandson. After six weeks, the pair went out flying together in Sandy's Cessna 172, and returned engaged. She still remembers the tense conversation with her mother, breaking the news. 'She nearly dropped the phone,' says Anne. 'She was surprised, and not terribly happy. But by that September, we were married.'

From the very first, Anne liked Windorah. Right in the heart of the Channel Country, it's watered by the pristine Cooper Creek, which is fed in turn by the Thomson and Barcoo rivers. Around Windorah – an Aboriginal word meaning 'big fish' – the desert river, in the bed of the vast Lake Eyre Basin, splits into a sprawling mass of creeks, ponds and gullies. When there's no rain further north, the area is often ravaged by drought. But when it's wet there, the creek beds are suddenly filled, the river bursts its banks and the town can be cut off by the advancing sheet of water from the convergence of all the channels; a flow that can even occasionally reach Lake Eyre. In 1939, the roads to the east and north of Windorah were cut for a record nine months by flooding.

As far back as 1861, search parties looking for the lost explorers Burke and Wills reported that the area had plenty of water and good grassland. With soaring demand from Britain for wool, and the government encouraging settlement by pastoralists, more and more people arrived to establish fledgling townships. Windorah was finally gazetted as a town in 1880.

Eighty-three years later, Anne fell in love with its atmosphere of early Outback charm and, with only eighty to 100 people, a post office, a hotel, a shop and a police station to service both the town and the outlying sheep and cattle stations, she found it a manageable size. 'It was a nice, secure, peaceful place,' she says. 'I liked it instantly. And it was a contrast with the city, even though Brisbane still wasn't much of a city in those days. People in Windorah were much friendlier, too, and the lifestyle was much more relaxed.'

It wasn't long, however, before the difficulties of life on a sheep station 10 kilometres away from a remote town became apparent. She found the heat of her first summer almost unbearable – temperatures have been known to peak above 47 degrees – especially as she'd quickly fallen pregnant. The floodwaters were high that year too, and the insects were terrible, especially her pet hate: the grasshoppers. In addition, Sandy regularly had to go off into the wilds of the family's sprawling 55 000-hectare property to pump water from the bores. She usually opted to go with him rather than spend so much time at home alone, and the pair would camp out, swim in dams, cook over a camp fire and then sleep under the stars . . . and the buzzing swirl of insects.

Goats still wandered across the main road in town, dust storms could come in as often as ten times a year, water was taken straight from the Cooper and, at home, laundry was done in a big copper with a blazing fire lit underneath. The only phone was a party line from the exchange that everyone else could listen in to and, since wireless, or radios, couldn't get a signal as far out as Windorah, there was a complete absence of modern music. 'I did miss music, and I completely missed the Beatles' era,' says Anne. 'When I left Brisbane, it was all Elvis and Bobby Darin. When

I eventually heard the Beatles and understood what everyone had been talking about, their music sounded very strange.'

Still, some of the biggest challenges were out in the paddocks. Anne soon discovered that the property's 15 000 sheep, 1000 head of cattle and dozens of horses were much easier to enjoy from a distance. While she didn't mind helping with the sheep, she was scared of the cattle and horses, and would do anything to avoid having to go near them. Necessity meant she eventually overcame that fear as she helped with drafting, branding and testing them for disease.

She didn't have much time to herself, in any case. With very few services available to the local population, and absolutely nothing for women having children, Anne saw a huge need for medical help. As a result, right from the first, she offered a hand to anyone who needed it, and soon found herself being called upon by everyone in town and from the outlying stations, and at all times of the day and night. The nearest doctor was 319 kilometres away in Longreach, while the Royal Flying Doctor Service would fly in from Charleville, 375 kilometres to the east – from where any prescription also had to come – to attend major emergencies and visit twice a month to hold a clinic. But for everything else, Anne quickly became the person everyone turned to.

'My training had been very good, and the nuns who taught me prepared me for standing on my own two feet,' says Anne, who had to learn to drive when she first arrived in town. 'Back then, we covered just about everything in our training, including children's wards where we'd look after babies at every stage of their lives, dealing with meningitis, croup, heart problems, feeding them with formula, everything.

'So here, I dealt with everything, too. There were kids with sore ears, people with something in their eye, sutures, pig rips, dog bites, injuries from people falling off horses at stations, car and motorbike accidents, home births, babies with diarrhoea, people wanting advice, tourists in trouble . . . and all with the minimum of equipment, not even a stethoscope! I had nothing. It was all guesswork and God. I'd have to work off the kitchen table for operations and boil saucepans of water on the stove. For night-time road accidents, I'd often have to get someone to shine a torch on their injuries so I could fix them up. That's, of course, until the batteries went – or the person holding the torch fainted!'

The locals' gratitude for Anne's readiness to help in any emergency quickly turned to respect for the young woman's determination to make the best of every situation, despite her obvious struggle with some aspects of Outback life.

Ross 'Chumpy' Ward remembers vividly the day he called her to ask if she'd fix him up after he crushed his hand unloading his truck. When he arrived at her place, she was as white as a ghost, and shaking. 'Turned out a grasshopper had come in through the window of her car while she was driving there, and she'd nearly rolled the car as a result,' he laughs. 'She was terrified of grass-hoppers. She was so shaken, she looked worse than me!'

Anne was born in Cunnamulla, a small country town in Queensland's south-west, the middle child of three sisters – Erin was five years older and Mary five years younger. Their parents ran hotels, usually living in the staff quarters, and as a result, the family moved around regularly. For Anne, it was never the ideal childhood. 'I hated it,' she says. 'We never saw my parents as they were always so busy working.'

At nine, and fast becoming something of a rebel, she was sent away to boarding school in Scarborough, on the Redcliffe Peninsula an hour north of Brisbane, in the care of the Brigidine nuns. At fourteen, her father died of cancer and her mother, together with her two sisters, then moved to Brisbane. Her mum worked in a number of jobs, including cleaning, to keep their heads above water.

Anne left school at fifteen and went to work as a clerk at an ice-cream company. It was a good job, but Anne wanted more. She decided she'd like to become a nurse, and started training as soon as she could, at seventeen. When she broke the news to her mum, she wasn't terribly pleased. 'She didn't think I would handle it,' says Anne. 'And she was nearly right. I don't know how many times I threatened to leave, but eventually I saw it out. It was very hard work in those days and it was hard getting used to the shifts.' She didn't much like some of her tutors, either; one Irish nun in particular was very strict and had an accent so thick, Anne often struggled to understand what she was being told to do. 'I made a lot of mistakes and got into a lot of trouble every now and again,' she says. 'But I made many friends, and it was good as far as companionship went. And I always liked the idea that once you learnt how to nurse, you could go off and do it and help people. That was always my driving force.'

After her training, Anne went to work at the Mater Private Hospital in Brisbane, with a plan to go to Sydney to do a midwifery course beginning in June 1963. It was an unsettled time, however. On her first night shift at the Mater, her mum appeared to tell her that Erin's husband Mick, a volunteer firefighter, had been badly injured in a sugarcane blaze. He died soon after. In the meantime, Anne was approached by one of the nuns from the children's hospital and asked if she'd like to go out west to do some work. She agreed, but was startled to discover the job began in two weeks. Hastily, she said her goodbyes and caught a DC3 to Windorah, to look after Sandy's grandmother.

She had no idea at the time, but she was about to enter the world of one of Australia's pre-eminent pioneer families. James Kidd, originally from Fife in Scotland, had come to Australia and looked after a number of properties in Victoria before working as a pastoral inspector for a bank in Queensland. In 1906, together with his wife Frances Hammond, the first white child to be born on the Cooper, he bought 560 square kilometres of land outside Windorah and built the homestead, Mayfield. Their daughter Catherine and their twins – a son, also James, Sandy's father, and his sister Margaret – were also born on the banks of the Cooper, with the help of an Aboriginal midwife. Three more children followed. James junior, with his wife Mary, became the next to work the property, with Sandy to later take it over as the third generation.

'We weren't sure how Anne would adapt when she came out here, but she fitted in very well,' says Sandy's sister Margaret. 'I think her childhood, moving about, helped her, and being from the country herself. But it was still very hard being so far from her family, and in such an isolated place. The year she came there was a big flood, too. But thankfully she stayed – and did an absolutely marvellous job.'

*

After Anne and Sandy married, they quickly carved out names for themselves in the region. Even though Anne had five children within six years – Catherine, Tom, Nicee, Helen and James – having to go to Longreach three weeks before each was due and then having to wait when inevitably they came two weeks late, she still managed to keep up her voluntary work as the area's nurse. She worked either from their new home, a cottage built for them by Sandy's parents on their property, or from an old shed in town, from which it was impossible to keep out the flies.

Her work could scarcely have been more diverse. She dealt with accidents at gymkhanas, camp drafts and rodeos, treating the patients and often driving them to town in the back of a ute or station wagon. It was hard: the patient could already be in considerable pain, quite apart from the bumping around they received in the vehicle afterwards. She'll never forget the day the flying doctor had to insert a catheter into a patient in the back of her Toyota. Then there were the accidents that happened on stations: everything from a stockman falling off a horse and injuring himself to a cook being scalded by hot water or boiling fat. Some illnesses were impossible to diagnose or treat without specialist equipment. One sick man came to her complaining about a shortness of breath. There was no way Anne could have discovered he had a lung abscess. She referred him straight to the doctor – who ended up saving his life at Longreach hospital.

But the road crashes were among the worst emergencies she had to deal with. There was the time she was driving to nearby Tenham Station with close friend Philomena Aspinall. The pair came across a car that had rolled, and found a young man close to death lying on the side of the road. Ever-resourceful, Anne rigged up a makeshift shelter out of wood she found in the scrub and an old blanket, to shade him from the burning midday sun while she tended to his injuries. Then there was that New Year's Eve when, in the middle of a party at her place, she received word there'd been an accident a long way out of town. Of course, she left immediately but when she arrived she found two men dead in their rolled vehicle. Having to confirm deaths was always one of the worst, although routine, tasks.

It was a more cheerful outcome the day she was summoned to another accident. This time it involved a Japanese tourist on a motorbike who'd been entangled in a minor bingle. Unable to speak a word of English, the tourist could not answer Anne's questions, and she ended up coming home with Anne for the night to be kept under observation, and until the phone interpreter service could be reached. 'I think she'd set off having absolutely no idea of the distances the Australian Outback involves, and the conditions out here,' laughs Anne, her blue eyes sparkling under her soft pale-blonde hair. 'There's a lot of overseas tourists like that. You wonder sometimes how they survive.'

Philomena is constantly in awe of her. 'She's saved so many lives,' she says. 'She went to a car accident once and saved the driver's life before the Royal Flying Doctor Service plane could land on the road. There was the other time a woman went into labour at the races. She's quite amazing. She's been the pillar of the community.'

In 1992, the doctor from Longreach visited town along with members of the board of the Central West Regional Health Services, and asked Anne if she'd like to have a proper clinic, and how she'd feel about running it. She didn't have to think twice.

Even better, after twenty-nine years of providing her services on a purely voluntary basis seven days a week, twenty-four hours a day, they finally offered her a paid, part-time position. 'I jumped at the idea,' she says with a laugh. 'After the clinic was built in town, we started by opening four hours a week, which soon increased to eight, then twelve, then twenty. Of course, I was still working all the hours anyone wanted me. But being supplied with proper equipment made a huge difference. Before, I was lucky if anyone sent me any gear. Now, I had the ability to properly check people's eyes and ears with all the right instruments, use proper dressings and have all the suture gear. It was wonderful.' In 1998, she was even given an ambulance for transporting patients – with Sandy often driving – something that, again, made a huge difference to everyone's lives.

Official recognition for Anne's amazing work also came in 2000, when she was awarded the Centenary Medal for her contribution to Australian society from the Commonwealth government. Two years later, her part-time position at last became a full-time one, so at least she was being paid an entire week's wage, even though she was on call twenty-four hours a day. At the same time, she was named the recipient of the Premier's Award for the Year of the Outback, presented by Premier Peter Beattie. 'That was really great,' she says. 'I thought, gee! That shows they appreciate me! But I'm nothing special. I just think, when things go wrong, a lot of people panic and don't know what to do. I do know what to do – but really that doesn't make me special at all.'

Sandy, too, was fast acquiring a reputation as someone who'd help anyone out, and give anyone the shirt off his back. During flood times, the gruff man with the battered hat, jeans and shirt invariably flapping in the breeze would tirelessly fly people and provisions back and forth over the river. He generously shared those skills as a pilot, particularly when anyone was reported missing. For decades he volunteered for search-and-rescue operations, finding patients from psychiatric hospitals who'd gone wandering, lost tourists, station hands in trouble, missing children. Nothing seemed to stand in his way and, once, during one dramatic rescue, he even landed on a sand dune. For his heroic work during the huge floods of 1963, he was awarded the British Empire Medal. He was also called upon regularly to teach pilots from the Australian Army how to navigate in vast, featureless, dusty regions. 'There are no landmarks out there other than the changing river course – which can fool people easily,' he says. He was equally concerned for the children of the region, and served on the state board for the Priority Country Area Program, which aims to improve the educational opportunities for kids in remote areas.

An outstanding farmer, moving from sheep to cattle in 1990, he also became famous Australia-wide as an outspoken defender of the Outback, rallying opposition when the proposal came to grow cotton in the ecologically fragile Channel Country. 'I'd just like to see no more tampering with the inland river systems,' he said. 'All this water has a purpose, and if you interfere with nature, you're going to get trouble.' Largely as a result of his efforts, not a single fibre of cotton has ever been farmed on the Cooper.

These days, Anne, now sixty-eight, still works just as hard as Windorah's nurse and the director of the Windorah clinic. Her dedication is still beyond the call of duty, however. She stays in the quarters at the clinic in town for three weeks at a time, then has a week off at home at her and Sandy's property Ourdel, an outstation of Mayfield, 13 kilometres from the main homestead. Sometimes Sandy, now seventy, will come into town to stay with her too. A relief nurse lives nearby, which allows her to have a week off every month.

'I work twenty hours a week, officially, but unofficially, I'm on call twenty-four hours a day,' says Anne. Her children are now aged from thirty-nine to forty-five, and she has eighteen grand-children who dote on her. 'I guess I'll start to slow down a bit one day, but not yet. Not while I'm still enjoying it so much.'

Indeed, it sometimes seems as if nothing will stop her. In 2002 she'd raced to the scene of a car accident to find one man dead and the other seriously injured. She tended to him at the scene and called for the flying doctor. By the time he arrived she'd begun having chest pains herself, and the pilot flew both her and the injured man to hospital in Brisbane. There, she was diagnosed with heart problems, and was eventually forced to undergo open-heart surgery in 2007. 'There's little doubt that she sacrificed her own health to help others,' says Philomena. 'The constant work with no set hours, being on call continually and having to race off at a moment's notice . . . it definitely affected her. But still she continues . . .'

The mayor of the local Barcoo Shire Council also believes her devotion has come at enormous personal cost. 'All those hours, days, nights, years she worked for us, and asked for nothing in return, took a great toll on Anne, physically and mentally,' says Bruce Scott. 'Words just can't express her contribution to this community. Her nursing care and concern for humanity and for the sick and injured shows incredible dedication. There aren't many people like Anne in this world. In the days when she had little medication or equipment, she had a wonderful knack of getting by, and never ever complained if it was too much. She's an amazing woman.'

In all the time she's worked in Windorah, the town has changed around her. Now the population is generally older, with only around eight kids at the primary school. Even when families do come to Windorah, they tend to be smaller. 'But the town will survive,' says Anne. 'It's surprising I suppose to some, but it will always have a future. For me, it's home now. I love it. I had my children here and my husband and all his family have always been around.' Life's much more comfortable, too. The electricity generators are much more reliable, the advent of phones in 1992 helped communications with the outside world and the introduction of the reticulated water system in 1995 made life a great deal more pleasant, leaving creek water only for the gardens. The provision of government funds for a sports shed and the town's information centre-cum-library also helped.

But despite the evolving world around her, Anne's passion for her calling has remained completely undimmed. 'Anne has always been dedicated to nursing and is always trying to work out ways of giving more and doing things better,' says Anne Maree Jensen, who for twelve years provided a pastoral ministry as 'the flying nun' in south-west Queensland. 'She's the real backbone of the Outback community, and of her family. She's a wonderful person.'

Yet Anne sees it in very simple terms. 'I do love nursing; this kind of nursing,' she says. 'I think I'd be hopeless in a hospital. Out here, you have a certain amount of autonomy, you're on your own. It's difficult at times, but it's good. And now you can ring the doctor any time you need him. I end up treating so many people, I start thinking that whenever I go anywhere, someone gets crook. But to help, you have to be determined and always have plenty of confidence in your own ability.'

And when the waters come and the town's cut off, and no-one can move without a fresh swarm of insects buzzing in their ears, darting around their eyes, getting caught up their noses and choking in their throats, there's always an upside. Anne smiles gently, with the patience of years of having to come to terms with the bug life of the region, and the contentment of having finally reached her peace with them.

'We do get cut off by floods just about every year,' she says, sorting out another jar of flour for a second batch of cream puffs for the party feast to come. 'But then it's a welcome sight. If the waters don't come, then we don't get good feed. You learn, in a place like this, to take the bad with the good. That's what it's all about.'

Anne's Cream Puffs

2 cups water

2 cups flour

4 eggs

whipped cream

chocolate sauce

4 tablespoons butter

Bring 1 cup of water and half the butter to the boil, then cool slightly and add 1 cup of flour; mix until it becomes a smooth ball. Then add two of the eggs and beat well with a wooden spoon. Place spoonfuls of the mixture onto a greased baking tray and cook in an oven preheated to 180°C. After 15 minutes, reduce the heat to 150°C and cook for a further 30 minutes. They should be golden brown when ready. Open each one to allow steam to escape and return to oven, still on the lower heat, to dry out for half an hour. Cool, fill with whipped cream and pour hot chocolate sauce over the top.

Then, because you missed something along the way, put the rest of the butter and the other cup of water in a saucepan and go to the local bar for a wine; return and heat, then add the remaining flour and stand to cool. Move to a shelf on top of the cupboard because Sandy thinks it is potato and starts to eat it.

Take it to another venue because the kitchen is too crowded, and add the last two eggs. Beat well, place spoonfuls onto a baking tray and cook. Don't expect to have any because the grandkids and Sandy will eat them all with custard and the cream and sauce.

5

Amazing Grace

RICKY GRACE, *Kalgoorlie and Perth, Western Australia*

Bounce, bounce, bounce. He sizes up the defenders, drops his shoulder and darts forward. Bounce, bounce, bounce. His run's been blocked. He feints left, spins past the opposing player and is gone. It's as if the ball's on an invisible wire as he heads for the corner of the court. He stops; his opponent keeps going. Bounce, bounce, bounce. Space and time meet power and agility.

He looks as if he's about to shoot, but instead the ball arcs through the air into the hands of his team-mate. After a split second, it's into the basket for another two points.

As the two players high-five, the crowd goes wild. The chant starts up in a deep rumble from the back of the packed city stadium. 'Rick-y! Rick-y! Rick-y!' The man of the moment laughs, cupping one hand around an ear to tell them to shout louder. They're happy, he's happy and his team is ecstatic.

Ricky Grace, star of the Perth Wildcats, is the absolute king of the assists. In terms of his willingness to help others look good, there is no-one quite like him.

That was then. Today, he's standing on the sidelines and it's a very different kind of game being played on an open-air court under the fierce sun in the Western Australian Outback. This time, it's between two teams of schoolgirls from the bush. Ricky, however, is no less animated. 'Come on!' he's calling. 'Pass! Pass!' There's a breakaway move, and he beams like a proud father. 'Yes!' he shouts. 'That's great!'

These girls might not be flying through the air and slam-dunking the ball through the hoop, but that doesn't lessen his passion one iota. It's still a team game and there are many life skills being learned.

Having retired from his own glory-filled days as a modern Australian basketball icon and Sydney Olympics star, with a leading record in assists, Ricky's now taking that record to a whole new level. He's become determined to provide the biggest assist of his life, this time to Outback kids who need it the most.

Ricky's drive to help others began when he was playing for the Wildcats and joined a bunch of team-mates visiting schools in their downtime to promote the game, and help run basketball clinics for their pupils. He found he absolutely loved it.

'I'm a big kid myself, still,' he grins. 'So I enjoy working with kids; there's a certain innocence that you don't get when you're dealing with adults. I liked working with the teenagers, especially. There are a lot of critical times in adolescent life, but I think those early teenage years are when they can make their biggest mistakes. You have a young adult's body, but a kid's mind. So you really need good positive role models, good mentors, and that's an area I've always been interested in.'

Ricky began getting so much satisfaction from that part of his work that, in the off-season, he started organising extra trips himself, and to schools farther and farther off the beaten track. In the south-west of the state, he visited Bunbury, Busselton, Manjimup, Albany, Esperance and Kalgoorlie. It went so well that he travelled north to do more of the same, in Geraldton, Carnarvon, Port Hedland, Exmouth, Broome and Derby.

The kids all seemed to respond well to him. The Wildcats were doing better and better in the National Basketball League (NBL), and Ricky, the African American who'd come over from the US to join them in January 1990, was the toast of the fans. In the more regional and remote areas, they adored him. With basketball having a huge following in Western Australia and many Aboriginal kids watching American basketball on TV – and seeing it as a game in which black people excelled – he had a ready-made fan base. He approached a few companies to fund his programs and they were keen to come on board.

After a few years, his trips began to cause a stir. He was approached by a chaplain from a Melbourne-based team, the Eastside Spectres, and asked if he'd consider visiting some remote Aboriginal communities in the Northern Territory. He happily obliged. 'I hadn't had any experience of Aboriginal culture at that point,' says Ricky. 'But while we were from two completely different cultures, I found I just connected very quickly with the culture and really appreciated, and enjoyed, it. I seemed to get on well with both the children and the adults. I loved being out there.

And then I started thinking I should do something like this in my own state, too.'

Early in 2001, he organised a meeting with Tom Stephens, the long-time Western Australian parliamentarian and Minister for Local Government and Regional Development in the Gallop Government. Tom wasn't convinced by Ricky's proposal but, about to leave on a trip to some isolated communities in the Kimberley, he suggested the basketballer accompany him. When they arrived, he was totally taken aback by the warm welcome Ricky received at each stop.

'He was a celebrity to these basketball-obsessed youngsters,' says Tom. 'Basketball is a highly prized and well-regarded sport in Western Australia, particularly among Aboriginal people, so Ricky built links with them very quickly. You're always looking for people who can connect and inspire, and he was able, very quickly, to do both. It was great to see the magic he spun with the kids.'

The pair also visited the distant 500-strong community of Balgo, halfway between Broome and Alice Springs, where the harsh Tanami Desert meets the vast Great Sandy Desert. The long-time priest there, Father Matt Digges, was sceptical. He took Ricky aside and issued him with a stern warning. 'Don't promise these kids anything you're not going to deliver,' he said firmly. 'They've been too disappointed in the past. We've had celebrities cycled through here with great regularity who say they're going to come back, and are never seen again. I've worked hard to build up my credibility with these young people. Don't say something if you don't mean it.'

Suitably chastened, Ricky held his basketball clinic, promising to return in five weeks to see how everyone had progressed. True to his word, he was back in five weeks to the day. And that happened again and again. Father Matt was forced to eat his words. 'He throws that back at me regularly,' laughs the priest. 'I'm sure, at times, it was very hard for him to keep his word and come back exactly when he said he would, but no matter what – I think he must often have had to shuffle everything else – he always came back when he said. In between, he even kept in contact with everyone by sending notes.'

Tom Stephens watched Ricky closely and, when they returned to Perth, asked him how much money he was planning to request from the state government, in order to continue his visits. He sat quietly while Ricky told him the planned amount, and what he intended to do with it. Tom shook his head, and Ricky felt his spirits start to fall. 'No,' said Tom, as Ricky feared the worst. 'Ask for twice that. I want you to go into these communities and carry on doing what you do. You do it so well.'

It was the start of a whole new chapter of Ricky's life. While he'd loved conducting the clinics, he wanted to have more of a long-term impact on the lives of kids at risk – the poor, those from broken homes, those most likely to slip through the net. He'd seen plenty of these kids during his trips out to the bush, both black and white, and wanted to be able to make a real difference. He founded his company Role Models WA in July 2004, with the aim of providing ongoing services, support and sporting and leadership programs to schools and communities in the Outback.

His first trips were to the Kimberley and Pilbara regions, each home to some of the most isolated townships in the nation. Rounding up a group of Indigenous sports stars to take with him, including AFL West Coast Eagles player Chris Lewis, basketballer

Jenny Bedford and state softballer Marisa Bradshaw, he set off to Halls Creek, 2900 kilometres north-east of Perth and 585 kilometres into the Kimberley from Broome, and then south to Mulan and Billiluna, then back to Balgo.

At first, Ricky concentrated on promoting healthy living and healthy lifestyle choices through sport. 'I believe team sport teaches you a whole lot,' he says. 'It teaches you how you've got to be able to get along with others, how to deal with both wins and losses, how to be disciplined, and the importance of eating right. For sport, you just have to take care of your body. My message was: if you put good things in your body, good things come out; if you put bad things in, bad things come out.

'But after a while, I started thinking that I wanted to incorporate an education message into this, too. It's good to have a beautiful body, but without a strong mind, it means nothing. So the importance of an education then became a huge part of it. It felt critical.'

At that point, Ricky devised his Up4it Leadership Development Program, designed to improve the school attendance rates of students in regional and remote Australia. In places like Halls Creek, low or erratic school attendance was a major problem for kids, their families and communities, so Ricky started tying regular attendance to sporting rewards: meeting favourite sports stars, being able to participate in basketball and other sports programs, and trips to sporting camps elsewhere.

As school attendances started to improve, everyone began to realise that this young man, originally from a land and a culture a world away from these kids, was on to something big.

*

Ricky Grace grew up on the streets of one of the poorest black neighbourhoods in Dallas, Texas, a city founded on the blood, sweat and tears of cotton and oil workers. While it had a fair share of the world's richest oil barons, the rougher side of the tracks at South Dallas was also home to a huge underclass, most of whom were black. Ricky was among them.

His dad Norvelous was a blue-collar worker in the farming industry, and his mum Earlie Mae was a nurse. They divorced when Ricky was nine and, from that point on, neither he nor his two brothers, David, five years older, and Michael, five years younger, saw much of their dad. They didn't see too much of their mum, either – she had two jobs just to make ends meet, working fourteen to sixteen hours a day, although always managing to keep a keen eye on Ricky's school grades, and planning work and sleep around his basketball games so she could attend every one. But besides playing basketball, Ricky spent most of his days hanging out on the streets and at his local sports centre, the baseball diamond and the swimming pool.

It was a time in his life when he knew he could choose either a good or a bad path. 'I was basically raised by the streets and there were all sorts of things thrown at you: drugs, stealing, robbing,' he says. 'But there was also sport, and I was pretty good at sport, playing gridiron, basketball and baseball, and loved it. I also spent a lot of time listening to the old guys at the centre, talking about what they used to do, and how good they were forty years ago. Even as a kid, I used to look at them, still stuck in that neighbourhood, and while I didn't know then how to get out of that place, I knew from them what *not* to do. I knew not to get caught up in drinking or drugs because that's what had happened to them.'

The man in charge of the centre, Simon O'Neil, felt sorry for the skinny, basketball-mad eleven year old with a slightly lost air about him, and took him under his wing. A positive role model who became something of a father figure to the boy, he'd chat to him whenever the two crossed paths. He'd talk to him about the importance of school and getting a good education, of staying out of trouble, and of working hard at his sport. His wise words made a huge impact on an impressionable kid.

'The American dream was to go to high school, go to college and get a good job,' says Ricky today. 'But I knew there was no way in the world I was going to be able to pay for college; I worked that one out early. Back then, most of us felt we had only two ways to get out of the 'hood: sport or music. And if you ever heard me sing, you'd know the second wasn't an option . . . So I focused on sport. My strategy was to get good enough in basketball to give me a college education, and then a good job. My only other ambition was for my parents one day to see me on TV!'

Ricky worked hard at school and ended up going to Midland Junior College, in Midland, Texas, the childhood home of one George W. Bush. It was a massive culture shock. Ricky had rarely ever seen white people before – his own neighbourhood, from which he had barely strayed, was 99 per cent African American and one per cent Hispanic – and he found it hard to understand what any of them were saying, and they sure as hell couldn't understand him. His first step, he decided, was to learn to speak in a way 'these white folk could comprehend'. His second step was to make sure he played American college basketball well enough that he'd be awarded a college scholarship and, hence, an education.

His third step was to stay close to the top of his class so he'd be able to continue with his basketball. 'That's always been the rule in America if you play sport: "No Pass, No Play!"' he says. That simple adage was later to provide him with the philosophical grounding for all his programs for struggling young people on the other side of the world, in Australia's Outback.

Going on to the University of Oklahoma in 1985, Ricky had intended to study law. His childhood hero had always been the fictional TV defence attorney Perry Mason, and he dreamed of growing up and becoming an African American version of the TV character. While there, however, he realised it wasn't for him, and studied for a degree in criminal justice instead, thinking he'd later be something like a probation officer. Whichever way it worked out, he knew he wanted to end up helping others.

'I think part of that is God-given and the other part is the influence of my mum,' he says. 'As a nurse, she's always looked after others – that's just her mentality. Even though she worked all those hours, she still found time for all the kids in the neighbourhood. They gravitated towards her, and adults always rang her for advice. She's always been caring and thinks of others – and that's just a trait I think I've also always had, of being unselfish.'

He was also extremely determined. In class, he strove to be the best at everything. When a classmate topped him in a spelling bee, he vowed to beat her and look at her in the same triumphant way she'd regarded him. The next year, he did. 'Only later did I learn to be a gracious winner,' he smiles. That competitive spirit was never more evident than on the basketball court, and he practised and practised for a shot at a career with a team in the prestigious National Basketball Association (NBA).

But even that was tempered by his need to help others. 'Whenever I've wanted to score the most points, and work myself up into an aggressive and selfish mentality, it's never worked for me. I'd go out and have the worst game of all time. Whenever I thought that I'm going out to be the top scorer and I'm going to score more than anyone else and show I'm the best, I couldn't make a shot. But if I was out there helping someone else to look their best, my team would win. They looked good, and I looked good as a result. I always made people look better, I was always good at assists. So at one point, I just had to accept that my strength lies in making people around me better!'

After helping the Oklahoma Sooners reach a championship game, the NBA called on him to try out for the Utah Jazz, based in Salt Lake City. His four scholarship years of free classes had run out, two classes short of attaining his degree, so he went to Utah for three months, making it into their last fifteen – but not, sadly, their final twelve. He then returned to college to finish his degree and was invited to try out for another team. Once again, he didn't make the final twelve, but was talent-spotted by an agent who asked him how he'd fancy playing for a team in Australia. He fancied it very much and, in January 1990 at the age of twenty-three, he flew over to see if he could make it in the Perth Wildcats.

Fitting in was tough at first. The club was going through tumultuous times with the death of one of its legendary players, the jailing of another and the firing of its coach. In addition, the new coach had his doubts about Ricky and resisted playing him in his natural position until the general manager insisted.

Gradually, however, things began to work out. The Wildcats ended up defeating the Brisbane Bullets to claim their first championship that year, with Ricky winning the title of Most Valuable Player (MVP). The next year, the Wildcats won again, defeating the Eastside Spectres, and he was selected to the All-NBL First Team. In 1993, the Wildcats lost to the Melbourne Tigers and Ricky became the only player on a losing side ever to win the MVP.

That year, he became an Australian citizen too. 'I found I really loved Perth, and I loved Australia,' he says. 'I enjoyed the fact too that it's English-speaking. Many professional basketball players go to Europe where there's more money, but the quality of life isn't so good. I just loved it here. There was also the chance of representing Australia in the 1996 Olympics. That didn't happen, but I did play for the Boomers at the Sydney Olympics in 2000.'

His basketball career continued to go very nicely indeed, and he ended up playing 382 games in the NBL, making six NBL grand finals, winning four, captaining the Wildcats over two years, winning MVP five times and coming first in the Perth Wildcats for assists, and first in assists twice in the NBL as a whole. His personal life was coming along well too, with his American girlfriend following him to Australia to become his wife. Three children arrived – their son Jerami, now fifteen, and daughters Jaida, twelve, and Jazmyn, nine.

But it was his growing commitment to kids in the Outback that was taking up ever-increasing amounts of his time, attention and imagination.

*

Ricky was always refining his Up4it program, with its three-pronged criteria: attending school for 80 per cent of the time; not getting into trouble; and trying your best when you were at school. Kids seemed to respond well to its simplicity, and the feedback from the schools was tremendously encouraging. When he introduced leadership camps in Perth as an extra incentive – the chance for Outback kids to come to the state capital to have what was usually their first glimpse of the sea and visit some of the attractions of a big city – school attendances rocketed.

Still, Ricky wanted to do more. He'd heard about the successful Aussie Rules football-coaching program at Clontarf Aboriginal College in Perth, established on-site to attract more students to the school and retain them, and wondered about the possibility of adding a basketball element. When he approached the principal, he was surprised by the warmth of the welcome. 'Ricky!' the man exclaimed. 'You're a godsend!'

Ricky felt confused. He'd been called many things in his lifetime, and his nickname was Amazing Grace, but he'd never been called anything like that before. The principal explained that, while there were plenty of activities for boys at the college, there was nothing for girls. Basketball could be the answer to that problem. Ricky was nonplussed; he'd never even considered coaching girls. 'So I politely pointed out that I was still playing for the Wildcats, that I'd only come in to see the place, and when I retired, I'd drop in and we'd sit down and talk,' says Ricky.

But the principal turned out to be a doer rather than a talker. At 8 a.m. the next morning, he rang Ricky. 'Ricky, I can't wait until you retire!' he said, his voice urgent. 'I need you now! These girls have absolutely no extracurricular activities to keep them engaged in this school.'

Setting up a basketball program for Aboriginal girls certainly wasn't something Ricky had ever envisaged doing, but the more he considered it, the more he thought, why not? After all, he'd earned his Masters degree in educational leadership at Fremantle's Notre Dame University in 1998, and had two daughters of his own. 'It really wasn't my vision at all, but I believe sometimes you don't choose your destiny; it chooses you,' he says with a smile.

As a result, Ricky's Role Models WA set up their Clontarf Girls' Academy in 2006 as part of Clontarf College to provide sporting, mentoring and leadership programs to girls aged thirteen to seventeen. Another girls' academy began at Kalgoorlie in 2008, and others have followed in Bunbury and Broome, as well as in Darwin, Alice Springs and West Arnhem in the Northern Territory, forcing him to change the organisation's name from Role Models WA to Role Models and Leaders Australia. The rest of the country could well follow one day. 'We're really now pushing out very strongly,' says program director Terry Boland, who has over thirty years' experience in education and more than ten years as a principal in government secondary schools. 'It's been very successful in engaging young girls in education through sport, and Ricky is very proactive and passionate about seeing his vision work. Girls grow up to be the cornerstone of good families, and it's important for them to be educated and to be allowed to achieve.'

The academies have a number of Indigenous staff who act as great role models for the girls; they have also introduced other incentives besides basketball, including grooming, deportment, cooking and art, and the results have been amazing. At Kalgoorlie,

580 kilometres east of Perth, for example, there have been a lot of successes to celebrate. One twelve year old, Lucy, arrived as an extremely shy student who'd barely talk and only attend sporadically, taking just 63 per cent of classes in 2008. But after participating in the team challenge activities and hanging out in the group room at lunchtimes, she started to build up friendships. After a year, Lucy emerged completely from her shell; she is self-confident, popular and the practical joker of the class. Her school attendance is now 98 per cent.

Cynthia was a tougher case. The thirteen year old started out attending just 20 per cent of classes and was violent and aggressive towards classmates and teachers. The next year, she was suspended from school – and its basketball program – after a vicious fight with another student. Finally, an individual behaviour management plan was devised for her, to include 80 per cent school attendance, zero truanting and regular checks on her behaviour. She stuck to the four-week contract, and has been achieving great results ever since.

Shamus Ballantyne, a former program manager, says the programs are working extremely well. 'They're a fantastic concept and the kids respond to them,' he says. 'Ricky's always actively involved, too. One time, he brought over Tania Major, made Young Australian of the Year in 2007 for her dedication to addressing youth welfare issues, who was great for everyone to meet. Ricky has a great rapport with all the girls.'

He also makes a great cheerleader for them when they play, says current program manager Sarah Ashwin. 'You see the pride in his eyes when they do well, and he's constantly encouraging, and chatting, to them. To have a legend like him talking to them makes them feel very important,' she says. 'It's great that he wants to help others. He's deadly.'

He isn't always perfect, however. On one trip to the US for the girls to play basketball, he gave them all a strict lecture upon arriving about getting up early the following morning to practise. Sure enough, they were all ready to start at 7.30 a.m.; he overslept.

Today, Ricky has just returned to the Perth academy after a trip to some Outback areas near Alice Springs. Tall, lean, handsome and looking much younger than his forty-four years, he does look tired, however, and he's embarrassed to explain that under his neat grey trousers he's wearing white socks with black shoes. They were the only pair that were left clean, he explains. Life is pretty hectic these days, especially since he only returned from the US a couple of weeks earlier; he visits regularly since his marriage broke up and his ex-wife returned to their homeland with their children. Even with all his other commitments, he manages to spend at least four months in total in the US every year, where he still has a house, to spend time with them. During his time there, he takes them to school every day, and is present for every basketball game, cheerleader event, science fair, parent–teacher meeting and hanging-out opportunity. The kids also spend one month of their summer holidays with him in Australia. Throughout the rest of the year, he won't go more than two days without speaking to them on the phone, keeps close tabs on their grades via their schools' websites and continually reminds them about exactly the same thing that he preaches to Australia's bush kids: the importance of a good education and wise life choices.

For now, in Perth, everything is going extremely well. The success stories just keep on coming. One of his pupils, twelve-year-old Tenesha, for instance, refused to look at anyone when she first arrived from her home in Kununurra, and clung to her grandmother. Now, after three months at the school, she represents it in cross country, netball and basketball. She's also a regular visitor to the academy office, constantly asking questions about what's happening and how she can be a part of it all.

Kirk Garlett, the father of two other girls at the academy, says they've both taken huge strides in their education, all thanks to Ricky's help. 'I've never met anyone like him,' says Kirk. 'He has so much time for everybody. He really is Amazing Grace!'

It's a moniker that's echoed again and again from the academies all through the Outback, where school attendances have risen between 17 and 26 per cent as a result of involvement in Ricky's programs. Even with some corporates, particularly mining companies like Barrick Gold, Xstrata and BHP Nickel West, coming on board to fund programs – they rely on one-third federal government funding, one-third state funding and, hopefully, one-third from sponsorship or donations – there's always a need for more money and more support. But few who are approached by Ricky can ever find the heart to refuse. Ricky's enthusiasm is his secret weapon, says Perth academy coordinator Narelle Henry, herself a stellar basketball player. 'He's so inspiring, so supportive, and has a very strong vision that he stays true to with a lot of hard work. All the girls love him.'

Almost on cue, a head peeks around the door of his Perth office, and two small girls peer in. 'Hello!' says Ricky. 'Come in. No shame here!' he urges them, knowing how shy they are. He asks them in turn about their day at school, and how their lessons went. By the time they leave, they're both smiling from ear to ear.

'They're great girls,' says Ricky. 'And it's great that we're able to help them here. Gone are the days when kids do things because "we say so"; kids now have to have incentives, particularly those in rural, remote and Outback townships. Those have to be fun and engaging, and sport is something most of them enjoy. A lot of these kids – both boys and girls – have the kinds of issues that remind me of when I was a kid. And they deserve the kinds of chances I've had.'

6

Stopping the Poison

Eileen Kampakuta Brown, *Western Desert Region, South Australia*

An elderly Aboriginal woman is sitting on a battered dining chair set in the glowing ochre dust of the stony desert beyond the remote opal mining town of Coober Pedy. She's gazing off into the distance, eyes half closed against the burning sun and swarms of flies, looking serenely content to be in the Outback close to her traditional homelands.

Softly, she begins to sing, a low throbbing sound that vibrates against the heavy afternoon air. Gradually, her voice starts to soar, then descend, like the two wedge-tailed eagles that are swooping overhead. Lifting her face to the sky, the tiny woman slowly gets to her feet and steps rhythmically in time to her song, her body swaying and her arms drawing arcs before her, as she determinedly walks her Country. It's a timeless march no-one, but *no-one*, has been able to stop.

For this is the extraordinary Mrs Brown, a traditional Yanku-nytjatjara woman who can neither read nor write, and who can barely speak more than a few words of English, but who managed to completely outmanoeuvre both the federal government and a massive American–British–Canadian–Swiss multinational conglomerate, to protect her beloved South Australian Outback. Along the way, she won an Order of Australia from those same politicians, and plaudits from across the world.

Eileen Kampakuta Brown was a young Anangu woman, working with her family at an isolated station in Walatina (known to non-Indigenous Australians as Wallatina) in the far north-west of South Australia, when it happened. In the middle of collecting firewood for cooking, she heard a deafening bang and felt the earth shudder beneath her feet. She screamed in fear and fell to the ground.

A few hours later, everything was enveloped in a terrible, hot stench. She thought a bushfire must be rapidly approaching, but the smell was much more acrid than anything she'd ever before encountered.

'It was a terrible smell, terrible,' she says in her native tongue. She shakes her head, puts a hand to her face and shudders at the memory. 'Then a thick black mist came. It swallowed us up. We couldn't see anything. We didn't know what it could be.'

Unbeknownst to Eileen, her family, friends and the rest of her community, that mist was actually a thick cloud of radioactive dust from the first British test of an atomic bomb on the Australian mainland, just 180 kilometres away on a flat claypan at Emu Fields, 280 kilometres west of Coober Pedy.

Scientists had warned that the unusual weather that day, 15 October 1953, was all wrong for the Totem One test and could prove dangerous for everyone in the vicinity and beyond. But with a number of postponements already – due to rain and wind – and mounting political pressure from a British Government increasingly anxious about its Cold War armoury, the scene was set. Protestations from Native Patrol Officer Walter MacDougall on behalf of the many Aboriginal people in the area had also fallen on deaf ears, with Chief British Scientist Richard Penney accusing him of placing the 'affairs of a handful of natives above those of the British Commonwealth'. As a result, the detonation was finally given the fateful go-ahead and with a deafening blast, the distinctive mushroom plume billowed high into the heavens and a dense cloud of radioactive particles drifted north-west across the northern region of the state, and into the lungs, skin, organs and lives of many, many people.

None of the Aboriginal families on their traditional lands were given any warning about the test and all were completely bewildered by the great explosion and the sudden mist engulfing them. Some older people were shouting, *'Mamu mamu!'* – Evil spirits! – and a few were throwing spears at the smoke to try to make it go the other way.

'The smoke caught us – it came over us,' recalls Eileen, then aged around twenty-six. 'Our eyes became red and itchy and painful. It was hard to breathe and everyone was coughing and choking. We were wondering what sort of sickness we had. There were no doctors, only the station bosses. They gave us Vicks Vapo-Rub ointment for our noses, and eye drops.'

At the time, Eileen was raising the children of her older sister

Pingkai Upitja, who was away working on stations, and frantically ordered them to stay inside their humpy in the hope that the smell and the mist might quickly dissipate. But her twelve-year-old nephew Yami Lester, who called her Little Mother and whom she thought of as her son in the way of traditional Aboriginal communities with their strong family ties, was instantly blinded in his right eye, and suffered blurred vision in his left.

'It was the worst time,' says Eileen, sadly. 'When we got up in the morning from the tent, we tried to open our eyes but we couldn't open them. We had red eyes and tongues and our coughing was getting worse. All day we sat in the tent with our eyes closed. Our eyes were sore, painful, red and shut. All people got sick right up to Oodnadatta.

'Everyone had headaches and people started to get really sick. It wasn't just us. The wife of the station boss got really, really ill and she was taken to Alice Springs and never returned. She must have died there. The ones who were weak, or old, just started dying. They were gasping for air and couldn't do anything without running out of breath. They used to walk a long way, but they were bruised up inside and couldn't anymore. Only the strong survived but even they got weaker. We buried a lot of people, and then we would move on to a fresh camp. It was a terrible time.'

Another nuclear test took place at the same site twelve days later. Ironically, it was then concluded to be too remote and later testing, in 1956, took place at the more 'accessible' Maralinga, 180 kilometres to the south and only 60 kilometres further away from Coober Pedy. That time, at least, there were attempts to move some Aboriginal people away from the area of the testing site.

Today, sitting in her camp at Ten Mile Creek, looking out over the vast red lands she's always called home, Eileen lifts her dress to her knees. The ebony skin on her legs is blotched with white. She pulls back a sleeve to show the same strange pigmentation on her arm. 'This is all over my body, and it started that day,' she says. 'My eyes have never been the same since, either. Those nuclear tests affected us all. No-one was spared.'

Forty-five years after the blasts, in 1998, Eileen was living in Coober Pedy when she heard startling news: the federal government had just announced a plan for a national radioactive waste dumping program in the South Australian Outback. It proposed building two dumps, mostly to take the waste generated by Sydney's Lucas Heights nuclear reactor. One would be a shallow burial site for low-level waste that would be radioactive for up to 300 years, while the second would be an above-ground facility storing intermediate long-lived waste that would require isolation for up to 250 000 years and would be a radiation hazard for around 10 000 years.

Eileen, together with other Aboriginal female elders living in the town, was enraged. The region pinpointed for the dumps was Billa Kalina, an area stretching from Woomera and Marree to Coober Pedy and very close to the Great Artesian Basin. The declaration immediately brought back painful memories of their first nuclear encounter. Many had buried children, parents, brothers, sisters and friends since then, and there'd been a huge increase in cancers – an illness that had until that point been virtually unknown among the Indigenous population. Many others, Eileen included, had never been able to bear children, while eye and skin diseases, asthma and birth defects had become commonplace.

Eileen's nephew Yami, who was by now totally blind, had gone from being a stockman to what he laughingly called a 'broomologist' – making brooms in the Blind Institute – to becoming a welfare worker, educator, interpreter and Indigenous activist. He had agitated for a Royal Commission into the British tests, visiting the UK to interview the scientists involved. Largely through his efforts, the Hawke government set up the McClelland Royal Commission in 1984. It found the decision to detonate on 15 October 1953, in those adverse weather conditions, knowingly exposed Anangu communities to extremely dangerous fallout. Most of the survivors were unable to claim compensation, however, since they weren't able to give times and dates of the bombs and their effects – since they possessed neither calendars nor clocks back then, and had no doctors available to chart their illnesses or to issue death certificates. In addition, Aboriginal culture often prevented them mentioning the names of those who had died, or any intimately personal issues such as gynaecological problems. As a result, the Commission only awarded minimal compensation to a few, including Yami. Thirty years on, many more were still struggling.

It was thus easy to understand why the government's latest plan, outlined in the local newspaper, caused so much consternation. Eileen passionately loved her Outback lands. At the edge of an ancient inland sea that had once filled much of Central Australia, they're a vast arid desert of rock, sand and spinifex, the atmospheric setting for movies like *Mad Max*, *Priscilla: Queen of the Desert* and *Ground Zero*. Craggy formations tower up, startling in colour at the Painted Desert and breathtaking at The Break-aways, while the ramshackle township of Coober Pedy itself produces an estimated 70 per cent of the world's opals. Alarmed by the thought that the area could again become contaminated, Eileen and the other women – or *kungkas* in their own language – convened a meeting.

It was no surprise that Eileen became one of the main driving forces for action. A respected elder well known in both her own community and beyond as a teacher of her Anangu culture, she was also much loved for her happy, optimistic outlook, and her wise countenance. Everyone looked up to her, and she commanded great admiration, and affection, from the whole community. Her adopted son Yami says her generosity of spirit endeared her to all. 'She cared about everyone,' he says. 'She ended up looking after a lot of children. To me, she was my second mother and really looked after me. She's a very good woman.' His eldest daughter, Rose, also has fond memories of how people were always drawn to her honorary grandmother, and followed her lead. 'Growing up, she was never strict with us children. She was always kind and gentle, and you instantly treasured her. She was always laughing, and finding something to smile about. She'd worked hard all her life, and had tough times, but she was always very positive.'

At the meeting, many of the other women agreed to join her and form a group to oppose the government's scheme. 'We've had enough poison, enough sickness, from the bomb,' said one. 'We knew about the poison from when we were young girls. We knew we had to fight it.'

Yet, to provide a credible and forceful opposition to the plan was an extremely tall order. The women were determined, to be sure: as the custodians of the Seven Sisters Dreaming – a narrative about seven sisters who moved through the ancestral landscape, creating natural phemonena – they vowed to protect the land for all Australians, their children and their grand-children. But with very little English language between them and few contacts, and being totally unable to read and write, their prospects of success looked dim. Yet they refused to be deterred. They recruited a local nun from an order founded by Mary MacKillop, Josephite Sister Michele Madigan, who'd been working with Aboriginal people in the area and spoke their lan-guage, as their 'honorary paperworker'. Then, through her, they issued a powerful statement.

> . . . We were born on the earth, not in the hospital. We were born in the sand. Mother never put us in the water and washed us when were born straight out. They dried us with the sand. Then they put us, newborn baby, fireside, no blankets, they put us in the warm sand. And after that, when the cord comes off, they put us through the smoke. We really know the land. From a baby we grow up on the land.
>
> Never mind our country is the desert, that's where we belong. And we love where we belong, the whole land. We know the stories for the land. The Seven Sisters travelled right across, in the beginning. They formed the land. It's very important Tjukur [the Law], the Dreaming that must not be disturbed. The Seven Sisters are everywhere. We can give the evidence for what we say; we can show you the dance of the Seven Sisters.
>
> Listen to us! The desert lands are not as dry as you think!

Can't the Government plainly see there is water here? Nothing can live without water.

There's a big underground river underneath. We know the poison from the radioactive dump will go down under the ground and leak into the water. We drink from this water. Only the Government and people like that have tanks. The animals drink from this water – malu kangaroo, kalaya emu, echidna, ngintaka perentie, goanna and all the others. We eat these animals, that's our meat. We're worried that any of these animals will become poisoned and we'll become poisoned in our turn . . .

All of us were living when the Government used the country for the Bomb. Some were living at Twelve Mile, just out of Coober Pedy. Everybody got sick, whitefellas and all.

The Government thought they knew what they were doing then. Now, again they are coming along and telling us poor blackfellas 'Oh, there's nothing that's going to happen, nothing is going to kill you.' And that will still happen like that bomb over there.

And we're worrying for our kids. We've got a lot of kids growing up on the country and still coming more, grandchildren and great grandchildren. They have to have their life . . .

It's from our grandmothers and our grandfathers that we've learned about the land. This learning isn't written on paper as whitefellas' knowledge is. We carry it instead in our heads and we're talking from our hearts, for the land. You fellas, whitefellas, put us in the back all the time, like we've got no language for the land. But we've got the story for the land.

Listen to us!

The statement caused an uproar not only in Australia but in the rest of the world. Everyone's imagination had been caught by the idea of Eileen and her friends, part of the oldest race on Earth, and also one of its most powerless, uniting to try to defeat their federal government. For Eileen, a cheerful, laid-back woman in her seventies – already beyond the average life expectancy of an Aboriginal woman – was the least likely political activist anyone could possibly imagine.

'But she's always been a fighter,' says Rose, who grew up call-ing Eileen 'little nana' as she was so small. 'She was always ready to speak up if she saw injustice and she was ready to speak loud. At the same time, she's always so calm and happy. She never took life very seriously. But with her lands and culture at stake, she felt very strongly that she had to protect the South Australian Out-back. She wanted to give it her best go.'

Becoming a political campaigner was a world away from the life Eileen had known. Her parents had followed traditional Abo-riginal ways in the arid, spinifex-dotted western plains of South Australia, travelling around Australia's largest desert, the Great Victoria Desert, camping and eating wildlife caught on the way. But by the time Eileen was born (around 1927) at Iltur (Coffin Hill), 280 kilometres into the desert west of Marla, Aboriginal Australia was changing irrevocably. Her uncle Peter used to go there regularly to buy dingo scalps from locals, which he would exchange for sugar, tea, tobacco, flour, and flour sacks (to be made into dresses), in the rations outstation of Sailors Well, just north of Walatina. Now he was intent on luring the family in from the wilderness to join the workforce there.

One day, he took Eileen's older sister Pingkai to Sailors Well to work, helping to care for the animals. Soon after, he persuaded the whole family, including Eileen's younger brother Pinnyna, to undertake the six-day walk there. They were never to return to their homeland.

Eileen grew up a feisty, independent little girl. She looked after the sheep kept by the reserve's boss, an Afghan cameleer turned storekeeper who brought the mail and rations from Oodnadatta, at that time an important stopping-off point on the trading route between Marree to the south-east and Marla to the north-west. When she was twelve she got another job, 40 kilometres down the Oodnadatta Track on a station at Welbourne Hill, again minding sheep and then working inside the house, washing dishes and clothes – always by hand – and cleaning floors on her knees with a cloth. It was all for no pay; in those days you just received food as wages. 'So tired!' says Eileen. 'We got very tired with the work. We even milked the cows. Yes, we were all growing up there learning whitefella work, but one of the bosses was a nasty person who was bad to Aboriginal people. I wanted to get away and leave work and go to Wintinna where some of my family were minding the sheep.'

One night, Eileen, then fourteen, filled a pillowcase with dresses, blankets, bread, salt bullock meat and black tobacco and, just before daybreak the next morning, slipped away and walked the 40 kilometres to Wintinna. Her mother was delighted to see her headstrong young daughter return to her side. Eileen began looking after sheep again until she caught the eye of a young man with a limp, travelling from Oodnadatta with camels. She'd been swimming in a waterhole and he shone a mirror at her to show he wanted to speak to her. Too shy to approach him, however, she tried to forget about him until he returned another day to deliver gifts: the mirror, a comb and a cake of soap. They talked, and Eileen's grandfather ruled they should be together. They were married by firestick, the customary Aboriginal form of wedding ceremony.

Her new husband, Tommy Brown, was a Christian, later to become a preacher. He'd had polio as a boy, but was as spirited as his new wife and wouldn't let anything hold him back. The couple set off together, with Eileen's nephew Yami in tow since his mother, her sister, had since died, and married again, formally, in 1960 at the Lutheran Church in Coober Pedy to satisfy the religious authorities. After their honeymoon, they went to work at Todmorden Station, then at Coober Pedy, Oodnadatta and finally at Mimili. 'We weren't in love at first, but I learnt to love him later,' says Eileen. 'But he was already in love with me. From when I was a young girl until he passed away, I had only that one love, nobody else.'

All through her marriage, as well as working to support her husband, Eileen kept busy teaching the children in the community about Anangu culture. She felt it was vital that the old ways not be allowed to die out, and she took it upon herself to keep the thread strong. After Tommy's death in 1989, she devoted herself entirely to her teaching. 'She's a dear lady, and she always had many friends through her teaching,' says Lucy Lester, Rose and Karina's mother. 'She's a very good singer and dancer, she's happy to share her story with people, particularly children, and she's brought a lot of very sacred things out into the community.'

Indeed, Eileen has always seen this as her calling. 'I teach everyone, I've been everywhere teaching people about Anangu culture,' she says. 'I'm the number one cultural woman for the Kupa Piti Kungka Tjuta (the Senior Aboriginal Women's Council of Coober Pedy). I'm the teacher of my grandmothers' and grandfathers' ways. I always get up for the culture; I'm the leader of the culture; I'm the teacher.'

It was this strong belief in the importance of her culture, its values and the central role of the land in her dreaming that gave her the drive, and the confidence, to fight for what she saw as the future of her country and its people.

The memory of the fallout from the nuclear testing weighed heavily on Eileen and she was adamant that no-one should face the risk of being poisoned a second time. 'We didn't want this being put into our country,' says Eileen, jutting out her chin. 'We had seen first-hand the damage it had done. We weren't going to allow this to happen again.'

The group decided to call on others for help, from all around Australia. Sister Michele was eager to support them. 'Mrs Brown is one of the most extraordinary people I've ever met in my life,' she says. 'As well as being a real go-getter, wise and well balanced, she's so full of love. She was so committed, everyone fell under her spell. I wanted to help support those women to save Country.' One of the first letters she wrote for the women, dictated by them, was to the organisation Friends of the Earth. 'Dear Greenies,' read the note. 'We are just dropping a few lines to let you know we want help. We're trying hard about this rubbish, the radioactive dump. We don't want that, we've got kids, we've got too many kids to grow up and see the country . . .'

It brought an immediate result. Some of the Friends of the Earth members had been involved with the campaign against the Jabiluka uranium mine at Kakadu, and met with the women in Melbourne. Two of the activists then travelled up to Coober Pedy to work out a plan of action, and ended up basing themselves there to help. 'We were struck by their experience of the bomb before, and they were old women with a lifetime of experience,' says one, Nina Brown, then aged twenty. 'Mrs Brown was a pivotal part of the group, being a senior woman and their cultural advisor. She was absolutely impressive.

'She was the one they deferred to as their cultural guide and she was the peacemaker of the whole community, the trouble-shooter, the person who always brought everyone back to what it was all about.' Nina, together with the other honorary 'Melbourne kungkas', became the women's helpers, setting up the website, organising fundraising, spreading the message and handling communications.

From that day on, their campaign, named Irati Wanti – 'the poison, leave it' – moved into top gear. Hundreds of faxes were sent out to anyone who might read them, Eileen signing them with a simple cross, and a contingent of the women travelled around South Australia and the entire country, spreading their message of opposition to the nuclear dumps in the Outback and asking for others to join them. Support came thick and fast. The South Australian government soon announced its active opposition to the waste dump construction, and polls found that 87 per cent of people in the state supported the stand.

TOP: Marian Gauci flanked by her new family, all sharing an al fresco Christmas dinner on the property outside Gulgong, New South Wales. *Left to right*: Cassandra, Alexandra, Marian, Tamara (standing), Bethany, Marian's husband Dominic and Josh. (*David Hahn, courtesy of The Australian Women's Weekly*)

ABOVE: Marian moved from a big city to a property outside the small town of Gulgong (pictured) so that the five orphaned children could remain in their home. (*Hamilton Lund, Tourism NSW*)

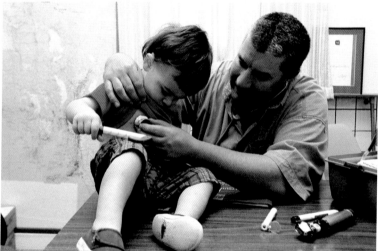

TOP: Alistair and Royal Flying Doctor Service nurse Trish Mansfield race to the aid of a patient after being picked up from a dusty runway in Outback South Australia. (© *Newspix, Kelly Barnes*)

ABOVE: Alistair examining one of his youngest patients in the clinic at Marree, South Australia (*RFDS*)

TOP: Marguerite Baptiste-Rooke taking some quiet time in the Outback landscape around Alice Springs, Northern Territory (*Kamile Georgious*)

ABOVE: 'I have very much to thank her for,' says Vietnamese refugee Dung Le at the restaurant she set up with Marguerite's help. (*Sue Williams*)

ABOVE LEFT: Anne Kidd at the clinic she runs for Windorah locals and those in the vast area surrounding the town. Anne is on call twenty-four hours a day, seven days a week.

ABOVE RIGHT: One of the windswept main streets of the tiny town of Windorah (population 80–100), in Queensland's Channel Country

FULL PAGE: The towering red sandhills just outside Windorah
(*All photographs Sue Williams*)

TOP LEFT: Ricky Grace during his term as a star player for the Perth Wildcats

TOP RIGHT: Ricky playing with the kids at his academy in Kalgoorlie. School attendances have soared since basketball was introduced as a reward.

ABOVE: Children and parents farewell Ricky at the end of another of his Outback camps, which he holds for kids living in some of Australia's most remote areas. (*All photographs Role Models Australia*)

ABOVE: Mitchell Litchfield is making a major contribution to regional life around Griffith, New South Wales, as a youth worker with Youth Off the Streets. Mitchell runs a host of activities with local kids, managing to educate, inform and entertain them all at the same time. (*Sue Williams*)

OPPOSITE TOP: To some it may look like dry, featureless land, but to Eileen Kampakuta Brown, the desert outside Coober Pedy, South Australia, is Country rich in life, tradition and legend (*Sue Williams*)

OPPOSITE BOTTOM: Eileen at Observatory Hill for the Australian ceremony to award her the Goldman Prize for environmental campaigning (© *Fairfax, Robert Pearce*)

TOP: Joie Boulter (right) has given her young charge Dion Beasley (left) a new lease on life at her home in Tennant Creek, Northern Territory (*Sue Williams*)

ABOVE: Dion spends every spare moment sketching the town's dogs, and his images now adorn his brand of merchandise, Cheeky Dog (*Cheeky Dog*)

The kungkas and their retinue, many of whom had never before left their communities, travelled long hours to state their case, to Adelaide, Alice Springs, Darwin, Melbourne, Sydney and Canberra. 'I met [then prime minister] John Howard and spoke right to him,' says Eileen, beaming. 'We said to him, "Do you have children, Mr Howard? And grandchildren? Do you love them, and are you concerned about them? Because we are concerned about our families." But he didn't answer our questions. It was more or less like he was being told off by a couple of wise old ladies. He was listening at the time, but I think he kept his ears in his pocket.

'I prayed a lot, though, and really asked for help to win this. I had faith and if you really believe in something, and put all your hard work into it, I believed we would succeed. We spoke from the heart. White people have books, but we have the book of the land in our hearts.'

The women – Eileen together with Eileen Wani Wingfield, Ivy Makinti Stewart, Eileen Unkari Crombie, Emily Munyungka Austin, Angelina Wonga, Martha Uganbari Edwards, Rjunmutja Myra Watson, Betty Nyangala Muffler, Peggy Tjingila Cullinan and Lucy Kampakuta Wilton – took turns to speak at functions, rallies, conferences, protests and schools. They organised a camp at their beloved Ten Mile Creek in the red desert outside Coober Pedy and, at one stage, had about 300 supporters come to stay. As well as constantly contacting politicians, they also invited any celebrities they'd heard of, such as the stars of *SeaChange,* to sign up.

'And when they ran out of words, they sang,' says Rose's younger sister Karina Lester, who often came along to interpret for the women, and accompanied a delegation to Germany in

2004 on their behalf after an invitation from the international nuclear campaign. 'It was always so moving hearing the beautiful voices of the old women, singing about their lives and their love of the land – *Inma*, or ceremonial song. It was astonishing. They never became overwhelmed by the enormity of what they were doing, or intimidated. They spoke in their own language or in broken English, and were always so focused. I think for the politicians and businesspeople, the nuclear dump was a case of "out of sight, out of mind", but these women spoke from the heart and their experience of losing brothers, aunts, uncles, sisters. If the dump was so safe, they asked, why couldn't it be on the east coast where it was coming from? They were so impressive, and Nana led the way.'

When the news was leaked that the South Australian Outback was also being considered as a possible repository for the world's nuclear waste, everyone's outrage intensified, and the campaign moved up a notch. Multinational nuclear waste management company Pangea Resources, an American-owned conglomerate comprising the British Government's British Nuclear Fuels Ltd, Canada's Golder Associates and the Swiss Government's NAGRA, was recommending the Australian Outback as the ideal dumping ground for the permanent disposal of global stockpiles of high-level nuclear waste. It said that around 250 000 tonnes of spent fuel and high-level radioactive waste would have accumulated by 2015, mostly from Europe, Russia and Asia, and the Australian dump could take much of this – as well as 20 per cent of future global production.

'They seemed determined to poison us,' says Eileen. 'Why do we want the world's poison dumped in the Australian Outback?

They want to dig a hole in our Dreamtime and fill it with poison. To other people, this land may look as though it supports no life but we know different. This land is a rich, beautiful land, and needs to be protected.'

The women faced plenty of setbacks along the way. Driving through the night to attend a public meeting in Adelaide, their van hit a bullock on the highway near Port Augusta. Happily, no-one was injured. It was a bigger blow, though, when the government decided on a site for the waste dumps near the rocket range at Woomera, then shifted it to the nearby old sheep property Arcoona Station, just 180 kilometres south-east of Coober Pedy. 'It's like our words went in the wind,' complained Eileen Wingfield, demanding a hearing with more politicians and federal officials.

Yet all victories, however small, were regularly celebrated. Coober Pedy was declared a Nuclear-Free Zone in 2000 after hundreds of locals signed a petition; the publicity from a three-month anti-nuclear camel trek by supporters drew even more attention to the cause; and Canadian author and activist Naomi Klein dropped by to become a friend of the campaign. The Australian Council of Trade Unions passed a motion acknowledging the kungkas' right to assert 'their lawful protection of Country', and singer Paul Kelly performed at an opening of their art exhibition. Another, almost surreal, high point was having *Batman Forever* actor Val Kilmer, in the area to film the 2000 sci-fi thriller *Red Planet*, call in to visit them at Ten Mile Creek. The women even featured on an episode of the TV show *Race Around Oz*, with film-maker Dahlia Abdel-Aziz winning the judges' prize in the competition for her five-minute story, *Following The Sisters'*

Journey, and they also travelled for two days by train to appear at the Sydney Olympic Games with a message about the importance of safeguarding and celebrating culture.

Plenty of awards came their way, too, including a South Australia Great Regional Award for their contribution to 'the building of a more positive and vibrant region', and a Conservation Council of South Australia prize. Eileen was always thrilled to have their struggle recognised but her proudest moment came on Australia Day 2003: becoming a Member of the Order of Australia for service to the community 'through the preservation, revival and teaching of traditional Anangu culture, and as an advocate for Indigenous communities in Central Australia'. To this day, she carries it in her wallet wherever she goes.

Yet there was still more to come, and from a most unexpected quarter. In April 2003, in the fiftieth anniversary year of that first nuclear explosion, Eileen and her friend Eileen Wingfield, whose grandson had just been diagnosed with a brain tumour that she believed was a result of the 'poison', were awarded the prestigious American-based Goldman Award for the Environment – the environmental version of the Nobel Prize. They'd been chosen, said the prize's founder Richard Goldman, because they exemplified 'how much can be accomplished when ordinary people take extraordinary action to protect the health of our planet'.

The two women appeared in a full-page story in the *New York Times*, being honoured for their exceptional courage and commitment to looking after the environment. It was the perfect platform from which to relay their message to an even wider audience. 'This award makes me feel strong,' Eileen told the waiting media at the presentation in Adelaide. 'Even though I am getting old,

I will keep going, still talking strong against the poison.' She is the fourth Australian ever to have won.

The award, and subsequent ramping up of Eileen's campaign, marked the turning point in the women's fortunes. Shortly after the parallel award ceremony in San Francisco, the Australian Federal Court ruled that the government's compulsory acquisition of the land earmarked for the dump, under urgency provisions – acquired just three days before the South Australian government was to approve the land as a park – was illegal.

With an appeal likely to cost millions of dollars and involve lengthy delays, and with the October federal election looming and three Liberal seats in Adelaide at risk, Prime Minister Howard visited Adelaide and admitted, on radio, that the dump was a 'no-win situation for the government'. After being heckled by protesters and being questioned continually by the media, he promised to reconsider the issue at Cabinet. Then, on 14 July 2004, six years after the start of the Irati Wanti campaign, the federal government announced that it had finally abandoned their plans for the South Australian Outback, and would start a new search elsewhere on Commonwealth land for a dump.

Eileen was at an Aboriginal Women's Law and Culture meeting near Ernabella in the state's far north when the announcement was made. She didn't find out about it, however, until three days later during a stop at the Marla Bore Roadhouse, when someone's mobile phone came back into range on the way home. She and the other kungkas sang for the next 250 kilometres home. Two days later, they all visited Arcoona Station to celebrate their historic – and quite astonishing – victory.

*

Now, Eileen, sitting on the chair at Ten Mile Creek, smiles as she tastes once again the sweetness of success. It was a long, hard battle, and these days she's relishing being able to take time out. Aged around eighty-two – although with no birth certificate no one can be sure of her exact age – she's living at the Aboriginal aged-care facility she helped establish at Coober Pedy, Umoona Aged Care, and is very happy to come out to her Country whenever she can. Throwing a kangaroo tail on the fire built before her is an extra treat.

'It's a good time for us now, and for our country,' says Eileen, dressed in her favourite pink, with a pink lace top, a pink checked shirt, darker skirt and pink socks. 'We can have a break now and camp out and pick bush medicine and bush tucker, and spend time with our grandchildren and our great-grandchildren.'

She's been able to help the other women from their campaign, and their families, too. When she was presented with her $125 000 Goldman Award, she came home, then sat down with Umoona manager Sonia Mazzone and asked her to write out cheques for her. 'I sat in my office for a week writing cheques, giving all her money away,' says Sonia, who came to Coober Pedy for a two-week holiday and has ended up staying for the past twelve years. 'If any of the Anangu people had passed away, she gave it to their children. She simply said, "What would I do with the money?" She just wanted to make sure everyone else was well looked after.

'She is so giving, and is an amazing woman. She's my teacher, and I've learnt so much from her. She's very, very special. She's a director of the facility, helped secure funding for it and is the first one to speak up if any rules are broken. Her chihuahua puppy Juju can be just as fierce. He barks if someone he doesn't know comes near, but is absolutely devoted to Mrs Brown. She's such a spirited woman, and a great fighter. When she knows she's right, she'll never back down.'

The remainder of the money Eileen won went to the anti-nuclear movement. 'She does look to the past as far as her teaching goes, but she's also always looking to the future,' says Rose. 'She wants to make sure the future is safe, too. I'm so proud of her. When she started out, we all thought, *How* is she going to win that? But it proves that determination, and persistence, really can win through.'

This hasn't been the end of her fighting spirit, either. She, along with Yami and Rose – who's developed a rare kind of arthritis in her hands and the same skin discolouration as her Nana – are still angered by the British government's negligence over the tests. They'd like to have an apology and hope that, one day, they'll pay to clean up the Outback lands that the Royal Commission ruled were still contaminated from the radiation. One group of locals are lodging claims in the British courts, with barrister Cherie Blair QC, the wife of former British prime minister Tony Blair, representing them. Of Eileen's role, Yami, now sixty-eight, says, 'She done a good job on the dumps and now she's still working on this. I worry about Eileen as she's a fair age now, but she still talks strong.'

As the afternoon sun begins to fade, Eileen gazes over to the distant horizon, beyond vast flat lands. 'Coming here gives you strength,' she says, pulling her stripy knitted hat down further over her long grey hair, flecked with blonde. 'Sometimes, you're thinking so much, you turn around and think you can see the Seven Sisters!' She laughs heartily and claps her hands.

'Yes, people said we could never win against the government,' she says, finally. 'We were just a few old Aboriginal ladies. But we were never going to give up. We had good spirit, and we still have good spirit. No matter how much power and money anyone has, good spirit will always win through.'

7

A Chance to Shine

MITCHELL LITCHFIELD, *Griffith, New South Wales*

A tiny child is trying to throw a tennis ball into a bucket that's a quarter full of sand to stop it tipping over. She tries and fails, and tries and fails again. A young man walks over to her, crouches down and speaks to her softly, then arcs his arm to show her how she should toss the ball towards the bucket. She tries once more. This time, the ball arches neatly into the bucket and the girl jumps in the air and claps her hands in excitement.

Mitchell Litchfield hands her another ball and this one immediately finds its way straight into the same bucket. As does the next. And the next. A small boy joins her and she shows him the secret of her success. Soon, the pair are making their way steadily over the whole course, throwing a ball into each bucket as they go.

Mitchell grins as he watches them. 'All she needed was someone to take an interest in her, and a bit of guidance,' he says. 'She's a quick learner. She would have worked it out for herself in the end.'

He then notices a fresh gaggle of boys standing shyly by a game with giant rubber arrows and a hoop lying in the grass eight metres away. 'Hi guys!' he says cheerily as he approaches. 'Do you fancy a go? It's really simple . . .' He demonstrates how to throw an arrow into the middle of the hoop and then hands the other arrows around. 'Now, try and get it as close to that one as you can,' he says. 'Let's see how well you can do.'

A few minutes later, some older girls come over and ask if they can play basketball. 'Absolutely!' he says. 'Here, I'll get you some balls.'

For any casual onlooker to the school holiday scene in parklands south of rural Griffith in New South Wales, it would be easy to assume that Mitchell, twenty-six, is always the leader of every group, the life of every party. But behind the smiling exterior and the bubbly personality is a young man who, for a while there, was completely lost.

Suffering terrible bouts of depression, he was drinking too much, fighting too much and in constant trouble with the police and the courts. He was banned from all the bars in town and seemed hell-bent on a path of self-destruction.

But everything changed dramatically when a local teenager was bashed to death on New Year's Day morning in 2007, another tragic victim in the cycle of youth violence that had been devastating the town. As the shocked community mourned his death, there were many who decided something had to be done to steer the area's young people away from trouble. And chief among them was Mitchell.

He took up the first post as a trainee youth worker in Griffith, a role offered by campaigning priest Father Chris Riley, founder of the charity Youth Off the Streets, who came to see how he could help after being invited by the local Aboriginal community in despair over the senseless killing. And since that moment, Mitchell's never looked back, working with kids in crisis locally and also travelling around a number of Australia's rural, remote and Outback regions counselling young people about their troubles and depression, and helping them integrate with their local communities.

'It's been very challenging, but a great experience,' says Mitchell, who has just won the Australian Defence Force Youth Leadership Award in the inaugural Australian Rural and Outback Awards. 'There are parts of my life that I'd really rather forget. But if it helps others to talk about what I went through, then I'm always willing to.

'It's wonderful to have the opportunity to work with young people, and help them feel better about themselves. And in doing that, I always feel so much better about myself, too!'

Mitchell was born in Griffith, 570 kilometres west of Sydney and 450 kilometres north of Melbourne, and is the grandson of one of the first pioneer families to move into the region in the early 1900s when the Murrumbidgee irrigation channels were being built. His father's family came from Ardlethen, a small rural town about 80 kilometres away, and his mother's from Narrandera and Leeton, south of Griffith in the Riverina, to work in what's now become one of the largest wine and vegetable production areas in Australia.

The younger of two boys to his dad Paul, a plant operator with the electricity board, and his bookkeeper mum Kathy, he had a perfectly happy childhood. In his teens, he had the usual family conflicts, fallings-out with friends and relationship difficulties common to all young people. 'But I just seemed to take them a little bit harder,' he says now. 'I didn't know what I wanted to do after high school and, while I wasn't happy there, I didn't want to leave either and end up in a job I didn't want. So I had pressures from school, from home and from a relationship I was in. Everything was building up and at around the age of eighteen, I started to suffer from depression and felt I had nowhere to turn for help. In a rural town like Griffith – as in many rural, remote and Outback areas – there's very little professional help for youth depression, which I've now discovered is surprisingly common, and very dangerous.'

Mitchell went to see his doctor who put him on medication, but these particular pills gave him shocking headaches and made him feel ill and, not wanting to try an alternative, he soon abandoned them. As the depression closed in, life became darker still. His mum despaired at how he spent so many days sitting in his bedroom, and started to fear coming home from work each day, terrified she might find him dead. At the time, she had a job at a funeral home and spent a lot of time counselling parents who'd lost their children to suicide. Soon, she was agonising over whether she might become one of them. 'It was a very scary time,' she says. 'There were moments when I thought he'd really reached the end. I knew he wasn't taking drugs, because he was very against them, but there was something dreadfully wrong; he said he didn't care whether he lived or died.'

For Mitchell, that period was no less frightening. 'I started to lose any care or thought about what I wanted to do,' he says. 'When I was at home, I had problems with my parents but didn't care about that either, and I became more and more reckless. By twenty, I felt I'd fallen to an all-time low and had nearly lost all hope of trying to build a life for myself. That's when I started getting in trouble with the police.'

He began drinking heavily, particularly on Friday nights and at weekends, and was caught drink-driving twice in the space of two months. When he was out, he'd begin to argue with people and the exchange of words would quickly turn into a fight. Late one night, he saw a young friend being hurt in an incident with the police and he went over to them and, in the heat of the moment, grabbed an officer and pushed him backwards. From that moment on, he felt like a marked man. It seemed that every time the police encountered him at night, they'd stop him and question him about where he'd been, or what he'd been doing. He'd react badly and often end up being arrested for noncompliance, resisting arrest or assaulting police. Officers drove past his house regularly in the evening. And they banned him from every bar in Griffith.

'By the end, I felt I couldn't live in the town, I couldn't show my face, I couldn't go out, I couldn't do anything,' he says. 'Sometimes, when I got into a fight, it was the only time I'd feel alive. It felt like my whole body would combust in this explosion of anger. And it's not you in control anymore.'

Desperate to get away from his problems, he tried a change of scenery: living in Canberra, working for a friend who owned an earth-moving business. After six months, he was so homesick he returned to Griffith. Then he tried working on a farm outside town but, without even mobile phone reception, he found it too isolated and lonely. On the one hand, he longed for family and friends to stop constantly asking him if he was all right; on the other, he needed someone to talk to.

Help eventually came in the form of family support worker Savin (Sid) Barone, whom the courts directed Mitchell to see. Savin says it took him a long time to penetrate the tough exterior Mitchell always projected, but eventually the young man began to open up as the two compared notes on the guitars they both loved. 'He's a keen musician and he brought along his guitar and we'd swap a few bits and pieces,' says Savin. 'With each visit, he'd open up a little bit more, and be a little more up-beat.'

Mitchell found it a great help to be able to talk freely about how he was feeling to someone outside his family and friends. Savin then asked him if he'd like to join a men's group that he ran. Mitchell wasn't so sure, but Savin offered him the chance to help at the group, cooking the barbecues and lending a hand organising activities, as an alternative option to the community service he'd been ordered to perform by the courts.

'There were a range of people there with different problems – things like deafness, schizophrenia, drug addiction, alcohol, people going through a divorce – but when you were there, you felt like you didn't have a problem,' says Mitchell. 'You were all the same, all equal, with no-one looking down on anyone else, everyone helping each other out. It started to make me feel much more positive.'

Savin noted his progress with pleasure. 'He endeared himself to all of the group, and he began to obviously enjoy coming along and getting involved. The rewards were about being a positive influence on other people's lives.'

At the same time, Mitchell started as the volunteer coach of a local kids' junior rugby league team. He began by helping them train, then took over as coach when a friend of his couldn't do it anymore. 'It was every Thursday and Saturday during the season with twelve, thirteen and fourteen year olds and I found I really enjoyed it, and was good at it,' he says. 'My old coach watched me one day and asked me how I got the kids to sit down and listen. I told him I always explained why we were doing something, and how it would help them to be better players, and help win the game. I'd also found you had to vary your training a lot as they had short attention spans and if you lost them, they'd be off chasing butterflies instead.

'While I was coaching, I found I forgot about the bad things, and I started getting over the issues that were affecting me. When you've got nothing to do, that's when you dwell too much on your own problems. But I was teaching these kids new things, they were looking up to me, it felt good. I felt a sense of pride as no-one had looked up to me before. At the same time, I felt the enjoyment of helping others. We started to win, too. In the end, we won the championship every year for three years. I started thinking I'd love to get into some kind of field of work where I could do something like this . . .'

Then, on 1 January 2007, the unthinkable happened: a seventeen-year-old boy was bludgeoned to death by two other boys at the taxi rank on the main street of town.

The shock of the killing hit Griffith hard. Police said the teenager was head-butted twice by one fifteen-year-old boy, and then king-hit from behind by a second. When it was revealed that the victim was white, and his assailants were both Aboriginal, allegations that the attack was racially motivated began to swirl around town. Some elements of the media picked up on this line and ran with it. The local newspaper, the *Area News*, gave space to the views of former local councillor Peter Day: 'Having non-Europeans in this country has failed,' he declared. A branch of the Australia First Party, with a core policy to 'abolish multiculturalism', was soon set up. Police seized a noose from someone waiting outside court where the boys were due to appear on murder charges, at the same time as the dead boy's school friends held a memorial service.

Police were anxious to hose down the racial ill-feeling, saying the problem was more to do with late-night violence among young people who were unemployed, bored, drinking alcohol and taking drugs, than to do with anyone's ethnic background. Such juveniles indeed accounted for 13 per cent of the 371 assaults the previous year. A close friend of the dead teenager's, who organised a plaque to be set in his memory at the base of a tree close to where he died, said there were fights every weekend, with groups roaming the town looking for trouble.

Mitchell agreed. 'It was a very random act of violence – it could just as easily have been an Aboriginal kid fighting an Islander kid, or a white kid attacking another white kid,' he says. 'An Aboriginal friend of mine in high school got into a confrontation with another Aboriginal person; he got hit and died, and the fight was a result of alcohol and stuff. I think it's more about hopelessness and violence, alcohol, depression and other problems. Throughout my school years, for instance, we had a lot of suicides all about my age, with two sets of brothers hanging themselves. I don't think the violence was racial at all. It could have happened to anyone.'

Indeed, Griffith had always been proud of its rich multi-cultural heritage. It began with the irrigation scheme and the decision of the New South Wales Government to commission Canberra architect Walter Burley Griffin to design the town. Then its first settlers were soldiers back from World War I, who turned the native scrubland into farms. From 1913, Italian migrants began arriving in force, recruited to drive the steam-boats on the Murrumbidgee and Murray rivers and help at the farms and wineries. It's estimated that today, 50 per cent of Griffith's 25 000 people have some kind of Italian heritage. From the 1970s, people from Turkey arrived to work in the vineyards, from India to work in the citrus industry, and from the Pacific Islands to work on the poultry farms and in food processing. By the end of 2009, Singh and Patel had become the most common names in the local White Pages.

Sensing Griffith's problems were more to do with some of the area's disaffected young people than race, Father Chris Riley announced he was going to set up a branch of his Youth Off the Streets charity there. He drove up within twenty-four hours of the death and had a meeting with some of the locals, and immediately began recruiting three young people to take on as trainee youth workers.

Mitchell Litchfield was the first candidate he interviewed, and the first person he took on. 'I did have some doubts about him at first, but he was very open about his past,' says Father Chris. 'What really swung me was his dedication to the rugby team he coached. He'd accepted a massive responsibility there and had obviously taken it very seriously and done very well. That impressed me, and gave me the feeling that I should be able to trust him.'

Not everyone was as enthusiastic. When Mitchell's appointment was revealed, to begin in April 2007, the local newspaper printed a comment from an anonymous source: 'One of the anointed has been banned from the hotels in Griffith'. That hurt.

Becoming a youth worker was a steep learning curve for Mitchell. Father Chris intentionally threw him into the deep end, too. Starting out, Mitchell had to organise basketball games for local young people and sausage sizzles to get them out together. Like other outreach services Father Chris had set up in Sydney's Campbelltown and Macquarie Fields, the idea was all about involving young people in fun, healthy outdoor activities and at the same time winning their trust and allowing them to get to know the youth workers in a relaxed setting. Then, if they did have problems, they'd know who to approach for help, and feel confident about discussing their issues.

It was exactly the kind of work Mitchell had been yearning for. 'I knew from my time with the junior rugby league and with the men's group that I wanted to do this kind of thing every day,' he says. 'I wanted to be able to give young people opportunities and experiences that they might not normally be able to have. I wanted to give them role models in life, someone they knew they could turn to for help. I came to really understand, and truly believe, Father Chris's mantra that there's never a bad kid; just bad circumstances. This work was everything I'd ever hoped for.'

Soon, he was organising sports afternoons in local parks, with basketball and simple throwing games for the younger kids, and a barbecue to feed them afterwards. Then there were evenings for older kids where they'd get together to cook a three-course meal – something many had never done before – and then eat the results. He brought in speakers on a variety of topics, such as a local police officer, drug and alcohol councillor, lawyer, school or TAFE teacher or career advisor, followed by pizza and soft drinks. He organised video nights and initiated discussions about anything and everything that might be bothering the young people. There were fishing and cultural camps further afield; day workshops on drugs, alcohol and living skills; and advocacy work for those who found it hard to speak up for themselves in the areas of housing, legal issues or finding work.

Mitchell also travelled to remote towns and Outback areas like Walgett, Narrandera, Coonamble and Aboriginal communities outside Echuca and Lake Cargelligo to organise sports days and showcase cultural crafts, games, music and dance. Occasionally, he would go to Sydney for extra training on outreach programs there. He also helped organise Reclaim the Night evenings in Griffith, with entertainment, music and dancing, drawing attention to people's strong desire for a safe community. Just before Christmas each year, he held a day in the park with food, basketball, volleyball and touch football – and gifts for every child who attended. More than a hundred people turned up each time.

'My first impression of him was that he was quite shy, but he's really blossomed since,' says Kathy McKenzie, the manager of the Youth Off the Streets outreach service in Griffith. 'He's really come a long way. I know it was a bit of a struggle in the beginning because of his past and his reputation, but he's worked very, very hard. Now, he's really taken a leadership role here, and he gets on with everyone. He shines when he's with the young boys. They all really look up to him.'

Late that first year, Mitchell was asked to sit on a panel at Westmead Children's Hospital to take part in a forum on youth lifestyles. 'I spoke about the high expectations I place on myself as a youth worker, about my depression and about what parents need to do to communicate with their children in times of need,' says Mitchell. 'I also talked about the lack of help available for young people with such problems.' Listening in was youth health expert Professor David Bennett, the head of adolescent medicine at Westmead Hospital and Sydney University.

'I was very impressed by this young man, and I thought how courageous he must be to stand up there and describe his pain and suffering before an audience,' says Professor Bennett. 'He seemed a very open-hearted person, talking about how he'd been on this one track in life, then had taken an amazing step to move on to another completely different one. There seemed to be a real altruism about him too, an eagerness to use his experiences to help others.'

At the close of the forum, he approached Mitchell to ask him to help film an educational DVD on rural youth health in the hope of raising more money to set up the country's first academic chair in adolescent medicine. At any one time, he said, up to 20 per cent of Australia's young people will suffer a mental disorder, and mental health and behavioural disorders account for more than half of all their problems. Yet there are very few resources put towards helping them. Mitchell did so well that Professor Bennett then asked him to take part in a forum held by the Sydney Medical School Foundation in Sydney. 'He did very well at both of those,' he says. 'His is a very powerful message about the service learning concept; that by helping people he could feel valuable himself. I hold him in very high regard.'

In February 2008, Father Chris invited Mitchell to an orphanage in the remote mountains of East Timor that he visits regularly, and fundraises for, on a 'service learning' project. One of the tenets of his philosophy is that, by helping others, young people often end up benefiting hugely themselves. Mitchell indeed found it one of the most transformative experiences of his life. 'It was one of the biggest eye-openers,' he says. 'It left me much more thankful for my own lifestyle, because these children had no electricity, hardly any food or water, and very little clothing. Yet they never stopped smiling all the time I was there. Seeing and experiencing this made me a much better person!'

Today, Griffith has settled back into a more peaceful, relaxed pace. The young man's assailants were both convicted of manslaughter and were sentenced, because of their age, to detention. The local council cleared some of the trees obscuring views into the park off its main street, near where the teen met his death, and installed CCTV cameras in the area. The black marble plaque, surrounded by bunches of dried and silk flowers anchored with rocks, sits under the shade of a claret ash tree, its bark bearing a cross painted in white and the bold letters RIP. Every autumn, its leaves turn blood-red. 'We should get past the things that divide us,' says the gold lettering on the plaque, 'and focus only on the things that unite us'. Just 20 metres away stands the town's war memorial, its tower inscribed with the words Lest We Forget.

Visitors to Griffith now not only visit the area's wineries and open-air museum Pioneer Park, and take photographs of the lush farmlands in the distance from the lookouts; they also ask about another aspect of the town made famous by the second series of the hit TV drama *Underbelly*: its past as a centre for marijuana growth and distribution in the 1970s. By driving west out of town, they can stare at one of the magnificent mansions where drug baron Robert Trimbole once lived, as one of the 'crims in grass castles', and ruminate on the tragic loss of politician and anti-drugs campaigner Don Mackay, murdered by the drug barons.

But on the other side of town, Mitchell Litchfield is helping build a quite different future. Now graduating as a fully qualified youth worker, and having passed another certificate in drug and alcohol work, he's exceeded Father Chris's expectations. 'I am so proud of the way he has developed, and his enthusiasm for the work,' says Father Chris. 'I think he is grateful for us believing in him and giving him the opportunity. Now he is thinking of doing further studies at university, and we will be happy to give him a job for as long as he wants it.'

It's easy to see why he gets on so well with the kids of the area. A thickset young man with the shoulders of a rugby league prop and very short dark hair, he has a large tattoo covering his right forearm, yet has a very gentle, softly spoken manner. The tattoo is of his surname, written in Gothic script. 'I've always been very family-oriented,' he explains. Kathy McKenzie overheard, one day, a young boy asking him why he chose the path he finally did. Mitchell replied that he'd once been in a lot of trouble but, when he'd gone to a youth counselling service to ask for help, he was told there'd be no-one available for four to six weeks. 'I hope that if someone needs help, I'll be there for them, and offer them help immediately,' he told the kid. 'And I hope my experiences will help me support them.'

Kathy smiles. 'Maybe he'll always have his knockers, as some people refuse to believe someone can ever change,' she says. 'But I know how far he's come, what great work he's doing now to help others, and what a passion he has for this work.'

Since the Outback award for rural leadership, Mitchell has also appeared in newspapers and spoken on radio about young people in rural and remote areas, and their future. He's appeared on TV with Father Chris a couple of times, too. One appearance wasn't so easy, when Father Chris's huge Great Dane insisted on trying to climb onto Mitchell's lap on camera, and then his pet bird bit the host.

'Looking at him now, and where he came from, he's done exceptionally well,' says Savin Barone. 'When he was younger, he could have gone either way, but he ended up finding a path that was very positive. Now he's using that to share his knowledge with others in similar circumstances. He's got a strong sense of character and self-belief to have achieved so much.'

Of course, it's sometimes difficult to completely shrug off a troubled past, and there are still two bars in Griffith that haven't lifted their bans from four years ago. Sometimes that can rankle but since they're still refusing to review their decisions, he says he'd rather not go where he's not wanted anyway. 'I used to get really affected by people looking down on me,' he says quietly. 'Some of those people won't ever believe that someone can change. And sometimes there's no point in trying to persuade them; they won't be swayed. But now I've changed my attitude. I think it's their problem; they can think what they like. I know what I am and what I've achieved over the last few years. Sometimes, it's hard to give yourself credit, but then you just concentrate on helping others instead.'

His mum says she knows how hard that can be for him when people refuse to believe someone can turn their life around – and so dramatically – but she hopes his actions will speak even louder than words. 'He's come such a long way,' she says. 'We're so proud of him. Visiting him in jail and sitting in a cell with him wasn't much fun, but I've told him you can never forget your past; you just have to learn from it. One of his strengths in the work he now does is that he can say he's been there. I think that's going to help him, too, in his ambition to help the most hardened cases who think there's no way out. He wants to show that it is possible to break the cycle. He's very passionate about that.'

Occasionally, Mitchell can still struggle with depression but now he has plenty of strategies to cope, and is always eager to help anyone else suffering similarly. 'I still have a huge drive to better myself, and improve my youth work and leadership skills,' says Mitch. 'I'm now doing work that I love, and it feels like a great privilege to have a second chance and to help so many other young people. I just want to keep doing this for as long as I can.'

8

Cheeky Dogs and Lost Boys

Joie Boulter, *Tennant Creek, Northern Territory*

As the car noses its way into a camp on the outskirts of the remote Outback town of Tennant Creek, a pack of dogs races up beside it, whining and barking their welcome. There's a squeal of delight from inside the car, and the window is rapidly wound down. Joie Boulter stops the car and hands the young man next to her a bag full of bones. 'Here you are,' she says, smiling. 'They're all yours.'

As he tosses bones out to the waiting dogs, Dion Beasley's grin is wider than the packed dirt road winding its way around the rickety homes. There's the odd snarl and spat as the dogs fight over the meatiest scraps but soon there's no sound except a steady, concentrated gnawing. Joie drives a few metres on, and Dion taps her on the arm, pointing to another dog in the distance. His hands flutter excitedly, explaining in sign language which dog he's seen.

'Ah, the grey one with the big head . . . he's your favourite,' nods Joie, signing back to him. 'Let's go and see him.'

They drive on a little further and more dogs appear as if by magic. Dion takes a second handful of bones and flings it out of the window. One narrowly misses Joie's head as he attempts – in vain – to throw it out of the driver's window. He looks apologetic. She laughs and scrabbles on the floor to find it, then jettisons it herself.

'You know, I'm not even all that keen on dogs, really, and I'm terrified of running one of them over,' she confides, as Dion gazes intently at the disparate group now all contentedly chewing on the bones, or carrying them off to safe hiding places. 'But Dion loves doing this, and I think it's good for him to be able to care for others. It helps them – and him.'

Dion certainly looks happy enough, and why shouldn't he? When Joie came into his life six years ago, he was a skinny, under-nourished little Aboriginal boy, at risk of becoming completely sidelined by mainstream society. With muscular dystrophy and profound deafness, as well as a degree of autism, and with parents who couldn't care for him, he was isolated in a silent world of his own, unable to communicate with anyone, and completely bewildered by life. A health worker who'd seen him a couple of years before reported that she didn't think he'd even make it into his teens.

But today, he's a happy, healthy, confident kid who's learning sign language and has become the toast of the town with his new-found talent for drawing enchanting cartoon-like pictures of dogs. With his work now exhibited in art galleries and adorning a range of T-shirts, aprons and tea towels that are about to go on sale all over Australia, he's become a minor celebrity, admired and celebrated in turn. Once, he was referred to only as 'Mad One'. These days, adoring children call out, 'Dion! Dion!' as he whizzes past in his wheelchair or on his electric scooter.

'I'm sure anyone could have helped him if they'd had the time,' says Joie, the woman who's completely transformed his life. 'You don't have to be a Rhodes Scholar to take on a kid like Dion. I'm no-one special. I just believe that everyone deserves to have someone care for them in their lives.'

Joie Boulter has always been a caring kind of woman. Growing up on a dairy farm in the Murray Valley town of Cohuna in northern Victoria, the second oldest of three girls and two boys, she decided early on that she wanted to help others. Teaching seemed the obvious choice and after training at Bendigo Teachers' College, she went to work at a primary school in Swan Hill, 80 kilometres north of her home town on the New South Wales border. She took to the profession with a passion. Three years in, she felt there were kids in greater need in more far-flung Outback locations, and applied for a job on remote Elcho Island, off the coast of Arnhem Land.

To Joie, it felt idyllic. Shepherdson College, a community education centre at Galiwin'ku, 550 kilometres east of Darwin, was accessible only by barge or a twice-weekly flight. All power would go off at 9 p.m. each evening and, during the school holidays, all the teachers were encouraged to work at a different job on the island, rather than leave. 'But the people were great there,' says Joie. 'The isolation didn't worry me at all.'

It was a profession that suited her perfectly, according to her youngest sister, Nancy O'Loughlin. Joie always liked to help others and to make sure everyone had an opportunity to thrive. 'She's a very supportive person, and especially loved to help the underdog,' says Nancy. 'And she's always opted for big, ambitious projects, and sees them through to the end. She's very capable, and I've always been amazed how much she can fit into a day.'

Doing some relief teaching for a few weeks on the mainland, Joie met carpenter Tony Boulter, from a Mount Isa miner's family, who was building houses for an Aboriginal community. Their courtship didn't exactly go smoothly. Travelling with a friend one afternoon from Elcho Island on a boat to meet him, Joie was dropped at the wrong spot on the Arnhem Land coast and the pair ended up driving through thick bush on their little motorbikes, up and down hills, steering around towering termite mounds, for hours to find their rendezvous. When her friend's bike broke down after sunset, he took her bike and said he'd return to pick her up. 'But take this gun,' he told her. 'There are a lot of buffalo around here; it could be dangerous.' He roared off into the night, leaving Joie in the pitch black, stumbling around the wilderness with no idea where she was. 'I just plodded along until at last some vehicle headlights came towards me,' says Joie. 'Then the driver yelled out, "What are you doing out here?" I'd been miles away from where I was meant to be . . .'

Despite those early hiccups, the couple married and went over to the Papua New Guinean capital Port Moresby to work, Joie teaching in an international school and Tony working for the harbour board. Later, they moved to Darwin, and then on to Tennant

Creek in 1979 where Joie again taught and Tony was offered a job with the Department of Transport and Works. 'I thought this would be another interesting experience,' says Joie. 'And I'm still here, thirty years on.'

It was an interesting time to be in Tennant Creek, a small township 500 kilometres north of Alice Springs, originally established as a repeater station for the Overland Telegraph in 1872. The scene of Australia's last gold rush in the 1930s, popular lore has it that the town proper grew up where a beer truck broke down in an area occupied by 600 miners. Before then, it was inhabited by the Warumungu, an Indigenous people famous for chasing Scottish explorer John McDouall Stuart off their lands by setting fire to the dense spinifex growing across their country. By the time Joie arrived, they'd just lodged their land claim under the Aboriginal Land Rights Act. It was to become one of the longest and hardest-fought court battles in Australia and only in 1993 were parcels of their land finally handed back.

Tennant Creek was a place, says Miles Franklin award–winning author Alexis Wright, where 'more stars than you could see anywhere on earth shine across the sky so brightly and so close. Where you could imagine that if you looked up long enough you could reach up to heaven. And the leaves of the konkleberry and wild orange glow from the moon moving towards the western horizon. The light from so far away strikes the trunks of bloodwood and turpentine to find the soft hues of grey and white and brown.' [Grog War, *Magabala Books, WA, 2000*]

At the heart of the 240 000 square kilometre Barkly Tableland, stretching from the Tanami Desert to the west, towards the border with Queensland to the east and covering an area more than that of the entire United Kingdom, Tennant Creek's remoteness was a charm for many. Black soil and red dust, with great flat plains of cracking claypans dotted with tussocks of Mitchell grass, it's a long way from anywhere. Tourists will often stop over at the Devil's Marbles, an area of massive granite boulders 106 kilometres south of town, which are bathed in a fiery red at sunrise and sunset, but will rarely give Tennant Creek a second glance. There are no commercial flights in and the Ghan train and long-distance buses all arrive and depart in the middle of the night, hardly conducive to stopping over.

Back in 1979, the 3500-strong community wasn't exactly cohesive. Of the 60 per cent Aboriginal population, the majority were struggling to come to terms with being forced off their lands by the pastoralists, moved again when the mines were discovered and then shuffled into substandard homes in the five pitifully overcrowded camps on the fringes of town. A number had been working on cattle stations but had been unceremoniously sacked when minimum wage legislation was introduced. With alcohol being pushed by fourteen retail liquor outlets – more per head than in any other area of Australia – many had began to drink, and rates of alcohol-fuelled violence, abuse, addiction, mental illness and early death were on a steep ascent.

The Julalikari Council was the main Aboriginal body in town, and as well as campaigning for better health and housing services, with good results, they also set up Australia's first Night Patrol, to pick up intoxicated people in town and take them home – an experiment that was later duplicated all around the country. When the council proposed limiting the amount of alcohol available on the streets, however, there was a massive backlash both from licensees and some members of the white community. It took two long years of court battles and challenges for the Julalikari Council to be allowed to introduce, from 1995, one alcohol-free day a week on benefits day – the historic Thirsty Thursday, when takeaway liquor was banned, the pubs' front bars were closed and sales of large wine casks were stopped.

Federal government changes later stymied the initiative, and alcohol consumption then increased again, with an average annual alcohol consumption equivalent to 15.8 litres of pure alcohol, compared with 9.81 litres nationally. Assaults in Tennant Creek rose by 39 per cent, and the region recorded a domestic violence rate two and half times higher than in the Northern Territory as a whole. In 2008, another scheme was put in place to try to control the problem, with no drinking allowed in public in the town, restrictions on the sale of cask wine, tougher controls on liquor service, and treatment and rehab programs. 'It's really improved things in Tennant Creek now,' says the town's police chief, Superintendent Megan Rowe. 'There's a lot less violence and drunkenness on the streets, and women are able to spend their money on food and the kids instead of having it taken off them for drink. Now I think it's time to look at having a new Thirsty Thursday regime again.'

While alcohol claimed many lives, it damaged so many more. Little Dion Beasley was one sad victim. His parents were both ravaged by alcohol and the Alywarre boy had spent time in the small 360-person town of Alpurrurulam (also known as Lake Nash) near the Queensland border, as well as in the 200-person settlement Canteen Creek, 300 kilometres south-east of Tennant Creek. In 2003, he turned up in the special unit of Joie's school. With welfare services keeping an eye on him, he was at that time living with an aunt until she returned to Canteen Creek, and then he moved in with his grandfather at Mulga Camp, at the northern end of town.

Joie's heart instantly went out to the child. He was very small for his twelve years, and the muscular dystrophy, an inherited progressive muscle-wasting illness, combined with his deafness, seemed to make life difficult to cope with. He always looked confused about what was happening around him. 'He was a bit wild to say the least. He had no language, no communication and didn't know what was going on,' she says. 'Because everything was strange, he would refuse to do anything. I'd say he was lonely and absolutely lost. The world was one big scary place.'

She wondered how she could possibly help him when she didn't even know any sign language but, as she started to spend more and more time with Dion, gradually he began to respond to the attention. He grew calmer and less anxious, and the temper tantrums and violent outbursts he displayed when he became frustrated at not being understood became much fewer. Joie retired from teaching in 2004 but kept up her relationship with Dion and, when his grandfather John Beasley had to go into hospital at the beginning of 2009, it seemed only natural that he ask Joie for help. 'There was no-one else there to care responsibly for Dion,' says Joie. 'Dion is part of a very large family but circumstances are such that it is difficult for him to have the appropriate care in that environment. One of the biggest challenges for lots of people is treating Dion as a normal boy who likes to be included in all the kinds of activities available to other children – to have fun and be loved. He can take a lot of looking after.'

After living for her first twelve years in Tennant Creek in a caravan, and then in a small house before she and Tony moved to their current roomy home on the outskirts of town, Joie was well set up to lend a hand. By May 2009, Dion had moved in with her more or less permanently. The pair began to make real headway. When Joie sketched out the order of their day – get up, shower, breakfast and so on – Dion seemed to become instantly much more settled.

'He latched on to that, knowing what was going to happen during the day and knowing that, at the end of the day, he would hopefully be in the same place,' she says. 'If we're going away, we work out how many sleeps before we come back and who we're going to see, so his world seems to make a lot more sense. You can only imagine what might be going on in his head. I would be scared to death if someone put me in a car and I didn't know if I was ever going to return or who I was going to live with, and it seems that his early life had been just like that.'

Dion's grandfather eventually came out of hospital but he was still very unwell, so Dion continued to live with Joie and Tony. 'I think Dion believes that when his grandad gets strong, he'll go back with him to live, but the reality is, that's not going to happen. He's an old Aboriginal man who's worked hard all his life, and won't grow any stronger. This arrangement is working out for us all.'

Following Dion's eighteenth birthday, Joie, John and the Public Guardian were appointed as his joint adult guardians.

*

A keen artist herself, and a seamstress, Joie always planned to spend time making wearable art and doing exhibition work when she retired. So when she saw the drawings Dion did at school, she recognised immediately how much talent he had. He drew pictures about his home life, which then provided an avenue of communication between the pair, and all his drawings seemed to feature dogs – fat ones, thin ones, happy ones, angry ones, each one with a personality completely its own.

'Then some *really* cute dogs started happening!' she says. 'They were just beautiful. I realised he'd been drawing all the dogs that are a permanent feature of life in the Aboriginal town camps. There are so many of them around all the time, and to be able reproduce their features so beautifully he'd obviously been watching them closely and committed them all to memory.'

Close friend Georgina Bracken, the manager of the women's refuge in town and the chair of Barkly Arts, was astonished when Joie showed her Dion's drawings. 'They were fantastic!' she says. 'They grabbed me straightaway. My first thought was: Mambo, eat your heart out!'

Encouraged by Georgina's reaction and realising how much Dion loved dogs, Joie then started buying him books about dogs, soft toy dogs and plastic figurines. Dion's eyes would light up each time he saw anything new about dogs, and he spent more and more time sketching. His enthusiasm then began to stretch to all animals – except frogs. After being startled one morning by a green frog in the toilet (a common occurrence in those parts) he insisted the bathroom always be checked before he went in. Playfully threatening to put a frog down his shirt became an effective way of persuading Dion to behave when he was determined not to.

But it wasn't long before Joie hit on an idea.

'Because Dion was getting older and he needed a job, I thought if he's got talent, he should be channelling it in the right direction,' she says. 'So we tried to put a few of his dog drawings on T-shirts, and they turned out to be a great hit. The girls in school bought them and loved them. So we puddled along from there.

'We then bought forty T-shirts from the local shop and we got them printed locally at the Julalikari Women's Arts and Craft Centre. Then we got on to Darwin graphic artist Stan Whiting to do our little Cheeky Dog logo, which we then trademarked. So we started the Cheeky Dog company in 2006. We now send the designs to the Queensland T-Shirt Company, who use them to make up and print T-shirts, as well as aprons, bags and tea towels, and send them back here for us to distribute. We really launched into it knowing nothing. We probably did lots of things back to front, but we were keen to do something at the time.'

Dion receives a royalty for each item sold, which goes into a trust fund that will help to support him if he needs it as his illness progresses. 'I think it's important he stays in the community he knows, and this will be a bit of insurance if he needs to pay any-one for help,' says Joie. 'His money keeps rolling in and, while it's not a lot, it'll accumulate over time. It's funny: he's now got more money than we have!'

Dion sits on the veranda of Joie's house, doodling dogs all over his pad. He smiles as he draws a particularly fierce dog, which is baring his teeth in front of a smaller one. He's drawn a simi-larly dangerous-tempered dog before, menacing a smaller one, with the line below it: 'Cheekydogs don't mix'. Another day, he drew a whole pageful of little dogs that became 'One hundred and one Cheekydogs'. A particular favourite is three dogs running: 'Cheekydogs race'. And in his 'Off to Canteen Creek', forty-odd dogs are crammed into the back of an old ute ready to go visiting.

Those same cheeky dogs won him the top prize in the annual Memento Awards in 2005, which showcase fresh, contemporary, commercially viable craft, art and design, and the starring role in a number of exhibitions. They also run and bark over the uniforms of the local council.

At home, in his bedroom, he's lined up fifty toy animals in careful groupings of species that would do Noah proud. His books on dogs line another shelf, while DVDs of dogs and other animals sit in piles on the side. His *Lion King* DVD, which he insists on watching religiously every morning, takes pride of place.

Joie's taken Dion to the Royal Institute for Deaf and Blind Children in Sydney, which organised for him to be seen by several specialists. While he cooperated with them over his hearing and sight, he wasn't quite so compliant when they tried to measure his intellectual abilities. 'I think he gets sick of doing medical examinations, and people saying do this, walk here, walk there, write it down, and then saying do it all again,' explains Joie, running her fingers through her short grey hair.

'But when the psychologists want him to do tests, recognising patterns in groups of numbers and then copying them on to different pieces of paper, he doesn't understand why it's necessary. He doesn't see any purpose to it. Then he starts playing games. He deliberately gives the wrong answers and can do that again and again and again, until people eventually give up. He does it with me sometimes, so I recognise it when he does it to others. He likes to do the wrong thing and turns it into a game. The psychologists realised he knew a lot more than he was letting on. He has so much knowledge locked away there.'

Dion, now eighteen, has a degree of autism too, with a sufferer's typical love of order, routine and repetition, and distress when something can't be done at its regular time or place. Always wanting to wear black socks whenever he goes out, he also has to take with him a number of sticks, all the same length, shape and colour, which he arranges meticulously beside him. 'He's got an incredible memory for things, too, and a remarkable skill for reproducing them,' says Joie, now sixty. 'One day, he drew the houses in Alpurrurulam where he used to live with his family, the streets of the town and the hospital nearby, yet he hadn't been there for at least ten years. It was an exact aerial view – yet he'd never been in a plane over the town. He's also fascinated with numbers, and remembers all the numbers of the houses where the camp dogs live.'

Superintendent Rowe says Joie has done wonders with Dion. 'I'm absolutely impressed with them,' she says. 'Joie is very giving, and she's obviously devoted to Dion, and I'm not surprised the Cheeky Dog label is taking off. They're a fantastic product, and his drawings of the dogs in the town camps are quite unique. He now seems so happy.'

Every day, Dion goes off to school – the school's said he can stay as long as he wants to – to make sure he gets to socialise with other kids, then Joie takes him off to the camps to feed the dogs. That can be a quick or slow process, depending on the number of dogs that turn up. Few will ever forget the day a whole horde turned up to see Dion, and Joie ended up having to break up a dog fight over the food, prising them apart with a shovel handle. After feeding the dogs, Dion goes to his grandad's home, where the table is always cleared to give him room for his pad, pencils and stick collection. 'I'm very proud of him,' says his grandad John Beasley. 'He is a good artist. His dogs are very funny.'

Later, he'll often go for a swim in the town pool where he can move around in the water more freely than he's ever able to on dry land. Sometimes he'll go in the car with Joie, at other times in his wheelchair, and now regularly on his new electric scooter, designed along the lines of a Harley Davidson motorbike, with Joie cycling behind to keep a watchful eye on him. 'When he saw one in a shop, he jumped on it and then we saw the huge plate glass display window in front,' says Joie. 'He was heading straight for it, so Tony had to dive in front of him. He ended up running up Tony's leg – but that was better than smashing into the glass! The shop staff then told us he should have a little old people's bike with four wheels, but he wanted the Harley. He loves it.'

Back at home, he'll sit and draw, play in the inflatable pool that's been put up in the front garden, and continue his and Joie's joint project of learning Auslan, Australia's sign language, from a book. Otherwise, his only means of communication is via a series of grunts and indistinguishable noises. 'But we talk lots and lots with our hands, each guessing to fill in the gaps between the signing, and we always have a bit of a laugh and a joke. The main subject of conversation, of course, is dogs. He's got lots of ideas and he knows what he wants and has plenty of opinions on things. He's extremely talented, is very curious about everything and he's got heaps of potential. We just need more communication skills and we're working on those, as well as reading and writing.'

At school, his sudden progress has delighted his teachers. With Auslan, he's now able to communicate with others much more than he could before, and many of the other kids are learning snippets in order to be able to talk to him. The day he sat at the back of the class, passing notes with two other boys and laughing rather than concentrating on the film being shown, teacher Jacqui Israel didn't have the heart to reprimand him.

'It was just so lovely to see him interacting with others so much more than he ever did before,' she says. 'In the past six months alone, he's become so much more open and communicative and we're seeing huge changes in him. You get the feeling his world is starting to open up before him now, and even his art is changing. Before, he'd just draw dogs. When he came back from Sydney, he actually drew a picture of himself sitting in the plane, looking down at a dog. Before, he seemed very isolated. Now, at the recent school formal, he was dancing away in his wheelchair and girls were dancing with him, and he had his hand on a speaker to feel the music. It's wonderful to see.'

Such progress, of course, is mostly down to Joie and her devotion. She shrugs. 'I'm very fond of him, we're as thick as thieves,' she says. 'We have differences of opinion but he's the most forgiving person. I used to hold grudges, but he's been good for me in that. He says, "Are you angry? Will I have to go back to Canteen Creek?" Then I feel super-guilty! He's generally a very soft, loving boy. But it would help if we knew more about his background; we still only have snippets.'

Dion's muscular dystrophy has, sadly, progressed over the past few years, with his mobility more and more impaired. He can walk only short distances with the aid of a walker, and must use the wheelchair or his scooter for longer distances. But Joie's sister Nancy has seen other changes in Dion in the time he's been with Joie. Now healthy and well fed, he's a lot more relaxed around people he doesn't know. 'He's so much more outgoing and he can interact with people, and play to his audience,' says Nancy. 'He's terribly endearing. I think he keeps Joie young, too. She can be frustrated with the lack of health resources to help, but she loves having him there, and she has made a huge difference to his life.'

Tony, now seventy-four and currently the deputy president of the Barkly Shire Council, with four children of his own from a previous marriage, has surprised himself too by so warmly welcoming Dion into the family. 'It wasn't until Joie became involved that I really took notice of him,' he says. 'As far as I'm concerned now, Dion is our son. He has become part of us. He does have very set ideas and likes to do things his way and, at times, tends to push the envelope, but that's the same with any child.'

Georgina Bracken remains touched by the relationship between Joie and Dion. While she says Joie is a very talented artist in her own right, she's full of admiration for how much time and effort her friend has put into the boy. 'There's not many people who'd do something like this, and even put all the time into learning sign language,' she says. 'But Joie's a very community-minded person, very creative, energetic and dedicated.'

A businessperson from Western Australia is now interested in taking Cheeky Dog to the next level, with a website and a far more comprehensive distribution and sales system, so hopefully the products, with Dion's two dozen-plus designs, will soon be available all over Australia. Dion will then start to have a national profile, too. Apart from the income, that's been Joie's main priority – that Dion is not forgotten. An Aboriginal kid with severe disabilities could so easily fall through the cracks; that's something that is less likely to happen to a talented artist with a successful business.

'I suppose I did meddle in his life, but for a very good reason,' she laughs. 'I couldn't sit by with a conscience and let him just fade away. Now I can see him indulging his passion in art, and his self-esteem is really growing. A lot of people tell me his art makes them laugh, too, and I think it's wonderful if you can put a bit of lightness into the world. And in the process, Dion's gone from being hugely at risk, at the bottom of the pecking order, to a happy boy who's achieved a lot publicly and is valued and important in the community. You don't have to be special to spend time with someone, and give them what they need.'

Beside her, Dion suddenly taps his leg to get her attention and points to his feet, wanting his socks. She smiles, shakes her head and asks him, in sign language, if he's perhaps broken a limb and therefore can't fetch them himself. He grins back at her, then pushes off in his wheelchair to find them.

'I've learnt lots from him,' she says softly. 'I was a crabby old schoolteacher, but he's made me think about a lot of things, and see things through new eyes. I've been in tears plenty of times but there are times when you're with him when your heart sings. Even though he's young and I'm old, we have a great rapport. Seeing his wonderment, when he understands something and the light goes on and the eyes shine . . . it's wonderful. It's been a remarkable journey.'

9

Angels Really Do Have Wings

Cheryl Arentz, *Brisbane, Queensland*

The young girl stands on the beach, staring at the waves lapping close to her feet, lost in wonder at her first ever sight of the sand and the sea. A smile slowly spreads over her face, and she dips one toe cautiously into the water. Watching her, Cheryl Arentz feels her heart overflow.

When Cheryl first met Kayla Graham, the child's future looked short and bleak. At just seventeen months, she'd lost both her kidneys to renal failure and, at thirteen, her body rejected the new kidney donated by her broken-hearted mother six years before. She'd had a catheter inserted into her body to allow waste to be filtered from the blood to keep her alive, was on dialysis at home six nights a week for thirteen hours at a time, and had to spend long periods in hospital. The doctors told her mum to hope for the best, but to expect the worst: heart failure could soon kick in.

So when Kayla's condition later deteriorated dramatically and she was rushed back into hospital, with a priest called in to baptise her, it seemed this could finally be the end.

But the frail teenager fought back and, against all the odds, she clung on to life. After six months in hospital, she had rallied enough for Cheryl to be given permission to take her out on little day trips. And when Cheryl found out that, at the age of fourteen, Kayla had never before seen the ocean, she drove her from the hospital to the beach for the trip of a lifetime.

'The look on her face was priceless,' says Cheryl softly. 'It was pure joy. She hadn't known what to expect. I held her hand because she wasn't sure about the surf. She wasn't allowed to swim as she was still a very sick girl, but she paddled up to her knees. It was wondrous.'

It's a day that will be forever seared in Cheryl's memory. The little girl had suffered so much in her life – and without a single complaint – it was thrilling to be able to do something for her that would take her mind off the constant series of medical procedures she was undergoing, and the pain and uncertainty of her future.

Cheryl had already been an incredible help in her role as a volunteer pilot with the charity Angel Flight, which flies people from remote areas to cities for non-emergency medical treatment, to save them driving the gruelling, lengthy and often debilitating distances. She'd flown Kayla and members of her family a number of times from their home in Chinchilla, 80 kilometres west of Dalby in Queensland's western Darling Downs, the 300 kilometres to Brisbane for regular dialysis and hospital care, in place of the four-hour road trip each way.

But for a kid, especially one from the Outback, that first

magical glimpse of the ocean, and the first sensations of hot sand between the toes and warm salt water on skin, are experiences to be savoured: stored and treasured.

'Moments like that make you realise that the rest of us really have nothing to complain about,' says Cheryl. 'If you have good health, you have everything. But for children like Kayla . . .' Her voice grows thick with emotion. 'I was just touched that we could give this little girl some hope for the future, that she could come back to the beach when she gets better.

'Every day was a challenge for this girl, and it had been all her life. So to see her happy . . . You end up feeling so much joy, too.'

Cheryl considers herself to have led a fortunate life. With a happy marriage and a good business that she manages with her husband Barry, she's come to share his love of flying and the couple have their own small four-seater plane, which they use for both work and holidays. Their first was a Grumman Tiger, then they bought a Piper Turbo Lance T-Tail. So when Cheryl saw an advertisement in the local newspaper, asking for pilots to volunteer for a new charity to help fly people from the Outback to cities for medical treatment, she and her husband Barry decided immediately to offer their services.

Angel Flight was the brainchild of Bill Bristow, a Queensland businessman and pilot who'd seen a similar group operating with enormous success in the United States. He felt the concept could work even better in Australia, with 30 per cent of its population living outside metropolitan areas, and often having to travel vast distances for medical services. Since those people generally suffer higher mortality rates and greater incidences of heart disease, stroke and respiratory illnesses, he felt a service like this was badly needed. 'On top of this, when they need to access treatment for these conditions, and others such as cancer and leukaemia, they have to endure extraordinarily long and uncomfortable trips by road, often on a regular basis,' he says. 'I felt an idea like Angel Flight could make a real difference to Australians.' In 2005, he won the Queensland section of the Australian of the Year Award for the scheme.

To Cheryl, it sounded wonderful. So many people in rural, remote and Outback areas are extremely long distances away from major city hospitals and medical facilities, and might have neither the funds nor the strength to travel so far for help. 'We thought it seemed a really good idea, and we both felt we'd been fairly lucky ourselves over the years, so we wanted to give something back,' says Cheryl. 'We've been blessed with good health so you really feel for those who don't have it. We wanted to make a contribution and it seemed here our flying skills were needed. So it made perfect sense.'

Cheryl's first flight for the charity was in January 2004. Her task was to pick up a pair of nine-month-old twin boys, Alister and Mitchell Keene, and their mum Rebecca in Brisbane, where Mitchell had undergone open-heart surgery. Four days after the operation, he'd had a stroke. Now he was finally well enough to go home to Thargomindah, a tiny town on the edge of the Strzelecki Desert, 1014 kilometres west of Brisbane. The drive would have taken the little family fifteen hours, with feeding and toilet stops. In Cheryl's plane, it would take just three.

However, the journey didn't unfold quite as Cheryl imagined.

Rebecca phoned the day before the flight and asked if she could possibly bring a carton of nappies on board with her. She'd found some for sale in the city at a very low price and, with two baby boys in the Outback, they were usually an enormous expense. Cheryl happily agreed. A little while later, she called again. They were *very* cheap; could she bring two?

The cartons were much bigger than Cheryl had thought and with the babies' twin stroller and the month's luggage on board, she had to tear the cartons open if they had any hope of fitting all the nappies in the plane. In the end, they flew to Thargomindah in an aircraft stuffed nose to tail with nappies.

They still laugh about it today. 'It's amazing how many nappies you can fit in a small plane!' marvels Rebecca. 'They were in the spaces under seats, everywhere. With little twin boys, you get through a fair few! That was our first experience with Cheryl, and luckily it didn't put her off.'

Cheryl later flew the family back and forth another five times, as Mitchell had to return for more heart surgery and regular treatment and Alister then had to be operated on for a urinary tract problem. Other Angel Flight pilots took them a number of times, too. But both boys are now doing well and, at the age of seven and now at school, Mitchell shows no signs of his earlier stroke. 'Cheryl and Angel Flight have been real lifesavers,' says Rebecca. 'She's one of those very genuine people who lives to help others and is really interested in humankind. We still see her whenever our paths cross. She's great!'

Rebecca was so grateful for all the help she received from Angel Flight, she became a keen fundraiser for them. She started out making breakfasts for tourists passing through town, and those staying in caravans locally, with her earnings donated back to help cover fuel costs. She's also done some public speaking on their behalf, trying to increase awareness about the service they offer.

Cheryl sees them often since Thargomindah is a regular refuelling stop, and the family makes a point of coming out to see her at the airport. The first time Rebecca brought the boys, then aged four, to see her, the twins immediately both climbed into the plane, assuming they had to go to hospital for more operations. 'It was automatic for those boys,' laughs Cheryl. 'But it was so good to be able to tell them no, not this time!'

Cheryl Quirk was born in Cunnamulla, the administrative centre of the vast Paroo Shire of south-west Queensland, 970 kilometres west of Brisbane and 120 kilometres north of the New South Wales border.

Her dad Neville was head manager of the 100 000-hectare sheep station Garramen, where he'd started working as a fifteen year old after a childhood in Lismore. Her mum Dorothy was a city girl from Brisbane, who'd met her husband-to-be while working at a big department store in town. Although she followed her heart to the Outback to be with him, she never really got used to living there. She worked hard, cooking for the staff and stockmen, as well as looking after the couple's first child Ian and then Cheryl, but always found it lonely.

It was little better when the family moved to another property, this time in Barcaldine, 110 kilometres east of Longreach. Another two daughters were born, Leanne and Rhea, and Dorothy found herself forced to home-school the entire brood. Because there were no other children around and they only spoke to adults, they all started calling their parents Nev and Dot. 'She had to get that out of us very quickly!' remembers Cheryl. 'Dad was away a lot working, and the isolation was always the hardest thing for my mum.'

When the oldest children were ready for high school, it was only a matter of time before they moved closer to town. The shift came in 1969 when Neville bought a small 40-hectare farm outside the beef town of Casino, beside the Richmond River 30 kilometres west of his Lismore home town in northern New South Wales, and made ends meet by working in the local meat-works and then the operating plant.

On finishing school, Cheryl went to the local TAFE college and enrolled in commerce and secretarial studies – back then, nobody had the money to pay for university. Afterwards, she went to work at a motor dealership, but took a part-time course in ticketing and sign-writing. It was while she was doing some sign-writing for the local Lions Club that she met the club president, Barry Arentz. Impressed by her drive, he offered her a job at his motor dealer-ship. In 1984, he married her.

Cheryl, then just twenty-six, had been swept off her feet by her good-looking, highly motivated and entrepreneurial boss. Dur-ing national service in the air force, he'd learnt to fly and had loved it ever since. With the couple now living in Brisbane, he used his plane regularly to fly back to Casino so Cheryl could visit her parents. He also flew around the country looking at cars to buy for his business, particularly as it started to grow. Cheryl had found a new job with a pharmaceutical company in Brisbane but even-tually left it to help Barry run his firm. In the meantime, Barry diversified by importing Lincolns, classic American vehicles, and converting them to right-hand drive, and then just bringing them in and selling them without the conversion. He'd fly over to the US to look at vehicles, or to various places in Australia that might have one for sale.

'For him, flying was a means of transport but was also a challenging sport,' says Cheryl. 'I wasn't born with a love of aviation but, because he flew, I decided to do a spouse course, which is where the partner learns to fly in case something happens to the pilot. I enjoyed the two-day course very much. The instructor said I had a natural ability, but I didn't really; Barry had been teaching me along the way!'

The course finished on the Sunday and the very next morning Cheryl turned up at the flying school with the plane, determined to get her own licence. 'I had the aircraft, I had a bit of knowledge and I had really enjoyed the challenge,' she says. 'I used to enjoy it with my husband, and now I thought I wanted to learn.' She passed her private pilot's licence in 1990, her night licence in 1996, her commercial licence in 2002, which meant that she was allowed to take paying passengers, and her instrument rating in 2008. 'I learnt to love flying,' she says. 'Every flight is different, every day is different. It keeps your mind active, you have to be fit and healthy, and it's rewarding.'

Increasingly, the couple started using the plane for pleasure, circumnavigating Australia and visiting Papua New Guinea for the challenging flying conditions, the magnificent terrain and the chance to deliver medical and school supplies to some of the remote villages.

Some of Cheryl's favourite flying, however, was always around

Australia's Outback. She fell in love, in turn, with Uluru, Alice Springs, Innamincka, Broome and Fitzroy Crossing, where a cow managed to wander onto the airport tarmac even after new security gates had been installed as a result of the September 11 terrorist attacks.

'The most amazing things always happen in the Outback,' Cheryl says with a laugh. 'I was born in the Outback and, although my family is now in Casino, I still love going back there. I think there's a different air about the people who live in the country. They are so friendly and so gracious about the hardships they have to put up with. They're accepting, somehow, whereas we complain in the cities if we don't have airconditioning! I just love that about the Outback.'

Since Angel Flight's launch in April 2003 as a not-for-profit charity, the number of volunteer pilots who donate their skills and the bulk of their aircraft operating expenses to fly people around the country for non-emergency help has increased from eighty-eight to 2200 nationwide – nearly half the total number of qualified general aviation pilots in Australia. Last year, they made over 2000 flights, passing the 8000-flight mark since the scheme began. In addition, there are close to 3000 ground volunteers, or Earth Angels, who pick up the patients from airports and drive them to hospitals, or vice versa. With doctors and hospitals becoming increasingly aware of the service, it's facing more and more demand.

For the first two years after Cheryl joined, pilots paid all their fuel costs, but Airservices Australia never charged air navigation fees and airports waived their landing fees. Now the service raises sufficient donations to cover the fuel, so pilots simply give their time – and the costs of keeping their planes in the air. By the start of 2010, Cheryl had made seventy-three flights for Angel Flight, and Barry fifty-four. 'It was something we could do to give back to society,' says Cheryl. 'With our own business, we can take time off when we want to, so it works out well for us.'

For those in the Outback, Angel Flight is proving invaluable. When some patients come in, they might be leaving children or other dependent family members behind, so the time saved by a return flight home straight after an operation can be critical. They can also go home after an operation and return for follow-ups relatively easily, rather than staying in hospital for months at a time. Many would have no hope of being able to afford to pay for such a service.

Some flights are for compassionate reasons, too. One of the saddest flights Cheryl and Barry ever made was for a seventeen year old with liver cancer who had just forty-eight hours to live. His last request? He wanted to go home to Goondiwindi, on the Queensland–New South Wales border 360 kilometres from Brisbane, to die. His mother accompanied him on that flight and an ambulance was waiting at the other end to drive him to his house. 'I remember putting the seatbelt across him and he must have had about 200 stitches across his chest,' says Cheryl. 'But he still said thank you so politely. It was so hard to believe he had so little time to live.' In the end, he died seven days later, peacefully and, just as he'd wished, at home.

Another time, Cheryl flew the four children of another cancer sufferer, David, to hospital with him from Charleville, as it wasn't known if he'd come home again. On the way, though, they managed to share a few laughs. One of his boys sitting at the back of the plane asked Cheryl through the headphones if it might be possible to bungee-jump out of the aircraft. Because the plane doors don't actually lock, the firm NO! came very quickly. His youngest brother then announced he wanted to go to the – non-existent – toilet. In the end, both were successfully distracted with a game of I-spy and prizes of jelly beans.

'Some of the flights are sad, but you try not to dwell on that,' says Cheryl. 'One of our regulars is a nine-year-old kidney patient, hoping for a transplant. But if she wasn't with us, she'd be facing her five to six hours in the car, and that's three times a week. Often, the people you're dealing with are very sick, and it can be hot and uncomfortable in the aircraft, so they're not feeling too good, and you have to be aware of their needs. But all of them are very appreciative. Generally, it saves them hours in travelling and gives them more time to be at home with their loved ones.'

There are a few, however, who tend to blanch when they see a woman at the controls of the plane. One very tall, solid man from Mungindi, a town spread over the New South Wales–Queensland border and cut off by flooding at the Barwon River, actually went white when he first saw it was slim, slight Cheryl who was to fly him to Toowoomba for medical treatment for his injured arm. 'I introduced myself as the pilot and I could see the look on his face,' Cheryl laughs. 'It was like Nancy Bird all over again: Oh my God! It's a *woman*! I assured him we are very qualified, and told him that my husband was also a pilot, which I think gave him some relief. But he sat at the back and looked straight ahead the whole flight. Most other people are fine with it – although sometimes you do get asked how many flights you've done, and you do wonder whether men get that too . . .'

Often, Cheryl's happy to go the extra distance to help people when she can. One passenger, Maggie Hartley, was only six when she contracted the worst form of dystonia, a neurological movement disorder with similar symptoms to those of motor neurone disease with its uncontrollable muscle contractions. She was nineteen when Cheryl first met her and couldn't walk, had very bad balance and was plagued at that time by a constant twisting and twitching of her arms and head. Living in Goondiwindi, it would take her mum Lesley and dad Peter seven hours, with the extra time needed to lift her in and out of the car for a toilet break along the way, to drive her to Brisbane for treatment each time. When they moved to Inverell, in northern New South Wales, the car journey took the same amount of time. With Angel Flight, however, it took just two hours, door to door. As well as the thirteen-odd times Cheryl has now flown them, out of their total of twenty-five with Angel Flight, Cheryl would also drive Maggie to and from hospital, and stop off at her favourite takeaway place, KFC, on their way. During the week she stayed, Cheryl would also take her and Lesley to their other favourite restaurant, Sizzler.

'Meals like that were always a big thing for Maggie, and her choice,' says Cheryl. 'She's a lovely girl, very spirited and extremely bright. A beautiful girl in a very cruel body.' After two years of lobbying a specialist to perform a groundbreaking operation on her, when Maggie was twenty she finally had the surgery and her condition improved dramatically. As a result, she only needs a wheelchair occasionally, and has much better control of her body. 'She's now twenty-two, and has improved a lot as a result of treatment, but her arms are still very twisted and her spine is bent when she walks. But she still manages to get those jelly beans out of the container! She's very determined,' says Cheryl.

For Lesley, Cheryl's involvement has made a huge difference. 'She's such a huge part of our lives,' she says. 'The savings in time driving there, staying and driving back has meant my husband is able to go to work and our other daughter, Casey, who's nineteen, can lead a much more normal life, and Maggie has access to great treatment. It's changed our lives hugely, for the better. While Cheryl is a pilot for Angel Flight, and also works as an Earth Angel, there's no doubt in my mind that she's a real angel, too.'

Angel Flight is still a very big part of the lives of both Cheryl, now fifty-one, and Barry, sixty-nine. She treasures some of the close friendships she's made along the way, and has found she just loves helping others. It's not only about improving the quality of their lives; it's also the simple pleasure that doing someone a favour brings.

'Cheryl, like many of our pilots, loves to fly, and also loves to help people,' says Angel Flight's operations manager Terry McGowan. 'She seems to be an extra-special sort of a person, though, because she's one of only a few female pilots, and she'll soon be only the second woman to pass the 100 mark in the number of flights she will have flown for us. She's an excellent pilot and is also unique in that she becomes very involved with the people she's helping. She gets very attached, and they to her. It's always wonderful for us to be associated with people who do so much for others in the world – they can be few and far between!'

Certainly, Cheryl's become much loved by many of her passengers; Kayla Graham, for one. 'Words can't explain how I feel about her,' says Kayla, now nineteen. 'She's a magnificent person, she's caring and she'll do anything for anybody. It's amazing that someone would take so much time out of their lives, and spend so much money, helping someone like me, who they didn't even know at first.

'I remember that day at the beach so well, too. It was amazing. It was big and blue and sunny and so warm. And it was lovely having Cheryl and Barry with me to share it. When you are sick like me, you remember all your firsts . . .'

Kayla's now had a total of 387 journeys with Angel Flight, but she always loves it best when Cheryl's her pilot. Over the years, she's spent a lot of time at Cheryl's Brisbane home, and Cheryl's also taken her to Sea World and Dreamworld, to movies, and to see the sights of Sydney. Often, Kayla's mum Amanda or grandmother Pam will come to the city with her too, and they'll also come along on the other trips Cheryl organises. And with a new kidney given to her two years ago, she's now much better than she's been for a while, although she's still on a strict diet and a lot of medication, and all the time faces the risk of her body rejecting the new kidney. Despite those problems, everyone's hopeful she'll have a long, happy future to enjoy.

'It's been a real gift for us, too,' says Cheryl, the stepmother of Barry's two sons, Nathan and Clinton. 'It sticks in our mind that she never thought she would turn seventeen, and now she's twenty this year! We take for granted every birthday we have, but in her position that's not something you can do. We've all been very touched by her, and with her health improving, hopefully it's going to be a very happy ending.'

Every flight Cheryl makes with the charity puts life into perspective for her. Daily hassles suddenly pale into insignificance when compared to the enormous difficulties some of her passengers are battling. 'We often think work is important, and what we're doing is important,' says Cheryl. 'But it really isn't.

'We both love Angel Flight, we love the way 100 per cent of the donations go straight into the service, and we'll continue working for it as long as we can. It's growing and more and more people are using the service. And for me, it's just great to be in a position where I have a skill that means I can give back.'

10

Broken Wings and Fading Frills

STEPHEN CUTTER, *Palmerston, Northern Territory*

It was the kind of emergency that would send most people flee-ing for their lives. But not Stephen Cutter. The moment the call came in to his wildlife rescue centre, he was speeding his way to the scene.

A two-metre brown water python had become caught in a con-crete manhole cover after trying to slither through an opening in the middle that had proved too tight for its yellow-bellied girth. Too late, it had discovered that it wouldn't be able to slide all the way through, and was now firmly wedged.

Standing there watching the creature writhe in agony and frustration, Stephen hastily worked out a plan of attack. Although water pythons are non-venomous, they do suffocate their prey by constriction and have been known to attack, kill and eat even small crocodiles. With sharp teeth that can deliver a nasty bite, Stephen knew he needed to take care. But he also had to act quickly to save the snake.

With the help of some members of a crowd of curious – but wary – onlookers, he managed to lever up the concrete slab and wrap both it and the python in a large hessian sack, then brought it back to his vet surgery in Palmerston, 20 kilometres south of Darwin. On the step outside, he carefully chipped away at the man-hole cover with a sledgehammer borrowed from a nearby building site until the python had enough room to escape. It gave him barely a second glance as it slithered off quickly.

'Snakes are incredible creatures,' he says with a laugh. 'They survive a lot of things that a lot of other animals never could. Once, somebody found a 3.5-metre olive python that had been run over on the road, with its intestines all over the bitumen. It was pretty squashed, and they felt sure it would die, so they put it in a garbage bin. A couple of days later, they took a look and saw it was still alive. Then they brought it to us and we stitched it back up and put everything back in.

'Eventually, it fully recovered and we were able to release it. There aren't many animals that would survive something like that!' And, to be sure, there aren't many people who'd risk their own personal safety to make sure they do, either.

From his The Ark Animal Hospital, with branches in both Palmerston and Humpty Doo, 20 kilometres further south in the Litchfield area, Stephen cares for a huge range of injured wildlife, as well as for the animals of his ordinary paying clients. When he opened the centres in 2004 and 2006, he made a conscious decision to create a vet practice with a difference – one that looked after wild creatures as well as people's pets. But even the pets aren't always what you'd expect to find. Close to the tip of northern Australia, plenty of households are home to an extraordinary array of animals, from exotic birds and baby possums to every variety of reptile.

At the Palmerston centre, for instance, the injured wildlife undergoing treatment take up nearly the whole of the centre – its yards and surgeries. In the emergency room, there are two red-collared lorikeets sitting gloomily in covered cages, awaiting assessment. Lethargic and definitely under the weather, they were brought in by a concerned householder who spotted them huddled on the ground in the shade of a tree, and worried they could be lunch for any passing predator. Stephen is now treating them for a virus they seem to have picked up, and letting them regain their strength before releasing them.

Nearby is a buff-banded rail, a small ground bird with an orange-brown band on its streaked breast, that was attacked by a cat; it still bears puncture marks on its chestnut neck. A couple of cages down is a pretty black-faced cuckoo shrike with a broken wing that's just had a splint applied. It's a species known for the curious habit of shuffling its wings on landing; it's hoped that, after a month's treatment, this one will be back shuffling with the best of them. In a plastic bucket on the floor are four baby green tree frogs, one of which was hit by a train. Its tiny injured leg has now been pinned and, when it's healed, all four frogs will be set free together. With frogs as a group disappearing worldwide, mostly due to a fungus that people have accidentally spread, and Australia having already lost several species, Stephen will go to any lengths to save them.

Outside in a shallow pit, is a frill-necked lizard whose frill is looking distinctly the worse for wear, actually cracking up and falling off. This little fellow was hit by a car – a common occurrence since lizards don't have too much road sense at the best of times – and Stephen's now fixing him up. 'You're all right,' he coos, picking him up and stroking his scaly back soothingly. 'I know you're not feeling so well now, but don't worry, you'll be fine.' A car also caught the monitor lizard sitting warily in another pit next door. He's now on anti-inflammatories, quietly improving every day.

Just along the way, in one of the largest cages is a brown falcon, with a magnificent plumage ranging from a very rich dark brown to off-white. He was found as an injured baby and nursed back to health by someone who eventually tried to let him go – but he wouldn't leave. In despair, they gave him to a truck driver who was about to make the long journey up to Darwin, and asked him to drop the bird at The Ark. 'We're now in the process of teaching him to be a bird again,' says Stephen. 'From here, he'll go to a bigger aviary, and then hopefully will successfully go back to the wild.' He walks over to another cage, where two baby tawny frog-mouths, silver-grey owl-like birds, are huddled. 'These two also need a bit more practice being birds. They left the nest a little bit too early, and they need more time, more food and more experience. It's the same for those Torres Strait pigeons over there.' He points to another cage where two small cream-coloured birds sit on branches. 'These pigeons fly from here to New Guinea, depending on where the fruit is ripe, but these are fledglings who also left the nest too early, and can't yet fend for themselves. But it's often the teenagers – as with humans – who do the stupid things, like running at cars and putting themselves in danger. They're simply not as skilled at life.'

It doesn't take long to understand why Stephen called his centre The Ark. He seems to have a vast range of creatures, in ones or twos, all being brought here at their lowest points and then being released again as soon as they're well enough. Curlews, orange-footed scrub fowl, a grey pied heron with a broken wing, bats, possums, snakes, crocodiles, stray cats, dogs . . . Over the years, friends have become used to thinking of Stephen as a close relative of Doctor Dolittle – the character who can talk to the animals and shuns human company.

'Stephen likes people, but it's safe to say that he's always happier in the company of animals,' says the manager of his practice, Lisa Hansen. 'When he's with animals, he's very relaxed and knows everything there is to know about them. And if he ever doesn't know something, he'll be like a dog with a bone until he finds out. But with people, he sometimes doesn't feel quite in his comfort zone.'

Certainly, Stephen has a quiet manner with people, and is self-effacing and subdued. With animals, however, he comes into his own, and is assertive and confident. Animals seem to react well to that, too. Everywhere he goes today, for example, he's followed by five bounding crossbred puppies. Two were given to him to be euthanised but, as they were beautifully healthy and loving, he couldn't bear to do so. The three others were dumped on the doorstep of the surgery. Now the five are devoted to him, barely glancing at all their animal patient rivals for his attention.

As someone dedicated to rescuing wildlife in trouble, as well as fixing their injuries before setting them free again, there aren't many creatures Stephen would turn away from his vet centre. All are treated with the gentlest of attention and either helped back into the wild, or found a good home. Cane toads are the only exception.

'They don't have a future here, so there's no benefit in fixing them up and releasing them as they'll go on to hurt other things,' says Stephen. 'But that's no reason to be mean to them; it's not their fault. So we euthanise them humanely by putting a couple of drops of something onto their skin, which is very porous. They have a right to be treated with respect, regardless of the ultimate outcome.'

Born in Melbourne, the second of six children, Stephen moved with his family to Alice Springs when he was three years old. For a kid who loved animals, it was heaven. Living on a large block, the family hand-reared baby kangaroos, had an emu and kept all manner of chickens, ducks and dogs. His passion came to the fore early on, and he began to care for all of the orphaned or injured animals that were regularly brought in to be looked at by his father Trevor, another keen animal lover, and the first doctor employed by the pioneering health service set up by the Central Australian Aboriginal Congress. He wouldn't even allow his father to kill any of the family's roosters or bantams for the dinner table, so they ended up with a fair few dozen feral chickens roaming around the place, too. It was a similar story when he went out hunting with local Aboriginal women. Anything he protested about killing, he got to keep. 'I just wasn't a very good hunter,' he admits. 'I didn't mind eating witchetty grubs and honey ants, but when it started getting to the bigger creatures, I wasn't so keen . . .'

His mum Pat, a former schoolteacher, became used to having animals everywhere, in the house and outside, and having a son who talked of little else. 'He was always so knowledgeable about animals and was always reading books about them,' she says. 'He didn't read much fiction; just an incredible number of books about animals. From very early on, probably around the age of ten, he could tell you about the habits of all sorts of obscure animals, and identify many by their Latin names.'

He had a hard time of it when his parents decided to move the family – Stephen, his older brother Michael, and younger siblings Joanna, Elizabeth, Jemima and Hannah – to New Zealand for a year. Based in chilly Wellington in 1983, the only pets Stephen was allowed to keep were two pet frogs. But he made the most of it. He started keeping flies too, to feed the frogs, as there wasn't any other natural food around for them, and everyone became used to him constantly playing with either the frogs or his growing swarm. He was relieved, however, when it came time to return to Alice Springs and his beloved menagerie. At school, when everyone in his class was told to list their pets, he wrote down the names of ninety – including his flies and the chickens.

But at fifteen, there was an even bigger shock in store: the family was moving back to Melbourne, both for the children's schooling and to be closer to their elderly grandparents. Trevor soon became the director of the Victorian Aboriginal Health Service, but Stephen didn't settle, and made his parents' lives a misery. He missed the wide-open spaces, the red dust and heat, and, most of all, the animals. He was only allowed to take a dog and two cats with him to their new home, and pined over the loss of all his other four-legged, two-legged and no-legged friends.

Although he'd decided he wanted to work with animals from an early age, being a vet held little appeal. As a small child he'd read books about animals, but always skipped the parts about disease as he only ever wanted to know about the healthy ones. Thinking about animals being sick was just too painful. 'He also knew that, as a vet, you have to euthanise a lot of animals, and he didn't want to do anything like that at all,' says his mum.

His father's death from cancer when Stephen was eighteen devastated the whole family. Shattered by the loss, Stephen embarked on a science degree at Melbourne University in 1990, burying himself in his studies, and started thinking about becoming a zoologist. But it didn't take him long to discover that this might not be the answer to his dreams. 'I started to realise that it's a great myth that zoologists spend all their time with animals,' he says. 'They don't necessarily even have a lot to do with animals; they have more to do with *bits* of animals. Even when they're studying animals in the wild, they're doing it from a great distance. So I finally discovered that being a vet is one way you can spend all your time with animals.'

Five years later, when he'd qualified as a vet, he went to Colac, Victoria, a major agricultural, dairy and forestry centre 80 kilometres west of Geelong. There, the twenty-three year old with the genius-level IQ worked as a dairyman, tending the cows. It was tough work – mainly animal obstetrics since the cows seemed to be constantly pregnant – and he seemed to be forever overseeing the birth of calves at 3 a.m. on bitterly cold mornings. The dairy industry was booming at the time, and there was a lot of money floating around, but Stephen quickly became disillusioned. To him, it felt like the cows were often seen more as milk-production machines than living, breathing animals.

After nine months, he moved on to do two kinds of work much closer to his heart: locuming for animal welfare organisations in Melbourne over the summer, which supplied free veterinary care for the pets of people who otherwise wouldn't be able to afford it; and then running dog programs in Aboriginal communities in Arnhem Land in the Top End over the winter.

The main aim of the programs was to desex dogs and treat them for parasites in the communities. It was paid for by the local councils, but was only able to be done with the permission of the owners. It was one of the greatest challenges of Stephen's life. He was often the first vet anyone in those remote places had ever seen, and the locals were – understandably – instantly suspicious. As a result, he'd explain what he'd like to do for the dogs, what it actually meant, and how their dogs would recover well afterwards. Even so, he often ended up doing the desexing surgery on the dining table of owners' homes, so they could watch and understand, and then spread the word to others, without having to risk him disappearing with their beloved pets and never seeing them, or him, again. After a few days, when the dogs had completely bounced back, many from the communities would then call him and ask him to return to desex the rest of their dogs.

'When you think of it, if you have a lot of puppies in a city, you have a whole lot of different options,' says Stephen. 'You can call the council to take them away, you can drop them off in an animal shelter, you can advertise for other owners, you can take them to the vet to be put down. But in Aboriginal communities, you just don't have any of those choices. If you did want a vet, you'd have to charter a plane to bring one out, which would often cost many thousands of dollars, and then his bill would be on top. So the chances are that you'll end up with a lot more dogs than you wanted, and that's very expensive, too, on a limited income.'

His mum saw his work in the program as carrying on his father's help for Aboriginal communities. In the past, non-Indigenous vets had flown in to the communities, rounded up and shot the dogs, then flown out, leaving their owners heartbroken. 'Aboriginal people were getting a pretty shoddy deal up to then,' says Pat. 'But Stephen wanted to do a decent job for them, listening to what they wanted, explaining the options and going with what they chose.'

In that way, he too became a pioneer, like his father before him, but this time for the dogs in Aboriginal communities. Together with Phil Donohoe and Tony English, he founded the national Animal Management in Rural and Remote Indigenous Communities organisation, and still serves on its board. Whenever he is able he'll travel to Aboriginal communities as far afield as Western Australia's Pilbara, the Barkly Shire, around Tennant Creek and up in the Torres Strait, kicking off his shoes as soon as he arrives and checking out the dogs. Vet Jan Allen, the program manager, sees him as a true visionary in the care of animals. 'He's like an absent-minded professor or a bare-footed surgeon,' she says. 'He's very down to earth, easygoing and a very charming, understated ambassador for the program. He's good with the communities, but he's even better with their dogs. He's absolutely fearless, so the dogs can never scent fear, and he's really quiet and calm. The dogs then react so well to him, even those unused to being handled. He's really unique.'

The executive officer of the program, Julia Hardaker, has also been enormously impressed with him over the years. He'll eagerly volunteer to handle a dog at any time, even when its Aboriginal owner might be a little nervous. 'He has an unbelievable way with animals and is so gentle in how he talks to the people in the communities. He's hopelessly disorganised, and he's daggy and unassuming, but he's the best vet I've ever come across. The only time he's ever been bitten was two minutes after I happened to ask him one day if that had ever happened to him and he said no. Luckily, we were working in the covered annex of a health centre, so he was able to go straight in and get a tetanus shot. He was very embarrassed about that!'

In 2000, Stephen eventually moved to Darwin permanently and set up a veterinary clinic with friends, while still continuing the dog programs. Later, in 2004, he set up Palm City Vets in Berrimah and in December 2006 the Humpty Doo clinic, both with Lisa Hansen, who oversees the clinics and helps him as a vet nurse. The next year, he moved to The Ark in Palmerston and the intention, from the start, was to make it a service with a difference. 'We certainly didn't want to be just the normal vet clinic,' he says. 'Now, a quarter to a third of our paying patients are the owners of unusual pets, such as snakes and birds. We also do wildlife rescues, and we see as many of those animals as we do from paying clients – and rescue jobs, of course, are non-paying.'

Most injured wildlife are the unwitting victims of human activities. They are run over by cars – hawks, kites and falcons in particular tend to swoop down on roadkill and have wings broken by speeding vehicles as they struggle to take off in time – they are mauled by domestic dogs and cats, they are pulled out of trees by kids raiding nests, and they are hunted. Reptiles such as snakes might end up injured when they find a quiet, cool place to sleep in someone's house, and are bashed by a frightened resident. As a result, most of Stephen's work involves giving them first aid and medical treatment, or removing snakes from places they shouldn't be. For their rehabilitation, they either stay at the centre or are farmed out to a network of carers.

Naturally, not all of the patients survive. Some are close to death when they're brought in and, if they can't be treated well enough to enable them to fly, hunt for food or evade their predators, it would be a death sentence for them in the wild, anyway. 'You could often save the bird if you amputated its wing, but for a lot of bird species, that defeats the purpose of being a bird,' says Stephen. 'I guess the harsh reality is that wild animals *are* wild, and they don't let a person catch them usually unless they're in serious trouble. On average, maybe 50 per cent of animals don't make it because they're so badly damaged. From a wild animal's point of view, people are the enemy so by the time you let a person catch you, it means you really don't care any more if you live or die.'

But the successes are always celebrated. With green tree frog numbers plummeting around Australia, it was enormously gratifying to be able to save one who'd been chewed up by a lawnmower and had his skin peeled off by the blade. He was released six months ago but has stayed around, so his progress has been monitored, with satisfaction. Bats are regularly prised free from barbed wire in which they've become entangled, too. Extremely intelligent, with soulful eyes that seem almost to show their thanks, their rescuers are often taken aback by the bats' reactions. 'It's simply extraordinary,' says Stephen. 'Bats are one of those creatures where you look into their eyes, and you worry that you're being out-thought!'

Another area in which Stephen is leading the way is with a prison program he's developed with the local Berrimah Prison. He first approached the prison to ask for their help to build cages for some of his patients in their workshops. Three years ago, that extended to a select group of inmates breeding crickets, cockroaches, meal-worms, rats and mice to feed The Ark's wildlife. Now they also look after some of the rehabilitating birds and injured and orphaned native animals, like possums and joeys. It's not an unusual sight to see a tough inmate, in his prison uniform, with a little pouch slung over his front from which a tiny baby animal peers out.

'Some of these people have never looked after anyone else, or anything else, in their lives,' says Robbie Miller, the deputy super-intendent of the Living Skills Unit at the jail. 'And it's been great. It gives them the opportunity to massage a softer side of their per-sonalities, as they're caring for something that demands their 100 per cent devotion. It's a fantastic program, and we've seen some dramatic results. We might have an otherwise tough, violent man looking after something very tenderly. One person here said he'd had a hard life and grown up doing a lot of cruel things when he was younger, but that he would never do anything like them again. He'd come in with a definite attitude problem, but had really changed as a result of the program. It was a wonderful idea of Stephen's.'

Some prisoners get very attached to their charges and, after nursing them as babies, feeding them every two to three hours in their pouches, they'll keep them as youngsters in cages in their cells. As soon as the animals are old enough, however, they go through a careful release strategy. When prisoners finish their sentences before their animals are strong enough to be set free, they'll say a fond farewell to their furry friends. No one – as yet – has begged to stay on in jail just to see out an animal's time there. It simply gives them something to do with their time, they feel as though they're making a contribution, and some really enjoy the contact with animals, their nurturing side finally coming to the fore.

Stephen also continues his links with some of the country's most remote Aboriginal communities, returning regularly, usually in two- to three-week blocks, for dog programs. 'I've been going to a lot of them for ten to twelve years, so I don't have to spend much time explaining myself anymore,' he says. 'You just turn up and the people are ready and waiting for you.'

In addition, the clinics undertake a lot of training – teaching people how to care for wildlife. Their website, www.thearkvet.com, has comprehensive panels of briefing notes and FAQs about every conceivable animal, and Stephen has a column each week in the *Northern Territory News* and is a regular on radio shows. He was also recently the star of the thirteen-part TV series *Outback Wildlife Rescue*, hosted by Ernie Dingo and aired on the Seven Network.

The program showcased the range of his work perfectly. He was seen flying to the Tiwi Islands, off the northern coast, to pick up a joey with a broken foot and an injured blue-winged kookaburra that had been rescued by a group of Aboriginal boys. He brought them back to Darwin for operations, before returning to treat a northern brush-tailed possum suffering stress dermatitis. He was also shown treating a hawksbill sea turtle found floating in the harbour and suffering from pneumonia, then rehabilitating it in his own swimming pool at home for three months; rescuing an echidna with broken spines from an entanglement with a car; cleaning up a sacred kingfisher who'd dived into a tray of engine

FULL PAGE: Angel Flight pilot Cheryl Arentz is now heading towards her hundredth flight for the charity as she helps the sick and injured in remote parts of Queensland (*Sue Williams*)

INSET: Cheryl (left) with one of her most frequent flyers, kidney patient Kayla Graham (*Barry Arentz*)

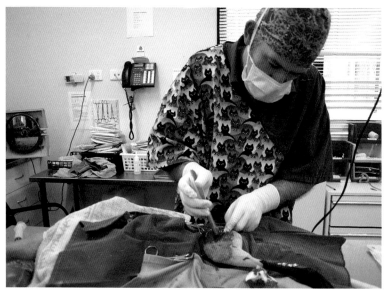

TOP LEFT: Vet Stephen Cutter tends to an injured baby turtle at his clinic for sick wildlife and pets in Palmerston, Northern Territory.

TOP RIGHT: Stephen frees a bat entangled in barbed wire on the Tiwi Islands

ABOVE: Stephen operates on a baby kangaroo with a broken leg at his clinic
(*All photographs The Ark*)

TOP LEFT: A member of Paul Pholeros's Healthabitat team installs kitchen cupboards so one family will have somewhere to store their food. Only one in twenty homes Paul and his team visit has a fully functional kitchen.

TOP RIGHT: Paul shares a laugh with one of the original Uwankara Palyanku Kanyintjaku (UPK) bosses, Nura Ward

ABOVE: Paul with some of his team in South Australia, taking a rare break from their work repairing houses in Aboriginal communities (*All photographs Healthabitat*)

TOP: Yvonne Evans in her cooking class for men, run from Mount Beauty, Victoria. It is aimed at helping men in rural and remote areas create supportive networks (*Regi Penn*)

ABOVE LEFT: Olga Havnen in Darwin, Northern Territory, where she works with the Australian Red Cross to close the gap on Indigenous disadvantage (*Sue Williams*)

ABOVE RIGHT: Remote area nurse Sue Le Lievre has helped to save many lives during her spell in the Kimberley's isolated Looma community in Western Australia (*Sue Williams*)

TOP AND BOTTOM: There aren't many people who could handle living in a place as isolated as Sandfire, 2000 kilometres north of Perth and halfway between Broome and Port Hedland. Fortunately for locals who become sick or injured, Royal Flying Doctor Service and St John Ambulance volunteer Mick Lanagan can. (*RFDS*)

FULL PAGE AND ABOVE: Elaine Crowder flies over vast swathes of the Outback in New South Wales, South Australia and the Northern Territory, stopping off in some of the world's most remote locations to help the locals. (*Sue Williams*)

TOP: Elaine with her good mate, ten-year-old Grace Dowton, whom she first visited as a sick toddler. Now Elaine always makes sure she visits Grace when she stops in White Cliffs, the old opal town in north-west New South Wales. (*David Hahn, courtesy of* The Australian Women's Weekly)

INSET: Paul Pholeros and some of his Healthabitat team set up camp in the mulga scrub, preparing to roll out their swags under the bright Outback stars (*Healthabitat*)

FULL PAGE: Red sandhills glow in the pale light—a timeless testament to the raw beauty of the Australian Outback. (*Sue Williams*) oil, thinking it was water; and saving a pregnant water python that had been run over by a car.

'Animals can get into all sorts of trouble, just like humans,' says Stephen. 'It'd be great if we all reached a point where we make decisions and think what impact they might have on wildlife. People are now starting to think about the environment, but its wildlife still seem to be further down the list.' And that's become Stephen's life purpose: to redress that imbalance.

Today, it's a typically busy day at The Ark. There was a big storm the other night and a flock of swifts became caught up in the weather; eight were brought in on one day. A baby crocodile is hiding in a pond in the yard, recovering from injuries sustained during a savaging from a dog. In a nearby pool, there are a couple of sea turtles, one of which was caught up in a fishing net while the other ate a plastic bag, mistaking it for a tasty jellyfish snack. It blocked his stomach and the danger is that when he tries to regurgitate it he could breathe in his own vomit, be unable to dive and then die of sunburn on the surface. Stephen especially enjoys saving these turtles. 'They have a very good success rate and they live for such a ridiculously long period of time,' he says. 'You feel like you're sending them back to have another seventy to eighty years. That's nice!'

Another large yard has cages all around its perimeter for thirty stray dogs, all waiting for new homes, and being trained in the meantime not to bark, to make them better pets. Another large shed houses twenty cats, luxuriating in their own airconditioned quarters inside or stretched out in the sun on the outdoor run. Then there are the cages of lorikeets, corellas, baby curlews,

Pacific bazzas, possums, wallabies, goannas . . . And even at home, Stephen is surrounded. There, he has a pet black cockatoo; a Waark (the Arnhem Land Aboriginal language Yolgnu matha word meaning crow); dogs Wundi, Mindil, Watu, Nyik Nyik and Maliki; cats Ari, Poppy and Bardi; and a variety of other birds, reptiles, frogs and native fish.

'Our animals come from all over the place, some from as far away as Alice Springs or Kunanurra in Western Australia – from all over Western Australia at times,' says Stephen, now thirty-eight, and also the chair of the Animal Welfare Advisory Committee in the Northern Territory, Wildlife Rescue Darwin and PAWS Darwin. 'While many come from the immediate region and the Outback communities, the nicest truck drivers will stop and pick up injured animals and bring them here. It's always great to be able to help them.'

His mum Pat looks on from a distance, admiring all the work he's doing – and most of it for free. 'He won't make his fortune from that, but he's doing something very worthwhile and something that's very valuable,' she says. 'I'm very proud of him. He's done something unique, all of his very own.'

Stephen prefers simply to get on with the job at hand. After all, that's what he does best, and it's what he's most comfortable with. 'Working with wild animals is a big challenge as not much is known about their medicine, so it often requires me to think outside the box,' he smiles. 'Animals see people as a threat, so they try to hide or run. They don't want people to know what's wrong with them, so I need to get through that barrier to be able to determine what is wrong.' He stops for a moment and strokes one of the dogs that nip at his heels. 'I guess I've always been obsessed with animals, and I'm really now living my dream.'

11

Taps, But No Water

Paul Pholeros, *Sydney, New South Wales*

The elderly couple politely but firmly rebuffs the offer of help from a visiting work crew to bring their house up to scratch. They never accept charity, they say. They've always worked for a living. They're doing just fine.

But behind the walls of their humble home in a remote community in northern New South Wales, the pair are obviously struggling. They're caring for their 22-year-old severely disabled grandson, yet have no hot running water – having to heat water on a stove to bathe him each morning – and live amid a tangle of electrical cables on the dirt floor that has visitors terrified for everyone's safety.

Finally comes the breakthrough. 'We know you don't need our help, but how about the young bloke?' suggests architect Paul Pholeros, the man in charge of this project, gesturing at the young man in the wheelchair sitting quietly to the side. 'Maybe he needs a bit of a hand.' It does the trick. The couple are too proud to accept any offers on their own behalf but, when it comes to their grandson, they want the very best for him they can possibly manage.

The crew at last gains admittance and sets to work fixing up the house: putting all the electrical cables inside the walls, installing a hot water tank and plumbing it to taps in the bathroom and kitchen. On the second day, a delegation arrives from the rest of the community. 'We want to thank you for what you're doing for uncle and auntie,' says the man at the front of the group. 'And we want you to know, we're all willing to pass up any work you were going to do on *our* houses, if you can help them and their grandson.'

Paul shakes his head at the memory. Their houses were just as shoddily built, and equally poorly maintained by the housing authority, but they were prepared to carry on living in the shambles created by others simply so they could see one family rise above it. 'Some of these situations absolutely break your heart,' he sighs. 'We see so many people living in abject poverty, and it can have a psychological toll even on those of us visiting – let alone the people themselves.

'You can give everyone all the statistics on the terrible state of Aboriginal housing, but it's the human stories that stay in your mind. And just spending a small amount on fixing simple problems with these houses, like fixing toilets that have never flushed, or providing a working hot water system, or making sure people have an area where they can wash and prepare food, can make a huge difference to people's lives. Improving people's living environments can lead to massive improvements in their health and wellbeing.'

It's a mantra that has occupied the collective mind of this Sydney architect and his large Healthabitat 'family' for twenty-four years now, and has led to a landmark not-for-profit project that has transformed the lives of more than 50 000 Aboriginal people across Australia. In the process, their work has come to the attention of health professionals all over the globe, who are now adapting its principles for their own use, as a tool for helping disadvantaged communities from the US to Scotland, South Africa to Nepal.

It all began when Paul Pholeros's dentist wife Sandra Meihubers embarked on pioneering work in remote Indigenous townships in central Australia. She set up the first ever dental health program on the 103 000 square kilometres of Anangu Pitjantjatjara Yankunytjatjara lands, to the south-west of Uluru in the great central deserts region straddling the Northern Territory, South Australia and Western Australia, providing care for people who had never before had a dental service. She suggested, at one point, that Paul come along with her and do some architectural work for the communities.

A few weeks later, he found himself in the windswept dust of the Great Victoria Desert, six hours' drive south-west of Alice Springs, turning a house in an isolated Aboriginal community at Fregon, on the compacted sand dunes and clay plains of northwest South Australia, into a clinic. He was then asked to design another small health clinic for a second community, then a third. When they were all finished in 1985, at the end of nearly two years' consultancy work, he was hauled in front of the then director of the local Nganampa Health Council, Yami Lester – the adoptive son of Eileen Kampakuta Brown – who was bemoaning the fact that, in two years of running the service and with the hugely improved treatment of illness, overall health still hadn't improved for local Indigenous people. 'We *have* to stop people getting sick,' he told Paul.

Three weeks on, Paul found himself in a room with two other people who'd been brought in by Yami: Dr Paul Torzillo, who was at the time the medical officer working at the Pukatja (Erna-bella) health clinic for Yami's health service and a leading thoracic physician, and Alice Springs anthropologist and community devel-opment worker Stephan Rainow, who'd been working in the area since 1977 and spoke the local Pitjantjantjara language. 'Yami told us he could employ 1000 doctors but unless people's living envi-ronments improved, there'd still be no change in their levels of health,' says Paul. 'He said he had no money and no budget and no plan, but that we should work together to come up with some ideas to stop people getting sick. He told us that, next door, he had eighteen Aboriginal people who would be our bosses on this new project – and that no-one would receive any wages. That day, he set us on a task that ultimately changed my life.'

For that landmark meeting launched the trio on a passionate crusade. They were set to work with the team of local Indige-nous people to 'stop people getting sick' – in the local language, *Uwankara Palyanku Kanyintjaku*. For years people had been doing work on how living environments impacted people's health, but Paul Torzillo set out to make detailed connections between differ-ent aspects of poor living conditions and specific illnesses. With the team of locals, and Stephan – who already had the trust and respect of many of the communities – all the different aspects of people's lives were documented, and the calamitous effects many of these factors were having on their health recorded, including identifying a number of Third World diseases that had popularly been assumed to no longer exist in twentieth-century Australia. Research results were compared with data collected nationally and internationally. Paul Torzillo then gave each of the nine aspects of living conditions a priority, so there was a clear plan going forward and tasks were prioritised.

Their UPK Report, published in 1987, caused a stir around Australia. For the first time, it had been comprehensively shown how poor living environments could have a devastating effect on health, and the way forward – also for the first time – had been clearly charted. Yet while the work was publicly applauded, there was little action. Frustrated with no signs of any perceivable progress, the trio decided on their next project: to actually undertake the recommended work in one small community to see if the health of residents would improve as they'd predicted. In 1991, they set up not-for-profit company Healthabitat in order to carry out their plans.

For the two Pauls and Stephan, it was the start of something big. And for those people living in some of the worst housing the nation has ever provided, their work was to prove epic.

What Paul and his colleagues found in the early days of Healthabitat startled them. In only one in ten houses they entered were the electrical systems safe. Only one in twenty had a functional kitchen. Fewer than a third had a working shower.

'So when people talk about diabetes in Aboriginal communities, they often don't think in terms of those people not having decent kitchens where they can prepare and cook food,' says Paul.

'And when they think of health, they assume most people will have a working shower to make it easy to wash themselves. The reality is very different.'

Paul Torzillo is even more blunt. 'A lot of the problems we're seeing today aren't about income but about being able to control your own environment,' he says. 'There may be a number of complex problems, but they're all being compounded by the most simple of issues to do with housing. If you can't have a shit in your own house, and wash the kids and put food somewhere you can keep clean, then your personal feeling is one that you're overwhelmed by your circumstances. If something's done about these conditions, and it's usually something that's very easy and straightforward, then lives can be improved exponentially.'

One dad, for instance, living in Condobolin, 460 kilometres west of Sydney, was in dire straits. In his house there was only a tiny amount of hot water and, with four children, it would only be the first up who could have a warm shower. The kids were all constantly plagued by chronic respiratory problems, while their dad, working long hours at a job outside town, never managed to get home in time to have a shower before the hot water ran out. The team removed the tiny hot water system and installed a big one. Since that day, the father reports his kids' health has improved markedly and having a hot shower after work has become one of the new joys of his life.

An elderly woman in a camp outside Tennant Creek was similarly impressed. When the work crew visited her house, they were mystified by the fact that all the taps were spindles with no handles. They wondered how anyone could ever use them. 'Ha ha!' she laughed, producing a single tap handle from her cardigan pocket. 'They all fell off and eventually they were lost or destroyed, so I made sure I held on to one so we could still get some water when we needed it . . .' The team discovered the original tap fittings had been of the very poorest quality available on the market and, in such conditions, it was little wonder they broke off very quickly. They left the house with a whole range of tapware – this time eminently more durable.

It's a theme that's repeated again and again in community homes throughout Australia. Stephan Rainow, sitting on a step outside the Nganampa Health Council clinic in Alice Springs, draws heavily on his cigarette. 'The authorities have always seen their housing stock as an asset-management exercise, and are more concerned about that than the people who are forced to lead second-rate lives living in such poor conditions,' he says. 'But we want those houses to deliver health benefits rather than sickness.

'It's terrible when you go into some houses and see uncovered, dangerous power points, and grandchildren crawling around on the floor. What if they put their fingers in them? You might go to another place and see septic tanks that have never been pumped out. People are having to live with the bad smell. They're horrendous situations to be in.'

At the beginning of their work for Healthabitat, Paul Torzillo remembers the three sitting down together, and Paul Pholeros saying he reckoned they could go into even more communities with small groups of skilled workers, recruiting locals to help them and training those locals at the same time. 'He said he'd had the idea of a housing program fixing around 1000 houses,' he says with a laugh. 'Stephi and I looked at each other and said, "Bullshit!" We refused to believe it could be done. But he had such a clear vision, right from the very beginning. And he was right.'

So far, with the help of a massive effort from a huge team, the last ten years have seen them employ and train more than 1200 Aboriginal and Torres Strait Islander people – and contract a further 300 tradespeople of all ethnic origin – to fix 98 872 defects in more than 6600 Aboriginal-occupied houses in no fewer than 170 locations, from the vast Outback to rural and urban centres across Australia.

It's a stunning figure, made even more extraordinary when you realise the three are still doing this work in their free time. Paul Pholeros, an award-winning architect since gaining first-class honours in his Bachelor of Architecture at the University of Sydney in 1976, works for his self-named company on projects all around the world. These have included designing the Nankun Crosswaters Eco Lodge in China, which has been promoted by the Chinese government as a model of sustainable development, and all manner of housing around Australia: Sydney, New South Wales's Kangaroo Valley, islands on the Great Barrier Reef, and South Australia and the Northern Territory. He's also Adjunct Professor of Architecture at the University of Sydney. Dr Paul Torzillo is the associate professor in the Faculty of Medicine at the University of Sydney, a respiratory physician at Sydney's Royal Prince Alfred Hospital, and medical director of the Nganampa Health Council, dividing his time between the hospitals, clinics and teaching in Sydney and Alice Springs. Stephan Rainow, meanwhile, is the public and environmental officer attached to Nganampa Health Council, which these days runs nine clinics that treat over 3000 people across a vast area of central Australia.

Any money earned by, or awarded to, Healthabitat goes straight into the work being undertaken, or to fund critical areas of research. 'We decided early on that we didn't want to profit from the work,' says Paul Pholeros. 'None of us want to make anything from other people's poverty and terrible living conditions. We want everything to be ploughed back into continuing to help.'

The reasons for such a poor state of public housing in communities are depressingly familiar. While popular myth has it that deliberate vandalism is the cause of much of the problem, the long years of careful research done under rigorous conditions has revealed quite the opposite: that the incidence of deliberate damage is absolutely miniscule. Instead, 65 per cent of housing defects are a result of normal wear and tear, often because poor-quality fixtures have been installed in the first place, and a lack of regular maintenance by housing authorities.

Paul and his team found that inferior products are regularly installed in kitchens and bathrooms in remote areas – flimsy fittings simply not up to the harsh environments in which they're used – and, in rural areas, the supply of bore water eats the heart out of poor-grade water systems. Pipes that no longer carry water as they've become so encrusted with salt, shower roses completely clogged and the cheapest of taps that simply fall apart when used regularly for more than a few weeks are very common stories. In most cases, there are much better, more suitable products available that could have been used to avoid most of the problems occurring.

The second major problem, accounting for 25 per cent of faults, is poor initial construction, and incorrect products or specifications. 'In one house, we found light switches on walls, but there had never been any wires installed,' says Paul.

'Those problems are probably a result of poor supervision, the fact that it's hard to get people to inspect work done in rural and remote areas, and self-certification, where trades certify their own work. A lot of contractors simply won't go back to finish off their work when they have to travel so far to do so, and they're waiting on the collection of only, say, 5 per cent of their total fee. They think it's not worth it. As a result of all these factors, some of the houses we see are highly dangerous.'

Over many years, less than 10 per cent of faults were found to be a result of overcrowding in homes, misuse, abuse or vandalism. 'When you have twenty people living in a two-bedroom house, you would expect it to fail quite quickly,' he says. 'And we found negligible evidence of deliberate vandalism to essential health hardware.'

These terrible conditions tend to prevail when they're coupled with residents who are too anxious to complain, who don't have money to spare – or permission from the housing authority – to fix the problems themselves, or who have grown up or lived so long in houses with toilets and showers that don't work that they simply think it's normal.

'There's no point talking about the bigger issues like better housing design if someone's standing in three inches of shitty water,' says Paul, matter-of-factly. 'We've found if you solve the simple problems first, then you can focus on the more complex problems later. The things that will kill you today, we fix first: electrical faults, bad wiring, crumbling walls; things that will affect you tomorrow we'll fix as a second priority. The problem is that many people believe the situation with Aboriginal housing is too complex to tackle, and that sense of hopelessness underpins much of public policy. But what should be done isn't a mystery. It can be very simple to improve people's houses in a very fundamental way and, in so doing, you can have a huge impact on people's health.

'And, of course, there's no better way than fixing problems in people's homes to start a meaningful discussion!'

When Mickey O'Brien first saw a photo of a man sitting, with a broad grin, by a fire outside his house in a remote spot in the South Australian Outback, he couldn't help smiling to himself. The man looked so cheerful, and what could be better than enjoying the cool afternoon air in front of a fire, with what looked like a bit of tarpaulin shade to shield him from the wind?

As he looked more closely at the photograph, however, his smile faded. The man was actually sitting in a wheelchair; he had a disability. Near him in the front yard sat a bedpan, a bowl and a walking frame. A young man in the corner of the frame – his grandson? – looked tired and anxious. Soon, the picture became clearer. The reason he was sitting out at the front of his house was because, in his wheelchair, he couldn't actually get inside. The doorway was too narrow and the steps up too steep. As a result, he was forced to sleep outside most of the time, under that very tarpaulin Mickey had been so quick to assume was his recreational windbreak. The bedpan and bowl: they were there because this man couldn't even get to his own bathroom.

'This man couldn't even use his house,' says Mickey, the South Australian manager for Healthabitat. 'It was totally unsuitable for a man like him with disabilities. It was a terrible, shocking situation. And it goes to show how many of us are so quick to jump to conclusions about people's housing conditions. It's only when we make the effort to find out what really isn't working that we're able to understand the whole situation.'

Healthabitat was able to help get the man rehoused in a place much more suitable to his needs, as well as going around his community and fixing the myriad problems that were dragging so many of his family and friends down with him. 'Other people might give you reams and reams of statistics and graphs and documents and talk about housing until your ears burn and your eyes bleed,' says Mickey. 'But the reason I love Healthabitat so much is that they look at a house, then straightaway get in and fix it up. Paul has always talked about solutions rather than problems, and we won't say we're going to do something unless we can do it straightaway. That's what makes him such a great person, and those three blokes together so inspiring. You feel so grateful they're around.'

And Sandra Meihubers, the partner who first started Paul off on this work, is equally admiring. 'It's extraordinarily visionary work,' she says. 'He's a man of incredible creativity and persistence and commitment. He's always trusted his instincts and his vision, and it's proved so right in this.'

From the most remote areas of the Outback in South Australia, New South Wales, the Northern Territory and Cape York, and even islands off the coast, where the Healthabitat teams have been working, the good-news stories are legion. There were, of course, those grandparents with their disabled grandson, whose quality of life improved 500-fold after Healthabitat fixed their house so they could care for him much more comfortably and effectively. The rest of the community was delighted when Healthabitat then insisted on moving on to their own homes and weaved their magic for them too.

One man living in a township outside South Australia's Maree, at the start of the Birdsville and Oodnadatta tracks, was struggling to cope as a single dad with five small children. With no hot water at all, the children were constantly sick with bacterial infections. Everyone was forced to wash in the backyard with the single cold-water tap that worked. There wasn't even any electricity to the outside toilet, so it didn't have a light. As a result, the smallest youngsters said they were too scared to go in there at night, and frequently wet their beds instead. By the time another of Healthabitat's area managers, Greg Norman, met him, he was almost at the end of his tether. 'The house had been built in the 1940s, an old-style mission house,' says Greg. 'It still even had the old coppers in the laundry, encased in concrete. It was an amazing place.'

The team went in, plumbed in a hot-water tank so the whole family could have hot showers, installed a light in the toilet, ripped out the coppers and put in a modern laundry. When the man saw what they'd done, his grin split his face from ear to ear. 'He was just so happy,' says Greg. 'He didn't say much; he was too overwhelmed. But now everyone would be able to wash properly, he could wash clothes – and bedclothes – quickly and their quality of life soared. It's situations like that which make this work so worthwhile.'

But despite all their experience, no-one was prepared for one sight that confronted them last year. A house in another remote community, this time in Outback New South Wales, had a partially collapsed roof, which a lot of workmen had inspected in the past but no-one had actually returned to repair. The timber frame of the house had also buckled, leaving it tilting at an angle that made everyone nervous. It was in the bathroom, however, that the greatest shock was in store. The shower had been leaking for so long, the water had softened the walls and had completely rotted away the floorboards. As a result, everyone who used the bathroom had to step over a metre-wide hole with a 1.8 metre drop.

'It was crazy that even going to the dunny could be so dangerous,' says Greg. 'It's amazing that such a house could ever have been put up and fitted out. I think it often comes down to a lack of supervision. If people think this work is never going to be inspected, it's no surprise that some might do such a bad job. They might say, "Oh, it's only a blackfella house." It's terrible. And we see, over and over again, people reduced to living lives in much more pain and discomfort and ill health than anyone deserves, just because people haven't done their jobs right.'

It's the dearest dream of Paul Pholeros and all of the Healthabitat team that, one day, this work simply won't be necessary. If, in the first place, suitable housing was built along all the right principles and to good specifications and decent standards, was inspected afterwards to make sure it was up to scratch and then properly maintained by housing authorities, then all their repairs wouldn't be needed. But after fixing those 6000-odd houses – which represent about a quarter of the Aboriginal-controlled housing stock – and transforming the lives of their 40 000-plus residents, he's not so optimistic that Healthabitat won't continue to be busy for a long time to come.

'In another ten years, we'll probably fix 7000 more,' says Paul, now fifty-seven and a member of the Australian Institute of Architects' Indigenous Housing Taskforce. 'But in that time, more shoddy houses might have been built, which will leave us with even more to fix up afterwards. We should be making it a priority that any new buildings are done properly and, after twenty years, you'd think that 90 per cent of our work should be in designing the very best houses to suit the locations, instead of 90 per cent fixing up bad work after it's done. People don't want a lot, they should just be able to demand the basic things: a good roof, taps and electricity that work, a place to wash themselves and clothing, and a clean place to prepare food. It's not much to ask for, is it?

'We're trying to recast this work not as an Aboriginal issue, but as a poverty issue. The fact that this is happening in Aboriginal communities isn't so important; it could be happening anywhere. Any of us would be struggling if we were forced to live in such poor conditions.'

That early UPK report dramatically showed the connections between poor housing standards and health, and also provided a simple, well-defined and easy-to-understand standard by which to judge work, and by which to formulate goals for the future. A healthy living environment, it argued, has nine principles. It should be a place that is safe from the dangers of electrocution from uncovered wires or water too close to electrical sockets, and of gas explosion or structural collapse; allows people to wash themselves, and particularly young children; allows them to wash clothes; has a system for removing waste safely; gives them the capacity to improve their nutrition with a safe, clean place to prepare and store food; helps reduce the impact of overcrowding;

separates people from the harmful effects of animals, vermin and insects; reduces dust; and gives residents the ability to moderate temperature. UPK also proposed immediate action, recommending that houses should be surveyed then fixed immediately, following the revered eye surgeon Dr Fred Hollows' principle of improvements *during* the work rather than *afterwards*, or as he put it in his mantra: 'No survey without service.' Finally, it said such projects should always be undertaken in partnership with local communities, so everyone knew what the work was about, and was actively involved in all aspects of the project. Accordingly, Healthabitat went on to insist on 70 per cent Indigenous involvement before any project was even considered.

Over the next three years, UPK became regarded nationally as a yardstick for environmental intervention in Indigenous communities. The final 1991 report of the Royal Commission into Aboriginal Deaths in Custody, for instance, referred to the UPK report and urged that its recommendations be widely adopted as it became the best-practice model. The two Pauls and Stephan then ran a research project in one of the small Pitjatjantjara communities to assess how well UPK would work on the ground. The results were remarkable and were published by the three in a 1994 book, *Housing for Health: Towards a better living environment for Aboriginal Australia*. It was launched in Parliament House by the then Prime Minister Paul Keating's federal health minister Carmen Lawrence, and the long-time Indigenous rights campaigner, lawyer Mick Dodson, who was to become Australian of the Year in 2009.

The book sold in great numbers, with all profits going to Nganampa Health Council, which had been involved from the beginning of the journey. Many copies were snapped up overseas, to be used as the blueprint for improving housing in other indigenous or impoverished communities. It was also awarded the President's Award in what was then the Royal Australian Institute of Architects.

None of the incredible work that followed the report and book, however, would ever have been possible without help from a dedicated core team of people, and the goodwill of the communities along the way. One of the proudest legacies of the project is the young people from the townships who've been recruited to help do the work, and are left with new skills afterwards. A number have since found jobs using those skills, or have chosen to go to college to pursue training and study for formal certificates to help them in the workforce. One man, Thad Nagus, who came from the mines to work for them, now has a degree in environmental health. 'For them, it can be very empowering,' says Geoff Barker, another member of the wider team. 'You're seeing them as equals and you're treating them with respect for their contribution. Then they start really enjoying the work, and sometimes that can be transformative.'

Sandra Newman, the CEO of the Orana Aboriginal Corporation at Wellington, 50 kilometres south of Dubbo, New South Wales, is unequivocal in her praise of the project team. 'We love them!' she declares. 'They make a real connection with the community and involve our young people as well as providing what the community needs in terms of fixing houses. Some of these houses are so bad, they can be unbearable to live in, with a lack of hot water, no flyscreens over the windows and nothing that works. But they do excellent work, and we're very grateful.'

At times it must be hard to keep going, but Paul says the toughest task is to convince people that these housing problems are solvable, and often for as little as $7500 a house – the average cost of repairing each one. And for such basic work, he becomes embarrassed when Aboriginal people sing Healthabitat's praises, often struggling to do so in English, which can sometimes be a traditional Indigenous person's third language. Yet in 2007, there was more formal thanks: Paul was awarded the Australia Medal (AM) in recognition for his persistence and outstanding service to the health and wellbeing of the Indigenous population of Australia and the Torres Strait Islands. He completely deserves it, believes Paul Torzillo, who was also awarded the same medal two years earlier. 'At first, I think my and Stephi's contributions were very important but Paul has now been the major contributor to this project,' he says.

Recently, there's been even more official recognition of the vital importance of Healthabitat's work, which could end up providing the template for improving living conditions of the poorest people internationally, too. In New South Wales, the health department completed a landmark study, *Closing the Gap*, which compared the health of the 9000-plus residents of 2200 houses that had been repaired over the past ten years with those whose homes hadn't. They found that the population exposed to the 'Housing for Health' program was a stunning 40 per cent less likely to be hospitalised with infectious diseases such as acute respiratory infections, skin conditions, intestinal diseases and middle ear problems, compared with the rest of the rural New South Wales Aboriginal population. The study also detailed the significant and sustained improvements to housing infrastructure brought about by the program, with nine-fold improvements in electrical safety, four-fold in fire safety, and a nearly four-fold improvement in the ability to prepare, store and cook food; while structural safety, waste removal and the ability to wash clothes and people all showed two-fold improvements.

Those remarkable health improvements as a result of the housing work are now detailed in reports submitted to several medical journals for peer review, both in Australia and overseas. 'It's all credit to the department for doing this work,' says Paul. 'Now it seems as though our Healthabitat work will be going up to a whole new level. That 40 per cent figure is incredible, especially considering that the money that's been spent on housing for this program has been chickenfeed compared to larger national programs.'

With hopes now high that such work could be extended around Australia, and adapted for poor communities internationally, prospects for major leaps forward in Aboriginal health look promising. Paul Torzillo is also optimistic, and gives much of the credit to Paul Pholeros.

'It's been huge,' he says. 'We always wanted to provide a high level of technical expertise and delivery on the ground, rather than ideology, and Paul has brought together a collection of people, mostly his contacts, which have enabled us to do that. He's always had a very clear vision for the direction of the program and his capacity for hard work is incredible. He's completely changed the rhetoric around environmental health.'

His rigour with the paperwork can sometimes be a pain, offers Geoff Barker, but it's all for the greater good. 'Paul's a really inspirational person,' he says. 'None of this could have been achieved without a very strong, committed team following his strengths and skills. He's a very special man.'

Stephan agrees. 'Without Paul's input, there wouldn't be Healthabitat,' he says. 'I think, as a professional architect, he felt some of these houses were an insult to his profession, the way they were designed and maintained in remote communities, and he wanted to help those stuck with these houses. He's been amazingly dedicated and energetic.'

12

Secret Men's Business

Yvonne Evans, *Mount Beauty, Victoria*

A group of twelve men is hard at work in a large kitchen in a small neighbourhood centre in rural Victoria. Some are busy chopping and dicing. Others are sweating over a vast selection of pans on stove-top rings. The rest are laying a long table with a crisp white cloth, polished cutlery, plates and serviettes.

As they're all performing their allotted tasks, each surreptiously takes a few seconds out every so often to sip from a wine glass, while the jovial banter between them never stops. 'More work, less talk,' orders the chef in charge. The rest of the men grin, and there's a short pause before the conversation restarts, at exactly the same volume and pace.

Yvonne Evans, looking on, smiles. The noise doesn't overly worry her, nor the amount of discussion. She's not even too anxious about how the delicate chicken risotto the men are supposedly concentrating on preparing will turn out. The most important aspect of this evening for her is how well the men communicate. For this is no ordinary cooking class. And while not all the men are completely focused all the time on producing a delicious meal, perfectly prepared and presented, the stakes are actually far higher.

This recipe can, and frequently does, save lives.

Every four days, an Australian farmer kills himself. It's an unfolding bush tragedy that's now reached colossal proportions, with the suicide rate twice the national average.

The reasons are as many as they are varied. The ongoing drought has exacerbated hardships being battled in rural communities, there's a crippling lack of alternative employment in small towns, the level of debt has been soaring, marriages have been breaking down under the pressure and depression has never before been experienced by so many men, with so few knowing where to turn for help.

The stark figures themselves are horrifying. Of the 2000 suicides a year in Australia, 80 per cent are now men; nearly five men are killing themselves every day. Rural men are particularly vulnerable, says Professor John Macdonald of the University of Western Sydney, who found that the rate of suicide for males aged 15–24 is twice that of similarly aged men in capital cities. One of the most common triggers is the end of a relationship, the Australian Institute for Suicide Research and Prevention at Queensland's Griffith University has found. Men are four times more likely than women to try to kill themselves after a break-up, particularly when it looks as though they're likely to have only limited access to their children.

The major difficulty for men is that they tend not to open up about their problems to anyone – male friends, wives, girlfriends, exes, families, colleagues – so they often simply can't see any way out of their troubles. Usually, men simply don't recognise they need help and, even when they do, there are few places in Outback communities that offer it anyway.

Yvonne knows that terrible syndrome all too well. One of the casualties was her own son, twenty-year-old Darryl. When he hanged himself thirteen years ago while she was away visiting his older brother, she became determined to do everything she could to make sure as few other mothers, wives, girlfriends and daughters as possible would have to go through the same agonising pain as she'd suffered, and still does, every single day.

'So I realised that I had to do something to help if I could,' says Yvonne, tears welling in her eyes once more at the thought of her son's lonely death. 'I had to find ways to help. Men need access to services, they need things to help them find some hope, things that will bring some joy to their lives, things to help them connect with others.

'I know when I get depressed I want to withdraw; you don't want to see people, you can't face them. I knew I had to find ways to help men form bonds with each other, to help them to talk, to encourage them to ask for help when they needed it, to become more resilient. If only this kind of project had been around for my son, he might still be here today.'

*

Yvonne Webster was born in a mining town in the north of England, her father the first of numerous generations not to have earned his living underground. Instead, he worked in the offices up top, then went to work for a brewery, managing different pubs around the country. As a result, by the age of seventeen Yvonne had attended no fewer than twelve schools. But then came the biggest upheaval of all. Just as she was about to go to university to study medicine, her parents, Margaret and Allen, announced the family was migrating to Australia.

Yvonne was devastated. Things didn't improve once they'd disembarked from the boat in 1970, either. The education authorities in Victoria decided she was too young to go to university, so she'd have to stay at school for two more years to make the adjustment to a different system – moving into a class of fifteen year olds. At that news Yvonne decided she wasn't going back to school, and instead found herself a job as a systems analyst in the early days of the computer industry, learning as she worked. She got married a year later and moved with her husband Andrew Evans to a rural area where he was working. After she had their first child, Mark, she found it impossible to get a job since no-one wanted to employ a mother with a small child. She then had two more children, Darryl and Cherise, and studied for a computing qualification by correspondence from home – and without a computer.

Andrew worked with the Rural Water Commission, and was, again, constantly moving the family as he was transferred around the country. 'We lived in ten or twelve different places just in those first few years,' says Yvonne. 'We were continuously moving. It was impossible to settle down.'

One of the places they lived in was Tatura, near Shepparton in the rich Goulburn Valley, 175 kilometres north of Melbourne – an area with 4000 hectares of orchards within a 10-kilometre radius and 4000 hectares of market gardens. There'd been a great deal of aerial spraying in the region to stop mosquitoes and prevent fruit fly when Yvonne arrived in 1985. In addition, a pest control officer called around to the house and, assuring Yvonne his chemicals were quite safe, proceeded to spray the outside of the house against spiders, with the fumes flowing freely inside the house, too.

Within weeks, Yvonne was coming down with all sorts of illnesses, including pneumonia and pleurisy. 'You name it, I seemed to have it,' she says today. 'My immune system seemed to be totally shattered. I just couldn't work out what had gone wrong with me.' The family then moved to Hoppers Crossing, just west of Melbourne, and Yvonne found that every time she passed by the petrochemical plant at Altona on the way to work in the city she felt queasy. Very soon, her health started completely breaking down.

A specialist finally confirmed what she was by now beginning to suspect: the chemicals in the environment were making her sick. But tests also found that her body was starting to react to most foods, and even the newsprint on newspapers could knock her for six. Very soon, she was so chronically fatigued that some days she wasn't able even to get out of bed to look after the children. She was becoming allergic to the world around her.

'I think I'd had health problems since I was a kid but it was after the spraying that my immune system just cracked up altogether,' says Yvonne. 'It was so hypersensitive, it reacted to everything.'

Much, much worse, however, was Yvonne's realisation that

Darryl, now nine, was suffering similar symptoms. He had wild mood swings constantly, in the depths of depression one minute, hyperactive another, angry and aggressive the next, and all often quite at odds with what was actually going on around him at the time. At eleven, the specialist diagnosed him as having the same severe problems with petrochemicals as his mother, as well as with different foods, additives in food, cleaning products used at school . . . pretty much everything. For Yvonne, that also explained why he was doing so poorly in his education. Psychological tests had shown he should have been in the top 2 per cent of his class; instead he was coming in at average or just below. 'He would get so frustrated,' says Yvonne. 'I know what that's like, because sometimes when something has affected me, I can't think, I can't even spell "and". It's ridiculous and I get so frustrated – whereas as a young boy, he couldn't understand why he felt that way.'

The pair were gradually growing sicker and, with Andrew getting a new job at the Victorian Alps ski resort Falls Creek, the whole family moved to Mount Beauty, 350 kilometres north-east of Melbourne and at the foot of Victoria's highest mountain, Mount Bogong. The air there was much cleaner, the water was chlorine-free and gradually Yvonne began to recover and function again. She also began to delve into mind–body medicine, studying hypnotherapy and neuro-linguistic programming among many other alternative healing arts, and grew more and more interested in colour therapy.

Yvonne began practising on Darryl, too, hoping to develop a method of helping him more and reading his moods. One day, when he was sixteen years old, Yvonne told him to pick a colour from her charts. He didn't hesitate before pointing to a colour known as double orange. Yvonne felt her heart lurch. It was the colour of suicide.

Darryl continued to struggle. A gifted artist, he'd set his heart on studying art at university but, because his grades at school weren't good enough, he was gradually seeing that dream disintegrate. Instead, at the end of high school, he was accepted into Wodonga TAFE for an architectural drawing course, but found he hated the confines of constantly drawing straight lines. As a result, he ended up dropping out, and started taking drugs, sitting around depressed most days. The only work he could get in Mount Beauty was picking tobacco, which was terrible for his allergies, or picking apples, where the fumes from the tractors would similarly overwhelm him.

'Every time he went for a job, it would end in failure, and that tormented him,' says Yvonne. 'He'd had to come back home, and that made him feel even more of a failure. It was soul-shattering for a young person. Then, my marriage to his father broke up at the beginning of 1995, and so he knew I was supporting him on my sole parent's pension, having to use my savings to break even. So, even worse, he started seeing himself as a burden and useless. I didn't know what to do. There were no counselling services in the local area, there were no experts, and the only thing the doctor would offer was antidepressants, and he didn't want those; in his mind he was only depressed *because* of his illness.'

As Darryl's twenty-first birthday approached, he seemed to sink deeper into despondency. He was planning a party, but at the same time was fearful no-one would come. Just before his birthday, in January 1997, Yvonne decided to visit her eldest son Mark, then twenty-five, in northern New South Wales. Darryl didn't want to come, but she took Cherise and her friend with her. Soon after she arrived, however, Yvonne started feeling oddly uneasy, and decided to drive back home immediately. Night fell halfway through the long journey and, exhausted and fearing she might have an accident in the dark with the two girls in the car, Yvonne checked them all into a motel so they could get some sleep and before starting out again early the next day. She woke sweating in the middle of the night after a nightmare, and set off in the morning full of dread. By the time she arrived home, Darryl had already killed himself.

'I kept thinking that if I hadn't stopped, I would have been home an hour before he made that decision, or if I'd not gone away, could I have done something? It's a question that never really leaves you. I think it's one of the hardest ways to lose somebody because you've got no-one to blame. It's so hard to understand and so hard to talk about. So you don't talk about it, and silently you just carry the guilt and the wondering: could I have done something, done more?'

Friends looked on anxiously as Yvonne struggled to cope with the shock and horror of her son's death. 'At one point there, I felt she could have gone either way,' says close friend Barbara Pyle. 'She could easily have gone with him, or used his death to gain in strength. Thankfully, she did the latter.'

In the weeks following the funeral, one man, introduced to her by Darryl six months before his death, proved a huge support.

Darryl had been working in a cafe in Falls Creek and had asked Yvonne to do a few shifts there to help them out. Michael Lacey happened to be working in the same building, and the other staff, saying it was about time she found a new man, encouraged him to ask her out, advising him he should buy her roses and chocolates to win her over. With snow covering the ground at the time, and no roses to be bought anywhere, he compromised with Roses chocolates. The couple got together soon afterwards and, throughout the terrible aftermath of Darryl's death, Michael became her rock. 'I couldn't have got through it without him,' she says now.

She was also helped by a number of Darryl's friends. They approached her to say Darryl had been very proud of her, and grateful for her efforts to help him with his illness and that he'd felt the colour charts she'd developed for the mind–body system had proved extremely useful. She was taken aback. Moreover, his friends started asking her to use the colour charts on them to help them understand their lives.

Despite still feeling devastated, Yvonne was touched by their faith, and set back to work on her project with increased vigour. Everything fell into place, and she ended up writing and self-publishing a book, *Mindcolour*, dedicated to Darryl. While she was pleased with the contents of the book, realising her vision had dire consequences. She'd spent all her money, and a bank loan, on publishing the book, and was soon faced with the threat of bankruptcy. With her divorce coming through at the same time, she felt she'd finally hit rock bottom. She could choose to either sink completely, or concentrate all her efforts on getting herself out of this mess. She went for the latter, taking every job she could to earn enough money to pay back her creditors. Eighteen months later, she'd gone a long way towards paying off all her debts, but was still fired up with the idea of trying to provide more help to people who most needed it. 'The book was one way, but I didn't feel it was enough,' she says. 'I knew I had to help by giving people access locally to services.'

Looking around the Mount Beauty area, Yvonne felt sure there was a huge need that simply wasn't being met. As a township established in 1945 by the Victorian State Electricity Commission purely to provide accommodation for the workers constructing the Kiewa Hydro-Electric Scheme, it suffered terribly when the project was finished and the 4000-strong workforce was scaled down to just eighty-five by the mid-1980s. Unemployment in the tiny town became a major problem, and the Commission was privatised in 1994, with drastic cutbacks in funding that slashed the amount of money coming into town. Then came a fresh series of heavy blows: the closure of the local timber mill, the largest employer in the region; the downturn in the tobacco industry; the devastation of the 2003 bushfires, which destroyed the tourist season and the seasonal work associated with it; and then the drought, crucifying local farmers.

Sensing an increasing air of desperation in the town, Yvonne joined the Mount Beauty Neighbourhood Centre, which at the time was in a similar state of crisis. Housed in a derelict building, branded an eyesore by the local shire mayor, it was hopelessly in debt and failing to deliver many services or much training at all. As pressure built up from the council to bulldoze the building, Yvonne set to work, together with the 84-year-old chairman Alex McCullough and her new partner Michael, who became the treasurer of the newly formed management committee, to see if they could turn its fortunes around and start providing the kind of services people needed. Alex had a huge network of contacts, having been a shire councillor for thirty years; Michael had a sharp financial brain; and Yvonne proved a skilled writer of funding submissions and sourcer of equipment for a fraction of its retail cost, on top of her determination to see her vision through.

'I thought we could do something from this place,' says Yvonne. 'We could bring Centrelink here instead of having to go to Albury-Wodonga or Wangaratta, and we could get some counselling services here instead of people having to travel and look for them.'

Yvonne often ended up working between fifty and sixty hours a week at the centre – even though she was only being paid for fifteen of those hours – setting it up, having it refurbished and teaching computer skills, despite continuing chronic health problems often sapping her energy. Always the one thing driving her on was her memory of Darryl. 'She's always done a lot with Darryl's problems at the back of her mind,' says her friend Barbara. 'She was so keen to help people so that they never got to the point he did. Even though she has all these health problems, and a lot of things in her life that could have broken her spirit, she has an iron will that kept her going, together with a big-picture vision, which enabled her to achieve so much. She's done a lot of things in her son's memory.'

Gradually, things started to fall into place and, in 2003, the same mayor who had branded the place an eyesore broke the news to Yvonne that the centre had won an Australia Day award for Organisation of the Year. The next year, the trio had a major break-through when they finally managed to have the centre accepted as a registered training organisation, with state and federal funding, and in 2005 the centre won the same award again. 'When I think of Yvonne, the term "fox terrier" comes to mind,' says University of Ballarat Associate Professor Barry Golding, a researcher in adult and community education. 'She gets an idea and won't let go, and she won't be beaten. I suspect she gets a lot of that drive and learning from difficult life experiences. Rather than squashing her, they brought out the best in her.'

The number of courses they could afford to run from the centre suddenly multiplied, and the services became much more diverse. 'Eventually, we've turned this place into a shining example of what can be done,' smiles Yvonne. 'It took seven years, but by November 2009, we'd brought over $2 million into town. And since we became a registered training organisation, we've been able to negotiate with the Wodonga Institute of TAFE and help skill local people, instead of having outsiders brought in, and this can lift people out of the rot. It means they can survive and live much more comfortably.'

The centre's fortunes mirror the massive impact it was able to have on the life of the community. In 1999 it was under the threat of foreclosure, had a membership of just seventy-three, a self-generated income of $4000 and a bank overdraft of $3000, and its building was valued at $10 000. It operated precisely nil hours of courses and teaching. In 2009, it had a membership of 1800 from a local population of 2400, self-generated income of $77 000, an annual income of $365 000 from all sources and long-term deposits of $40 000, and the building was valued at $565 000 – a more than 5000 per cent increase. In 2010 its membership numbered 1927, or three-quarters of the local population.

Most importantly, in any one year it now delivers around 19 000 hours of courses in partnership with Wodonga TAFE.

All through the centre's expansion, Yvonne's priority was always trying to help men going through difficult times. She knew there was a huge need, but the battle always lay in trying to reach them. The answer came almost by accident.

Before meeting Yvonne, her partner Michael had spent twenty years as a bachelor, yet still couldn't cook. Yvonne often commented on it but now, slowly, the seeds of an idea began to germinate. There would be many men in the same position, it occurred to her. So why not try to get them together, teach them to cook and at the same time polish some of their other life skills, while helping them to create networks with each other?

The first class had just four men, tutored by chef Roi Rigoni from local restaurant Roi's Diner. The five of them worked together to prepare a meal, learning, and getting to know each other, as they cooked. It worked so well, word went around, and the classes, dubbed 'Secret Men's Business', grew bigger and bigger. Soon there was a long waiting list of men wanting to do the course.

'It's certainly not your average cooking class,' says Yvonne. 'We have all sorts of men, aged from twenty up to seventy. Many of them said at the beginning that they found recipes frightening but, by the end, they've completely overcome any fear they had of preparing food. But it's so much more than that. They socialise, they build their confidence, they suddenly don't mind making mistakes, they're able to accept criticism without being floored by it, they open up, and they form strong bonds with each other. All sorts of things are discussed around the table.'

One regular at those first classes was Duncan McDonald, a retired Shell safety officer who'd moved to the area ten years before but still hadn't got to know many people. In addition, his wife Irene was sick with breast cancer. When he joined the class, he said he'd only ever presided over the barbecue but was now needing to learn to cook for his ailing wife and himself.

'It was a wonderful experience,' he says today. 'It was very helpful with the cooking, since I now have the confidence to walk up to the stove and see what's in the fridge and make a meal. I can also pick up a recipe and cook. My wife died four years ago now, and I cook for myself.' Even more than the cooking, however, Duncan, sixty-nine, found himself a great new network of friends. They proved incredibly supportive all the time he was looking after his wife, in her final days, and then after her death.

'Before, I would have passed a lot of chaps in the street nearly every day and wouldn't know who they were,' says Duncan. 'But now I can walk down the street and the men I now know stop for a chat, and we get together often for a meal. We each bring a dish and a bottle. It's wonderful to have their friendship. There was a lot of suicide and depression in the valley, and I think this course has really helped a lot of men.'

Somehow, the cooking done in the course becomes a metaphor for life. If the men taking part learn not to worry when the gravy gets lumpy, but instead to look for ways of fixing it or search for an alternative, that's a lesson they might one day be able to apply to a personal crisis. They learn to ask for help with a dish when they get into trouble halfway through, how to have the courage to be creative, to work as a member of a team, to solve problems, to take the initiative and to formulate a goal. And, as a bonus, they learn how to cook, too, and often end up throwing dinner parties for family and friends, which can provide an enormous boost to their confidence and self-esteem.

'It's the "men's shed" concept, with men getting together,' says Yvonne. 'It could be anything – woodwork, metalwork – but food is also a survival thing. Some men might be trying to look after a child or they might just have their children for weekends if a marriage has broken up, or they've lost a partner, so they need to be able to cook. For young males, it's another life skill, or it might lead to a job in hospitality. With the mix of ages, it's that mentoring thing too. I'm amazed by the way it's taking off. There are endless possibilities for it.'

Others have been quick to see the potential, too, with the centre winning a 2008 state government award for innovation in adult and community education. Inquiries from training organisations now coming from all over the country, as well as New Zealand. Some have duplicated Yvonne's methods for their own programs, and she's now designing a template for the course for others to adapt, and producing a package of materials and teaching aids. She would love, one day, to see such courses being offered everywhere there's a need, and even in lots of places where the need hasn't yet made itself known. 'The programs she's developed for men are very good at welding disparate groups of men together,' says Barry Golding, who specialises in the field of informal learning by adult men. 'Yvonne is very good at understanding the nature of community.

'She brought the men together in a place where they could

learn shoulder-to-shoulder, which they do really well, rather than being taught at face-to-face. They're not intimidated by the tutor or by stereotypes or even by recipes, and all kinds of magic can happen. In cities, people have many sorts of options for learning and socialising but in rural areas, the need for these kinds of networks is acute and critical for survival.'

For men in rural communities particularly, routinely faced with struggles over drought, running out of water, stock and crops dying, fluctuating prices for products and few services in the bush to help them cope with problems, everyone feels the course has enormous value. Chef Roi Rigoni is amazed by how successful they've proved, particularly when men who've completed earlier courses drop in on current classes from time to time, often just for the company. No-one's ever turned away – especially when they bring a bottle – and demand has far outstripped the number of men that can be comfortably accommodated.

'I think the courses have really helped a lot of people,' says Roi. 'At the end of the day, there is a need for one-on-one counselling, but this is a good step forward. Once the men are on the course, I can deal with most situations that arise. I've had to deal with a bit of stuff myself, like depression, cancer, a heart attack, a triple bypass and a pacemaker. So when people come on the course feeling bad, I tell them you can pull through anything. But Yvonne is really the heart and soul of the courses. She puts an incredible number of hours into them, and she's the world's biggest taskmaster, getting you to do things you never wanted to. But she's wonderful, and I love her dearly.'

Roi's democratic way of teaching and his understanding, have proved integral to the course's success, believes Yvonne. It's also helpful having a male as the tutor. 'Men have just never been taught how to ask for help,' says Yvonne. 'We bring up our men to believe that men don't cry, they shouldn't ask for help, counselling is for sissies, only failures ask for help. Most men don't find it easy to talk about things anyway; they can tend to be quite silent. Men at the moment, especially in the country areas, are really doing it hard. But where's the help, where's the support?'

Already, Yvonne knows the courses she runs have helped turn men's lives around. 'Yes, a number have come back to say how much they were helped,' she says softly. 'I know of a few lives that have even been saved along the way.'

These days, Yvonne, now fifty-six, still has health problems – especially when she works too many hours and ends up exhausted and drained. But what keeps her going is the knowledge that she's doing so much to help one small rural community and, with her example, so many others far into the Outback and beyond.

'She's just unreal,' says local Andy Shuttleworth, who teaches art at the centre. 'She gives up so much time to help other people, it's really wonderful to see. She might have 10 000 things to do that day, but whenever you ask her for help, she'll drop them all immediately to help you. The neighbourhood centre was just a shack when she took over, but now it's a great big place, offering so much stuff to do. There are often not that many diversions in the country, so it's great to have. There's been a lot of depression here at times, and we've had quite a high suicide rate in the past, but she's really helped a lot of people.'

With so many people struggling, she's also run a similar program for women, 'Saucy Shielas', and plans another for younger men. 'The earlier we can teach boys that it's all right to ask for help, that it's simply a part of growing up, the better,' says Yvonne, now with six beautiful grandchildren. 'We teach boys how to use a drill or how to do trigonometry, but we often don't teach them how to live, how to cook, iron clothes, care for themselves, look after children. Then we're surprised when they start to struggle. Boys are dropping out of school like nobody's business, especially in the country, and are bored and disruptive, and they grow into men who might not be able to cope when the going gets tough. So we should start now with trying to help them, not wait until it gets too bad.'

As a physical demonstration of how it's never too late to learn, and that often the experience taught by life is the greatest lesson of all, Yvonne has now obtained diplomas in Community Development, Community Education and Project Management, and advanced diplomas in Community Services Management and Management. In 2009 she was inducted onto the Victorian Honour Roll of Women for her services to the economy, community and families, and also won the Premier's Community Volunteering Leadership Award the same year. In addition, her project with Wodonga TAFE aiming to have community development skills – often acquired through volunteering – recognised by a qualification won an award for innovation in training and assessment from the Community Services and Health Industry Training Board. She hopes it will encourage many more people to volunteer in their communities. The neighbourhood centre was also a finalist in the 2009 Victorian Small Training Provider of the Year, a first for a neighbourhood house.

Yet while undoubtedly being able to help so many people,

particularly men, has also helped Yvonne come to terms with her grief over the loss of her son Darryl, he will always be with her. 'It's thirteen years [since he died], but I still find it hard to talk about it,' she says, her voice breaking. 'I wanted to give up when he died. But when his friends came to me for help, I realised I had something to offer.

'I understand some of the pain and despair being faced by those who are affected severely by the drought because at that time I lost almost everything: my home, my marriage, my businesses, my savings, my self-worth and finally my son. Since then, it has been a struggle, and I know the despair I have felt and how hard it is at times to get out of bed and face another day. Now, I just want to help others in ways I was unable to help my son.'

13

Ready for Anything

MICK LANAGAN, *Sandfire, Western Australia*

The scene was one of utter carnage. With crumpled bodies lying over the road and verge, the smashed-up hull of a ute quietly smoking in a culvert and pools of blood seeping into the red dust, Mick Lanagan went, without hesitation, straight to work.

He raced from casualty to casualty, assessing injuries, working out whose lives he could save and who was just too far gone. Even as he was calling on the satellite phone for backup, he knew that, at 270 kilometres from the nearest town on one of Australia's loneliest Outback highways, it could be a hell of a long time before any other help arrived. Calmly and efficiently, he administered emergency first aid to those he knew stood a chance, tried to stop their bleeding, bandaged their injuries, placed them on their sides and soothed the panicked.

'You have to be a little bit hard sometimes to do triage,' he says.

'But you've got to concentrate on where you can make a difference.' In this case, he knew his work could prove critical. A ute being driven by an unlicensed minor and crowded with people, both in the cabin and in the tray, had careened off the road, hit a ditch and rolled over, flinging passengers in every direction. Many were either unconscious or writhing in agony.

By the time Mick took a breath to look up, five ambulances had arrived at the scene, midway between Port Hedland and Broome on the edge of Australia's second-largest desert, the Great Sandy Desert, in the country's north-west. A Royal Flying Doctor Service (RFDS) plane had also landed on the local airstrip since it was too windy to attempt to put down on the road, ready to airlift patients to Perth. But by then, Mick had been working for a couple of hours in blistering 47-degree heat. 'I'd started to feel ill myself, but I hadn't been able to stop,' says Mick, who has diabetes and chronic back problems. 'But with others on the scene, I slumped down in the shade and a young paramedic came over and said I looked like I should eat something. He gave me a couple of biscuits to get my blood-sugar level back up again so I could carry on. I suppose I'd forgotten to look after myself, but I was all right.'

Thanks largely to Mick, just one of the thirteen people involved in the horror smash was pronounced dead at the scene, and only two died later in hospital. The rest survived. 'You have to be ready for anything when you live in a place like this,' says Mick, sagely. 'The Australian Outback can be a tough place, so you have to be prepared for it.'

And Mick's spent virtually his whole life getting prepared for absolutely anything that can go wrong in one of the most remote spots on earth, and making sure he's first on the scene to help.

There aren't many who could handle living in a place as isolated as the Sandfire Roadhouse. Two thousand kilometres north of Perth, halfway between the romantic old pearling town of Broome to the north and the iron ore exporting harbour of Port Hedland to the south, it's as far away as they come. But then Mick Lanagan isn't like most people. He loves the wide-open spaces of the vast, flat ochre dust plains that stretch out as far as the eye can see in every direction, and is eager to help others appreciate their wild beauty.

'I had a young couple call in once who said there was nothing here,' he grins. 'But I told them this is a place where you have to look more carefully for the beauty to reveal itself. In one square yard you can see maybe ten different sorts of native wildflowers. Then there's so many birds and so much wildlife – although unfortunately a lot of it without legs! – it's just incredible.

'As well, out here, at night, it's so silent you can actually *hear* the stars. It's magnificent. If you listen hard, you can hear the night talking to you. I can't imagine a better life.'

Along with the beauty, however, comes a fair amount of savagery. The two-lane highway that runs past Sandfire is so straight, countless drivers have fallen asleep at the wheel and ended up in horrific accidents. Many of them overdose on carbohydrate snacks out of boredom, then become drowsy. In an accident, sometimes they're at risk of choking on what they've just been eating.

The area is also so empty and windswept that Mick has to

deal with numerous tourists who get into trouble far from their comfort zone in their usual cushioned city haunts. People living on stations inland, towards the coast 20 kilometres away, and just about anywhere along the 600 square kilometre stretch of lonely Outback that Mick looks after, all turn to him for help when sickness strikes, accidents happen or someone gets bitten by a snake. And that's not to mention the sizzling 51 degree summer temperatures and the deadly bushfires and fierce cyclones, which can strike without warning at any time, day or night.

But as a forty-five-year volunteer with the RFDS and St John Ambulance, and constantly either on his radio liaising with those organisations or driving the highway in his ambulance – he once covered 1900 kilometres in one day's shift once – Mick's are always a safe pair of hands . . . whatever happens. 'He's unbelievably helpful and his skills are highly regarded,' says Lyle Gilbert, the St John Ambulance station manager at Port Hedland. 'Without him we would certainly have seen much worse outcomes, with people having to go a long, long way for help. He started with a genuine concern to help others and he now provides the best care possible for people. He's real salt of the earth, his heart is definitely in the right place, and he's a great part of the team.'

One Christmas two years ago, a young mum collapsed at the caravan park at the roadhouse, and Mick managed to haul her back from the dead. An asthma sufferer, she turned out to have a severe respiratory problem resulting from a chest infection.

Another time, a man who'd already been sick for a week stopped off at Sandfire, having driven past five hospitals on his way there. He asked for help and Mick took him to his place. Once there, the man crumpled. 'He basically died on my dining-room floor,' says Mick. 'So I brought him back to. I got him cranked up again and then I told him what a clown he was for not looking after himself, and not going for help earlier. Some people are real stupid.'

But there's often a lighter side to his work, too. One afternoon, a German family rolled their car and Mick rushed to their aid to find their little girl with blood pouring from her mouth. He examined her hastily, expecting to find terrible head injuries – until she spat out a tooth that had become loose.

A rugged kind of Outback bloke, Mick's origins are from hardy Irish-Australian stock.

His mum Eileen O'Connor was born in 1910 in Cork, the Republic of Ireland's second-largest city. It wasn't an easy childhood: her dad Gerald was killed in a hunting accident six weeks after her birth and her mum, also Eileen, a nurse during World War I, then married an Australian soldier stationed in the UK. At nine years old, the young Eileen junior set sail with her mum and new stepdad Septimus to his homeland, settling in Perth.

But it wasn't the fresh, happy new start they all hoped for. Septimus turned out to be a heavy drinker, and her mother suffered ill health. Both died the same year, leaving Eileen, who'd been nursing them both, penniless and having to look for work. She ended up in a variety of jobs, as a cleaner, as a cook and as a child-minder. In 1926, she had a daughter, Kathleen, and in 1936 left the city to become a cook and companion to the wife of a wealthy Outback sheep-station owner at remote Turee Creek, between Paraburdoo and Newman in the Pilbara. It was there that Eileen met George Lanagan, a New South Wales–born head stockman who was also enormously skilled at erecting windmills, looking after cars and generators, sinking bores, making saddles and tending horses.

The pair married in 1938 and went to manage a station near Wyndham, 55 kilometres from Kununurra near the Northern Territory border, and then in Billiluna, 150 kilometres south of Halls Creek in the Kimberley. 'Working around the sheep and cattle stations was a hard life, but Dad knew no different,' says Mick today. 'Dad loved the Outback, and Mum grew to love it too. She was an extraordinary woman to adapt so well to such a completely different way of life.'

Twenty-five years before their arrival, surveyor Albert Canning had been asked to find a route Kimberley cattlemen could use to take their stock to markets down south to supply the eastern goldfields at Wiluna, 180 kilometres east of Meekatharra and 764 kilometres north-east of Perth. It was too expensive to ship cattle from Wyndham, and driving them south through the deserts would prove a way of avoiding the cattle tick that was plaguing much of the cattle in the tropical north. So with a team of eight men, twenty-three camels, two ponies and a series of Aboriginal guides kept in chains, Canning trekked, mapped and sank fifty-one wells in some of the most inhospitable terrain in Australia, through the Gibson Desert and the Great Sandy Desert. In doing so, he created the Canning Stock Route, one of the toughest and most remote last-frontier tracks in the world – and its longest historic stock route – covering a distance of 1780 kilometres from Halls Creek to Wiluna.

During the 1930s, at least one mob of cattle a year was brought down this treacherous track and George Lanagan, as one of Western

Australia's most experienced stockmen, drove cattle down the track no fewer than four times. In 1940, on his last trip along the full route with its vast expanses of sand dunes, spinifex plains, salt lakes and steep hills, thirty-year-old Eileen came along too, making history as the only white woman ever to traverse the Canning Stock Route with a full mob of cattle. Since the track was pitted with the graves of so many men who'd died en route, to complete the four-and-a-half month journey was a remarkable achievement for any man, let alone a woman. But Eileen rose magnificently to the task, and each day would ride ahead of the 800 cattle, fifty-five horses and twelve camels on her horse Nully, prepare camp and burn any poison bush before the cattle could graze on it.

Despite the hardships, the snakes and the packs of dingoes that howled all night, she coped well and carried only five possessions with her: a diary, a pencil, a camera, a gun and a jar of face cream. Today, her beautiful black-and-white photos are stored for posterity in the JS Battye Library of West Australian History, an arm of the State Library of Western Australia. They also keep the cookbook she wrote as president of the Kimberley Division, much later in 1979, with its myriad Outback recipes, including one for Stock Route Bread. 'First, catch your camel,' it recommends, so the would-be cooks can find the ingredients carried in its panniers. After making the dough mixture, they're instructed then to put it in a dish that will fit into the boxes on the camel's back without slipping out. 'There is no need to knock back dough as the movement of the camel has this effect.'

In the years after running the stock route, Eileen and George had two children, a daughter, Mary, born in 1944, and a son, Mick, born in Geraldton in 1946. Their youngest child was a chip off

George's block. By the age of four, with his dad managing Carnegie Station, some 500 kilometres east of Wiluna, Mick was riding horses like he'd been born on one, and mustering 500 sheep on his own. He was also a bright kid and excelled at the correspondence course lessons he studied at home.

But at nine, there was a rude shock in store: he was sent off to boarding school in Perth. 'I didn't know what a football was or what a cricket ball was for, and I was teased mercilessly,' he says. 'I just couldn't handle it. I didn't belong there and I absolutely hated it.' He was a rebel all the way through school. Joining the school air force cadets, he took revenge on an officer who bullied the smallest boy in his class by filling his boots with honey – something that saw him locked up overnight in a cell. Two weeks after his thirteenth birthday, he gave his parents an ultimatum: either they let him leave and go out to work or, he vowed, they'd never see him again. He won. He quit school and got his first job at the Elders saleyards, working with both sheep and cattle.

When George was offered a new job back in the Kimberley, managing another station near Derby, Mick returned with his parents and began learning the business. While his dad was a fabulous cattle man, however, he wasn't a great teacher. Quiet and introverted, he had a terrible stutter that made him even more self-conscious. Instead, George sent his son out to work with a windmill man, to learn how to build them for himself, repair them and sink bores. After that, he was sent to an engineer to learn from him how to work with engines and pumps. Watching his dad with the stock also taught him a great deal, and soon he had become a huge help around the stations. When the family moved to another station at Myroodah, between Broome and Fitzroy Crossing, Mick was routinely left in charge. One time, during the 1967 rainy season when Mick was twenty-one, his parents went on holiday. He was out cutting yard posts with the workers between rainstorms when the head of the axe he was using flew off as he swung at a tree. It caught him on the inside of his right knee, cutting it badly and leaving it a mess of blood and bone. Mick wrapped it up tight with rags and then someone drove him back to the homestead through the mud on the tractor.

There, Mick radioed the RFDS. The doctor on call, hearing him describe the injury, said he'd have to go to the hospital at Derby for repairs, but the river was up and the airstrip was soaked. He was left with only two options: ride a horse the 140 kilometres to Derby, or undergo repairs at home. 'I know all station men are saddlers – so are you?' asked the RFDS doctor. Mick said he was. 'Well, can you stitch it up yourself then?' Mick knew there was little alternative. 'So I packed the wound with sulphanilamide and threaded a needle,' he says. 'The first stitch took some doing, but it wasn't too painful as it had gone pretty numb. The next few days were a bit ordinary with a bit of pain, but it healed up pretty well. I would have done anything for a bottle of rum, medicinally speaking! But when my dad returned home, he got up at me not so much for the accident – my fault as I hadn't secured the axe head properly – but because the stitching wasn't as neat as he'd taught me . . .'

Yet Mick was nothing if not resourceful. Few people in the area will ever forget the time, the year before, when a man fell ill and lapsed into a coma on neighbouring Nerrima Station, south of the Derby to Fitzroy Crossing road. The airstrip there was again wet, so Mick knew he'd have to be taken to the strip at Myroodah,

70 kilometres north, for evacuation by plane. But there was one huge problem: lying between Mick and Nerrima Station was a big, boggy blacksoil plain, impossible to cross by vehicle.

The plan Mick hatched was strange, but simple. A stretcher was lashed between two mules who were led, belly-deep, into the bog. When Mick, his helper and the mules reached the unconscious man on the other side of the plain, they tied him onto the stretcher then urged the mules back, trudging through the mud to rejoin their vehicle on the other side, and drove him straight to meet the RFDS plane.

'Mules are tough, reliable, never-give-up animals,' laughs Mick. 'They're also pig-headed buggers. The weather was closing in and the Queenair was coordinated to get to Myroodah at the same time as us, and took off again just in time, with rain splattering on her. Turned out the chap was diabetic, and would have died without the mules and the RFDS – and us, I suppose.'

One summer night that same year, Mick's dad was struck by severe abdominal pain. The emergency button was pushed on the RFDS radio to alert the base operators in Derby, who immediately dispatched a plane, guided to the strip by the headlights of four trucks. 'It turned out he had a ruptured ulcer, which was bleeding badly internally,' says Mick. 'He made a full recovery thanks to the RFDS. The alternative would have been a five-hour trip on the back of a truck over gravel roads. He mightn't have made that.'

It was the beginning of Mick's lifelong love affair with the RFDS.

The Outback could be a rough kind of companion, but Mick never wanted it any other way. He went contracting for a while, building fences and installing tanks and windmills, but was never any good at the money side of running his own business. He then went back to working on stations, where his wide variety of skills were always in great demand and, at one point, even tried to set up a school outside Derby for the bush kids who simply weren't getting any education.

He tried living back in the city once, in Perth, when his sister Mary fell ill and needed support and help with her kids. There, he started driving trucks. Absence hadn't made him any fonder of city life, however. 'I hated waking up in the morning, knowing I was in a city,' he says. 'People in the city don't seem to have any manners; they push past you, they're rushing and they're always walking around with their heads down. In the bush, you don't have those kind of routines. You work with the seasons, you fix things when they go wrong, and you're master of your own destiny.' Eventually, his sister told him to go back to the Outback; he was making her miserable, too. Sadly, she died in 1986, at the age of just forty-two.

By then, Mick had started having health problems of his own. He'd had two bad horse-riding accidents and then in 1989, also at the age of forty-two, he had a third. He'd been riding a big galloper on a station when it hit a hole in the ground, fell over and rolled on top of Mick, concertinaing his spine and crushing discs. The horse had to be shot to put it out of its misery, and Mick was raced to hospital, courtesy again of the RFDS.

Things there went from bad to worse. At the local hospital, he was simply offered some Panadol and sent away. But still in pain, and sure there was something seriously wrong, he flew down to the hospital in Perth where his sister Kathleen was working as a deputy matron. A battery of tests revealed he had cancer in his spine. He was in the hospital for the next six months, enduring numerous laser probes with no pain relief possible, in case anything went wrong with his spinal cord during the operations. 'Fortunately, I'm so pig-headed, I can turn pain off,' says Mick. 'You feel pain and know you can't stop it, so I've learnt to ignore it and blank it out.'

Eventually, though, Mick couldn't cope with being confined to the hospital for so long, and discharged himself. 'I decided I'd go back to the Outback for some peace and quiet and see how I went there. And I managed to cure myself, with the power of positive thinking. Being out there always helps.'

That kind of mental resilience when the chips are down never fails to impress those who know him best. 'He just willed himself better through sheer determination,' says Meredith Earnshaw, who, as the medical-chest officer for the RFDS's Western Operations, looks after the medical kits left on all stations. 'He makes the best of absolutely everything. He's an old-style bushie, incredibly self-reliant and strong-minded.'

Unable to go back to riding horses to do station work, however, Mick found himself at a loose end. It was then that an old mate, Ken Norton, the owner of the roadhouse at Sandfire, called. Ken's father Eddie had set up the roadhouse in 1970; his truck broke down there with a load of fuel drums on the back, so he simply started selling fuel pumped from them, the first few litres for a carton of beer. Ken and Mick had got to know each other when Mick was working at the station at Wallal Downs, 45 kilometres away, and Mick had become godfather to Ken's daughter Karina. 'Mick seemed to be vegetating up Broome way and didn't know what to do next,' says Ken. 'I knew he's a man who can turn his hand to anything and is sharp as a tack. He's also pretty good at all the medical stuff. So I thought he'd be pretty handy to have around here.'

Ken invited him down and asked if he'd be willing to do a course in looking after engines, bowsers and lighting plants. Delighted, Mick said he would, got his certificates, then went to Sandfire to live. It was the start of a whole new phase of his life.

Nestled between the last two monster sand dunes of the Great Sandy Desert, the Sandfire Roadhouse is the only fuel stop in 610 kilometres of road running through the barren landscape. Today, it doesn't look too impressive. In 2007 a blaze roared through the roadhouse – famous for its collection of single shirt sleeves hanging from the ceiling, left by people passing through for a $10 donation to the RFDS – gutting the building and causing $1.5 million in damage. Fire investigators believe it was started by an electrical fault. Then many of the trees that provided shelter to the site were flattened by the ferocious Cyclone Laurence, which hit the west coast in December 2009 with wind gusts of up to 285 kilometres per hour.

Mick Lanagan, however, remains philosophical. 'No-one got hurt, which is the best thing,' he says. 'And while I think the cyclone blew our airstrip windsock probably to Alice Springs, these kind of things happen in the country. We do choose to live here!'

Shortly after an earlier cyclone struck back in 1994, his father and mother both died. That wasn't his only source of sadness. He had a daughter, Rosemary, but she left with her mum when the relationship broke up and, twenty-two years later, they tragically lost her to drugs. He's always been close to his sisters' children, though, and has 'adopted' three more daughters over the years. They were troubled girls who came to him for help in their teenage years and, later, when they'd got over their problems, each asked him if they could keep him on as their surrogate 'dad'. 'I guess after my own daughter died, I just wanted to help others who were having difficulties,' says Mick, quietly. 'People seem to know I like helping others, so it goes with the territory.'

His goddaughter Karina Turner, says he's a real softie who's always there for everyone. 'When people want a bit of a hand, or guidance, or even someone to talk to, he's such a good bloke,' she says. 'He has great stories about life and the people he's met along the way, and he's fantastic to sit down and have a yarn with.'

Mick's 'adopted' daughters, Annette, Rachel, and Rosemary – with the same name as his late daughter – all now live happy lives of their own, and have given him the joy of nine grandchildren and one great-grandson. 'It's funny, but everyone says he even looks like me!' laughs Mick. 'It's the power of thought!' They're also just as keen on the RFDS as the man they all call 'Dad'. When Annette suddenly had complications with a pregnancy, the RFDS picked her up from her station near Wubin, 250 kilometres north of Perth, to take her to the city's hospital where she made a good recovery and proceeded to have a daughter at full term. Years later they also came to the rescue of that daughter, Barbara, when she had a gall bladder emergency at her home in Augusta, in the Margaret River area, flying her to hospital in Perth, 320 kilometres away. 'So I guess the RFDS really saved her twice,' grins Mick. It was similarly good news when Rachel was bitten by a snake on the ankle ten years ago. In that case, the RFDS's training program for such incidents stood him, and her, in very good stead.

'Dad comes across as rough and gruff, but he's the most genuinely nice bloke I've ever come across,' says Annette Nix. 'He helped me out in a difficult time and, to me, he became my dad. He gave me a huge hand, and he's always been there for me, he's been the saving grace. He's very self-effacing, yet he's an amazing man. He'll get up regularly in the middle of the night to help anyone, and he still gets so many letters, emails and even visits from people he saved, years later.'

Mick simply believes in giving back, and he's tireless in his devotion to the RFDS, looking after all the region's medical chests. Meredith is full of admiration. 'He's a very giving person and is always ready to help out anyone who needs it. We rely on people like him, but such exceptional people are few and far between. He's very proactive in finding out if he can be doing anything better and is always ready to train anyone or advise them, or help if they have difficulties.'

Sandfire itself is gradually recovering from its own misfortunes, too. A two-piece transportable has opened on the site of the old roadhouse, providing travellers once more with food, drinks and a shop. A tavern next to it is also being built, in the style of an old bush pub, with 44-gallon drums serving as tables. The accommodation – both the motel units and the caravan park – survived all three calamities, both cyclones and the fire, intact.

'There's just nowhere I'd prefer to be,' says Mick, now sixty-three, who bought his house from Ken for a nominal single dollar – just to avoid having to fill out forms saying he was renting. 'It's what you're born to. The suburbs are nice, but I couldn't live there because the back fence is too close. My back fence is Alice Springs – 1400 kilometres away!'

For Ken, having Mick as one of the five people who live at Sandfire is a constant delight, he says. 'We can't work together, but we get along just famously,' he chuckles. 'We paddle our own canoes. For someone to truly enjoy the bush, they need a bit of solitude about them and to be self-reliant. But he's great company and his medical work comes in very useful.'

It's that medical work that Mick loves, too. Finally swapping his Akubra for the peaked caps of the RFDS or St John Ambulance – depending on the job he happens to be on – he's happy to be the man everyone turns to for help in that part of the world. 'Over that 600-kilometre gap between Broome and Port Hedland, they rely on me and my ambulance,' says Mick. 'It's just a way of life. There's always something that goes wrong in a remote place like this and there's never time to get bored.

'I first came across the RFDS as a four year old when one of the stockmen on the station I was living on got injured and the plane was summoned. I remember how scared I felt when I saw the plane starting to fall out of the sky, and land in a cloud of dust. It was only later, when I learnt to fly myself, that I discovered that every landing is a controlled crash! But I love helping them; they're part of my family. I just love people, and it's fun to help. And I love living here. How can you ever get lonely in the bush? There's always plenty of people travelling through, there's the native wildlife and you have your pets. There really is no place like it.'

14

A God-given Desire to Fly

ELAINE CROWDER, *from Bourke to Broken Hill,*
Oodnadatta to Alice Springs

She was a young kindergarten teacher in a town being built around
an iron-ore mine deep in the wilds of Western Australia; the other
woman was someone who'd been running an outlying Outback
station for the last twenty years, and had never even been near a
town before.

It was an encounter that was to end up changing 23-year-old
Elaine Cleal's life.

'She walked up and I was so shocked by her appearance,' says
Elaine. 'She had these deep, deep furrows in her face from working outdoors for so many years. Life had been very hard for her,
and she'd never even been to a hairdresser's, let alone imagined
going to a beautician. She had to put orders in for food months
in advance, as the traders only delivered every so often, and fresh

fruit and vegetables were a rarity. I was so impacted by that. It made me realise, suddenly, what an uneven playing field it was in Australia. I learnt, for the first time, the effect of isolation on families and how tough life is for many people in the Outback.'

It was hardly a picnic for Elaine either, back in 1968 in Tom Price, the new town settled after mining magnate Lang Hancock discovered rich deposits of iron ore in the Hamersley Ranges, 1564 kilometres north of Perth. Although the site was being rapidly developed by Hamersley Iron, with housing, streets and bars for after-work drinking, there were precious few other facilities. And with people arriving from all over Australia and the rest of the world to work at the mines, life was absolutely chaotic.

'It was a community plonked in the middle of nowhere and everything was very, very basic,' says Elaine, then setting up, and working as director of, its kindergarten. 'There were no facilities for people being counselled, or advice services, or anything like that. There were always going to be problems and breakdowns of some kind. It just seemed that people in the Outback often needed these services more than anyone else, and they were always missing out.'

By the time Elaine returned to Sydney to live with her newly widowed mother, she'd developed both a close affinity with the Outback and a real concern about what she regarded as a grave social injustice in the lack of resources available there. When a major report was released years later by the Australian Human Rights and Equal Opportunity Commission, revealing that more than 800 000 children and young people in rural and remote Australia 'suffer educational disadvantage that verges on discrimination', she was shocked.

That same year, 2000, the now married Elaine Crowder launched her own charity to try to help right some of those historic wrongs. In her United with God (UWG) Aerial Ministries Inc. plane, she makes regular flights to Outback areas to provide any struggling locals with goods they might need, services they long for, educational help for their kids, counselling or even simply a chat. If they ask her for spiritual guidance, she'll give that too. 'People have to cope with isolation, running a property, looking after their children, helping them to learn by satellite computer – when some parents are illiterate themselves – and often in conditions of ter-rible hardship,' says Elaine. 'We assist any person in need in these rural, remote and Outback communities. And often – irrespective of drought or eventual rain – the needs are great.'

Whenever Elaine lands in White Cliffs, the dusty old opal town (population 210) in the north-west of New South Wales, 90 kilo-metres north of Wilcannia, one of the first people to greet her is little Grace Dowton. As a baby she suffered convulsions, which left her with cerebral palsy, and Elaine first met her when she was three. Grace is now ten years old; the pair are firm friends, and her parents count Elaine as one of their greatest supports. Mum Wendy Dowton says she's become an incredibly valued ally. 'There are those times you put out to the universe or whatever that you need support and Elaine just came along,' she says. 'She gave us support in so many different ways with Grace. She would give us help in any way we needed it, in whatever capacity she could.' Husband Neville says she's simply a great person to have around. 'She's just so nice and she's a very, very kind-hearted sort of person. She's helped Grace and she's really someone you can rely on.'

The help Elaine offers other families is as varied as it is valued. One woman on a remote Outback station in the far west of New South Wales asked for some counselling as she was very depressed and lonely. Elaine talked to her for hours, then presented her with a beautiful basket of lavender soaps donated to her by one of her local Sydney churches. 'She was overwhelmed that others could be so caring to someone they'd never met,' smiles Elaine. 'Tears were running down the lady's face – but this time, tears of happiness!'

A family in the same region was devastated at the loss of their baby, and their grief was made even worse by the knowledge that they didn't have enough money to provide her with a proper funeral. The day Elaine delivered funds for the ceremony was another she'll never forget.

It was a much happier occasion when Elaine phoned ahead to find out what another family on an isolated property near Bourke might be wishing for. The answer took her completely by surprise: a pizza. Not prepared to disappoint anyone, she ended up flying in with five frozen pizzas for the family to warm up their own takeaway feast.

More often, she delivers clothes, shoes, books, toiletries and DVDs to families, although once she even donated a four-wheel drive, driven there by one of her team of volunteers to transport the goods. The practical help, along with counselling, educational assistance – for which she is extremely well qualified after a lifetime of teaching – financial advice or anything else anyone might need, is delivered not only by her but also by others of her group of people with varied, and complementary, skills. The day she was asked to help out in a motel, peeling potatoes, to give the staff time to sort out some of their issues, won't be forgotten for a long time.

'But every time you are able to help anyone, it's an amazing experience,' laughs Elaine, now sixty-five, who also takes Bibles and Evangelical Sisters of Mary Christian literature for those who ask for it. 'Outback people are so generous themselves, and they can find it hard to accept a helping hand. Yet some of them are doing it so tough, they really appreciate a bit of help. And some of us in the cities are so keen to offer it.

'I feel very blessed to be doing this. I love to fly, and I have a real passion for the Outback. In a dream, God instructed me to buy the charity plane, and then He taught me what I should be doing with it. And as soon as I started the charity, people came from everywhere to help: web designers, accountants, aviation people, ministers, pastors, people wanting to give away things they don't need . . . It's been amazing!'

Elaine grew up in the north-western New South Wales farming town of Warialda – which translates as 'the place of wild honey' – 602 kilometres north of Sydney in the Gwydir shire. She was the youngest of six children, and the only girl, to her parents, Herbert, a shearing contractor and weekend bookmaker, and Mary, a staunch Presbyterian, who did the paperwork for the business. All the children – Don, Greg, Ken, John and Frank – learnt to live with their dad's mantra, 'We are no better than anybody, and nobody is better than us', and became used to sharing their house with various workers who came to stay at times, from every religion, race and walk of life.

'Dad would give anyone the shirt off his back,' says Elaine. 'He was extraordinarily helpful to everyone, loving, and very generous. We would have Indigenous people staying at the house, shearers, wool pressers, cooks, everyone. It was a great lesson in life.' It also made a huge impression on a young girl who came to embrace similar values of fairness, egalitarianism and humility.

After boarding school in Inverell, 128 kilometres away, she did her nursery school diploma, which she then converted into a Bachelor of Education specialising in early childhood. She taught at preschools in Parkes, in western New South Wales, and in Moree in the north-west of the state. Then she took the job of establishing a preschool at Tom Price. She was appointed by the Australian Inland Mission (later to become Frontier Services) founded by the Reverend John Flynn, who started the Royal Flying Doctor Service. It was a seminal move. As preschool director, she was also expected to be teacher, family advisor, bookkeeper, accountant, nurse, counsellor, fundraiser, public relations officer, Presbyterian representative, and much more besides.

There were many other things Reverend Flynn's successor, Reverend Fred McKay, didn't mention when he appointed Elaine. 'Like the difficulties of being only one of six single females among a population of thousands of men!' says Elaine, who was also featured in Ivan Rudolph's book, *Flynn's Outback Angels*. Rudolph likened her work to that of Reverend Flynn himself.

Elaine's father had died the year she'd gone out to Tom Price, so in 1970 she moved to Sydney to keep her mum company, working in a selection of nursery schools around the city. In 1974, she married the English-born marine engineer David Crowder, whom she'd met on a cruise around the South Pacific, and the next year took up a job with the New South Wales Department of Youth and Community Services as an early childhood advisor. As well as conducting workshops in child-care centres in Sydney, she also spent time educating people in childcare in the far west of the state: in Bourke, Walgett, Brewarrina and Lightning Ridge. In 1977, she and David had a son, Philip, and after that taught part time in TAFEs around Sydney and the Central Coast. Then, tragically, David was struck down with non-Hodgkin's lymphoma. In December 1988, after spending a year in and out of hospital and with Philip having turned eleven, he died at the age of just forty-three.

'It was one of the toughest years of my life,' says Elaine. 'After my son and I had worked through great grief, all this helped me to really prioritise what's important in life: quality time with my son; having a real appreciation for those less fortunate; laughter; quality relationships; and all those things money can't buy. After all, how many chairs can one sit in at one time, and how much materialism is wholesome?'

Elaine and Philip went on a number of trips together, back home to Warialda, to Melbourne, Cairns, the Gold Coast, Byron Bay and Bali. When Philip was eighteen, mother and son even did a parachute jump together to mark the day. However, when Philip finished school and said he wanted to spend a year in Brazil as an exchange student, Elaine started thinking seriously about what she wanted to do with the rest of her life. She'd been teaching at the Meadowbank TAFE in western Sydney, but began thinking of learning to fly. She'd always loved flying, having longed to be a pilot since she was shown a photo of her father in air force uniform when she was little. She'd even taken a couple of flying lessons in Moree. Now she decided it was time to rediscover her passion, 'my God-given desire to fly'.

In between working full time, as well as teaching an additional two evenings a week, she managed to fit in an extra three nights a week of TAFE study in aviation theory, and could afford flying lessons in a Cessna 150 once a month at Bankstown, and then in a Cessna 172 at Bathurst. Learning to fly in outdated, ancient aircraft, often more fitting for the scrap heap than for beginners, proved a real test of her nerves. The doors flew open on her first solo circuit, knobs on the dashboard routinely came off in her hands, there were radio failures in the training area and front wheel tyre blow-outs, and she had to become used to a pilot seat that bounced forwards and backwards as she was roaring up the runway at full speed, getting ready to lift off.

Elaine's dream was still to be able to fly solo and gradually an idea began to form: starting up a charity involving flying to the Outback. All the dramas of learning to fly, she knew, would prove great practice for the uncertainties that no doubt lay in wait well beyond the eastern seaboard. After seven years, at the age of fifty-four, she finally achieved her pilot's licence. It felt like the start of something big. 'Next came the dream from God in regard to getting the charity plane for His work in the Outback,' she says.

Her son, Philip, now thirty-three and a Sydney teacher of kids with behavioural issues, was amazed that she'd embarked on such a new direction in her life at a comparatively late age. 'I think she found her true calling then, a time when all her skills came together to enable her to do something like this,' he says. 'She's always been an extraordinary woman, setting up early childhood centres around Australia, but this was a major new challenge. I'm sure many people questioned what she was doing, but she's so determined, so driven, and all she wants to do is help people in the Outback.'

Elaine used her and her late husband's superannuation, with her house put up as collateral, to be able to afford to buy a four-seater Cessna 172SP Skyhawk plane in the US, which was delivered and reassembled in Sydney. She then began setting up her nonprofit tax-deductible charity. The objective was to visit those in need to give educational support, provide social and emotional counselling, and make donations.

'It was to show the love of Jesus in a compassionate and caring way to those in isolated and remote locations in the Outback,' she says. 'It seemed this was the path I was being led along. I became a teacher, then I learnt to fly, and I had always had a passion for the Outback. It all came together in the voluntary work I'm now doing.'

So far, Elaine has flown to the Outback nineteen times, fourteen of them alone. Destinations include west and north-west New South Wales, visiting places like Wilcannia, White Cliffs, Tilpa, Narromine, Cobar, Dubbo, Ivanhoe, Bourke and Broken Hill; she's also visited part of south-west Queensland, the south-eastern corner of the Northern Territory and northern South Australia, close to Innamincka. Many of these places haven't seen rain for years, which has contributed a great deal to families' hardship.

When she's there – either by herself, or with volunteers – she'll often offer counselling, one-on-one language and literature sessions with the children, music and movement sessions, after-school care and respite care, and will network with charities, community groups, churches, schools, hospitals, libraries and services such as the Royal Flying Doctor Service (RFDS). 'For our volunteers, it can prove a real education, too,' she says. 'Especially when they're fighting off bush flies or they find a snake near where they're sleeping. I've found city slickers generally don't like outdoor showering with snakes and spiders, or getting covered in red dust. But for me, having been born in the bush, I like all that, and I never mind getting some dust up my nose.'

The journeys are rarely without drama. On Elaine's first trip to the Outback, with fewer landmarks to help with navigation over the wide-open spaces and with the sun in her eyes almost all the way, she managed to get lost. As the sun finally began to sink below the horizon, she knew she'd have to land somewhere soon. Spotting an airstrip on a station, she made preparations to land and the owner, noticing she was coming in with darkness looming, parked his four-wheel drive with its lights on at the end of the runway to guide her in. As she climbed out of the plane, he bounded up to shake her hand and told her he had dinner ready. The next morning, to repay the favour, she flew him over his station, which he'd never before seen from the air. She's visited him and his family many times since, but always with plenty of notice.

She's often found herself battling whirly-whirlies, spiralling gales that whip across the plains, and once, on the way from Wilcannia to Cobar, a wind that did a 180 degree turn and left her performing involuntary aerobatics, with her head most of the time up against the plane's roof. Another time, the plane's alternator wasn't working properly and she even considered a forced landing on the Moomba oilfields off the Strzelecki Track in north-eastern South Australia. Luckily, she was able to make the plane limp into Innamincka, with all unnecessary electrics turned off, so as not to drain the battery.

But the people she meets make every adventure worthwhile and, generally, she'll start one conversation that will lead to many others. One time, a rural doctor told her about a family having a tough time; another couple she was visiting told her of someone else who needed a helping hand. 'It's like a rolling stone,' Elaine laughs. 'You start off, and you soon find out where there's most need. And we'll always follow up on people, send parcels or call them on the phone, and keep detailed notes and records. That's a very important part of our service.'

One young man, living alone in the shearing sheds at an isolated Outback station, happened to mention that he'd love a couple of videos to pass away some of the time he spent on his own. A child in another family was having trouble at school, and needed some extra coaching. A father had been given access to his young daughter by the family court, but couldn't find any way of getting to her mother's home. Two boys having to live with their grandparents while their mum was in Sydney looking after their young brother in hospital revelled in regular visits, showing Elaine their school certificates and sports trophies. A victim of domestic violence needed some emotional support after making the decision to leave her husband. A mum with an intellectually challenged child needed some guidance on his future schooling. Another woman simply wanted to chat, since she hadn't seen any-one outside her immediate family for weeks.

Volunteer helper Bruce Robjohns, an ex-RFDS radio operator,

met Elaine first in White Cliffs, where he was a community worker, and she was flying with a hairdresser-beautician to visit some of the most isolated women in drought-ravaged areas. 'They got a facial and their hair done, which would be so novel and wonderful for them, even though no-one was going to see them!' he laughs. 'That's Elaine. She's always about practical help that will make people feel better, rather than making them fill out forms and talking about help that'll never come. I always think of her very much in the ilk of Reverend John Flynn: flying around and really helping people out with their practical needs.'

She grew even more determined, too, after the report by the Australian Human Rights Commission, which found that children in rural areas were much more likely to be significantly educationally disadvantaged than those in the cities, with inferior service and much lower educational success rates.

'It's just not a level playing field for people in the Outback,' says Elaine. 'I just feel that some of us in the cities have so much, and others have so little. I like to help everyone, white, black or brindle, to help everyone to reach their full potential, and the charity is non-denominational and non-governmental. Some people just need a leg up from time to time.'

Pastor Scott Lamshed, with churches in Wilcannia and Broken Hill, says she's really helped everyone she's come into contact with. 'She's brought us many donations that we've been able to give out to meet some of the needs in our community,' he says. 'And always, when she says she's going to do something, she does it. She's very genuine, empathetic, and feels where people are at. I now consider her a close friend.'

With each trip costing around $4000, Elaine has to limit them to one every three months, raising funds through speaker nights, trivia evenings, a stall at a flea market, donations from supporters and businesses, information on her website (www.uwg.org.au), and hiring out the charity plane. In 2007, she even put her house on Sydney's North Shore on the market to raise more money, but it failed to sell. Instead, she converted it to create a self-contained flat on one side, which she could rent out for extra cash for the charity trips. At the moment she's caring for an elderly woman with Parkinson's disease, with that rent earmarked for the next flight, too.

But whatever happens, Elaine's adamant her mission will continue for many years. 'We do need to remember that if these people didn't live where they live in the Outback, the city supermarket shelves would be very depleted,' she says. 'We depend on them, and we should make sure they're living the best life they're able to while they're providing us with so much.

'The average person on the coast has absolutely no concept of the Outback and the life it entails. They live in cities, they have good schools and all the facilities, and they holiday overseas. But it's such an uneven playing field, many people need extra help. My son and I have been very blessed by God, and I believe it is now time for me to bless those less fortunate who are doing it tough in Outback Australia. And, along with others who are prepared to volunteer, or assist financially, as long as I'm able, I'll keep offering that help.'

15

The Power of Humanity

Olga Havnen, *Darwin, Northern Territory*

The situation quickly grew desperate. In the small community of Beswick, about 100 kilometres east of Katherine in the untouched wilds of Arnhem Land, the only local store in the area had shut up shop.

The manager had become embroiled in a bitter stand-off with the locals: he wanted his rent reduced; they said the rent was eminently reasonable. So he simply closed down the sole source of food, clothing and basic necessities in the remote Outback area, locked the doors and drove home to nearby Barunga.

Members of the Jawoyn community called the Fred Hollows Foundation for help. They explained the situation to Olga Havnen, the Foundation's Indigenous manager, and asked her advice. She was appalled. 'In a really crude way, it was having the effect of starving people into submission,' she says. 'And I don't think store management was this man's particular area of expertise, either. I felt the quality and availability of supplies in the store was not terribly satisfactory.'

The store had already been closed for two weeks, and Olga knew she'd have to act quickly. She told the locals the Foundation would provide them with an interest-free loan to restock the store and find someone as a new, short-term store manager. She then approached Woolworths, to see if they'd donate some of their old shelving and refrigeration equipment to a good cause, and second one of their store managers to work with the local committee to train them in what needed to be done.

In a very short time, the store was completely restocked with goods showcased beautifully on new shelves. It wasn't just fruit, vegetables, meat and bread, either, but also fridges and washing machines – and for sale at $50 less than in the nearest town, Katherine. Even more impressive, within six months the community had repaid the loan in full to the Foundation. In addition, it had paid something like $120 000 in wages within the community.

Olga was thrilled. 'It was such a good example of how, if you provide the kind of support and expertise that people ask for, you can get some really good outcomes,' she says. 'So much of it is about giving people the skills to help themselves, rather than foisting on them what others think they need. People in these areas are very keen to take the initiative and run with it.'

It's become a philosophy that's guided Olga throughout her life's work helping to improve the lot of Australia's Aboriginal population, her people. She's done it every which way, too, through a number of community organisations and government bodies, as well as in senior roles working for the Fred Hollows Foundation and now the Australian Red Cross. And even though she's probably done just as much voluntary work in the area as she has worked in paid positions, she's never regretted a moment of the years struggling to bring Aboriginal issues to the forefront, and doing whatever she could to help build stronger communities and support their initiatives to solve problems.

'There's a hell of a lot of goodwill and determination to see things done better out there. I think it's inevitable that things will improve. Aboriginal people are incredibly resourceful and always cope and survive. It's just a question of degree . . .'

As a kid, Olga Havnen never thought of herself as Aboriginal. Her mother, Peg, a respected Aboriginal elder, and her Norwegian father, John, both believed in the value of a good education, and the fair-skinned young girl started school in her home town of Tennant Creek. She continued her studies at Alice Springs, staying with her grandmother, and was then awarded a scholarship to study as a boarder in Townsville.

One afternoon, when she was fourteen, a couple of her classmates came to her to say she had a visitor waiting at the reception area. As homesick girls, they were always playing pranks on each other, pretending they had visitors, so she just laughed and carried on with what she was doing. Later, they came back again and assured her she really did have a woman waiting to see her – and what's more, the woman was *black*. Olga was confused. 'I remember thinking, I don't know any black women,' she says. Finally, she wandered through to reception, and was startled to see her mum sitting there. 'I suppose I just didn't have that sense or consciousness of colour. People were just people, and this was my mother and you didn't think of it.'

But for Olga, it was a revelation about how others thought about race. Even more bewilderingly, after that afternoon, the other kids never treated her the same again. They weren't particularly nasty or unpleasant towards her, but she could feel a shift in their attitudes; a new demarcation line being drawn. It was as though they were telling her, 'We didn't know you were Aboriginal! We didn't know you were *black*!'

About the same time, Olga started realising that not all people lived in the same way. At Tennant Creek, most of the locals she knew lived in similar housing: rough and makeshift, hot in summer and cold in winter, with corrugated-iron roofs. In Queensland, she noticed people lived in brick homes. 'Wow!' she exclaimed the first time she saw their houses. 'They must be so rich!' As she saw more and more of exactly the same standard of housing, it slowly began to dawn on her that it probably wasn't so much that they were rich; it was more that she, and everyone she knew, was poor.

Later that year, she began to read Germaine Greer. That was the third lightning strike. Not only was she black and poor, but she was female too. Could things be worse? 'I guess it wasn't this great tectonic shift, it was more just like, okay, I've got that light bulb going on now, and you understand things a bit differently,' she says. 'You get to notice things that you might not have noticed before, like the way people were treated in shops or by taxi drivers, and a sense of outrage when they were treated much worse than others. When you're fourteen or fifteen, you don't understand why, but you have a sense of justice, and you just know it's not right.'

After all, Olga did come from an extraordinary family. Her

Western Arrernte great-grandmother Ranjika, from the Alice Springs region, married a Chinese man, Ah Hong, who came to Australia in 1873 as part of the gold rush but instead went to work on the railway. He later became a cook and opened an eating house and market garden in Alice. The couple had three children but Ranjika died when her youngest, Gloria – Olga's grandmother – was three. Heartbroken, Ah Hong took the children back to China with him, and the family lived there for ten years, becoming fluent in Cantonese. Finally, the rigidity of China became too oppressive and they all returned.

Gloria married an Englishman and had four daughters, among them Olga's mum Peg. Born in Alice, they spent their early days on the lonely mining fields of Hatches Creek, 100 kilometres along a dirt track east off the Stuart Highway, 170 kilometres south-east of Tennant Creek in the Davenport Ranges. But all the girls went to Catholic boarding schools in Queensland's Ipswich; Gloria, knowing the importance of a good education, made sure of that.

Peg won a scholarship to continue her education, but didn't take it up, working as a cook and going to live in Tennant Creek with her mum. It was there she met her husband-to-be. John was a sailor in the Norwegian merchant navy who liked the look of Australia and, with three of his mates, jumped ship in Adelaide in the early 1950s, intending to make for Sydney. They decided they'd do better to split into pairs but, possessing no English, John and his mate panicked when they saw the uniformed guards at the railway station, fearing they were police. Instead, they jumped into a taxi, and asked the driver to take them the 320 kilometres to Port Augusta. There, at the railway station, they caught sight of more guards, so told another cab driver to take them as far north as their money would last. They ended up in Oodnadatta. From there they got a lift to Tennant Creek, where John had a friend who was working as a prospector, and he found a job in the copper and gold mines. He met Peg at a country dance and liked her immediately. New European migrants didn't take any notice of the kinds of barriers most white Australians put between themselves and Aboriginal Australians at the time, and the couple were soon married, and had four children, with Olga the eldest.

Olga's was the typical small Australian country town childhood: wandering off from daylight to dark, hanging around the bush, catching snakes, birds and lizards, and making games out of anything she found. After sunset, with all the other kids, she'd move from household to household, playing with friends and eating. 'It was like having one huge extended family, except you weren't related, but you all accepted each other and treated each other as family,' she says. 'There was so much freedom. You'd eat at one place, but might end up sleeping at another. All the women would cook in big pots and there was never any question of not having enough food around for extras. I remember, at our place, it used to drive my father nuts. All the kids – maybe thirteen or fourteen at one time – were like a hoard of locusts moving in, and creating so much noise while he was on shift work.' On stinking hot evenings, they'd often all sit outside and listen to ABC radio with her grandmother Gloria, and usually sleep outside, too, to try to stay cool.

'She was a very bright, brave and responsible child, yet always willing to take risks,' says Olga's mum Peg. 'She was intelligent and capable but had a lot of courage with it.'

After leaving home to study, finishing Year 11 and 12 as a

boarder at Charters Towers in Queensland, Olga had the chance to go to university. She'd been a brilliant student, full of ideas and sailing through all her final exams two years younger than her classmates. Both her teachers and her mother had high hopes that she'd go on to study law. When Olga visited the school careers office, however, the counsellor had very different ideas. 'She advised her to do flower-arranging, and perhaps become a florist,' says Peg, flatly. 'It was hard to believe, I know, especially when she's now considering going back to university to do a PhD!'

Back then, Olga had quite different plans, however. She decided she was too young to go to uni and, in any case, she'd had enough of lessons for a while. She liked the idea of moving somewhere bigger than Alice, and perhaps near the sea. So she decided to try out Darwin, and moved there to do the bookkeeping for a small, family-run business, living in an old hut that had been used during the war as a hospital room.

It was December 1974.

Cyclone Tracy struck Darwin like a battering ram in the early hours of Christmas Day, 1974, with winds gusting at 217 kilometres per hour. Seventy-one people were killed and 650 injured. More than 80 per cent of the buildings in the city were destroyed or seriously damaged and only 400 out of 11 200 homes remained intact. After the six-hour storm came the largest-ever evacuation and reconstruction operation in peacetime Australia, with 35 000 of the city's 47 000 people evacuated by air and road, including many of the 41 000 left homeless. The damage bill was $837 million.

Olga was one of the people who stayed on. Her hut, with

flyscreen netting across the top and bottom of the walls, was perfectly designed for a cyclone. The wind roared in and then straight out again, and there was hardly any damage at all, apart from water damage. 'But trying to drive around the next day, it was just unbelievable,' she says.

She went on to work in a number of different fields, including real estate; she also married and had three daughters, Rebecca, Alexis and Kate. Then she joined the Aboriginal Development Commission, organising housing loans. It was from that point on that she became actively involved in Aboriginal issues. When the organisation was amalgamated with the Department of Aboriginal Affairs, she went to the Department of Foreign Affairs in Canberra, doing mainly human rights work. It was 1992 and the time of the Mabo decision in the High Court, the recognition of native title and the final, official repudiation of terra nullius – the idea that Australia was empty when white people first arrived – to be followed by the Native Title Act (1993). Olga was frustrated that, despite the historic decision after a decade of litigation, not much seemed to have changed.

Her grandmother Gloria, who'd been a young woman at the time of the Coniston massacre, the last recorded mass killing of Aboriginal Australians by whites in which up to 100 people were killed, chided her for her impatience. 'She was quite savage about it,' smiles Olga. 'She pointed out that, in the space of her lifetime, we've gone from being shot down and hunted like dogs, to the 1967 referendum, and now the Mabo decision. She said, "This has all happened in my lifetime – so don't tell me things haven't changed!" She was quite adamant about putting things in context. But having seen those landmark decisions, I think she was right.

Sometimes you don't think things are changing when they aren't readily apparent or obvious. But other times you know they're not, and you can get angry and outraged. I think that's why I've been drawn in to getting involved in mobilising groups for action and for change.'

There was always plenty to mobilise over, too. In 1996 the High Court delivered its Wik decision, that native title could coexist on pastoral leases but that pastoral rights would prevail if there was a conflict. The Howard Government tried to amend this so the two sets of rights couldn't coexist and Olga, at the time working for the Central Land Council, went to a meeting in Canberra for two days and ended up staying eighteen months. She spent her time putting together information kits, having talks with the trade unions, non-government organisations and churches, until the legislation was finally passed with independent senator Brian Harradine's support. But the networks she'd built over years of working for government and with opinion-makers and communities all came into their own as, now working for the National Indigenous Working Group on Native Title, Olga, together with the social justice campaigner Phil Glendenning and a number of others, set up Australians for Native Title and Reconciliation (ANTaR) and launched a massive information campaign.

The Sea of Hands, a colourful public art display representing the thousands of Australians in support of reconciliation, went up at Parliament; a series of talks was held all over Australia; and the historic walk across the Harbour Bridge for reconciliation was held, with a plane commissioned to write the word 'Sorry' in the skies above. 'They were only engaged to fly for an hour and a half, but they ended up doing three hours, which was terrific!' she says.

The Fred Hollows Foundation approached Olga soon after, and asked her to talk to them about what they could do for Indigenous Australia. Few were surprised. 'Olga was someone known for having a strong voice, and a voice of reason, and she had a great understanding of Indigenous affairs – what was happening, and the way forward,' says great friend and former *60 Minutes* TV journalist Jeff McMullen, who, as the CEO of Ian Thorpe's charity Fountain for Youth, is also involved in working for the better health and education of Aboriginal children. 'She's a person I've always been so impressed with. She has a great grasp of the issues, and what's going on on the ground. I put her in the same class as Pat Dodson and Lowitja O'Donoghue, the fine intellects who remain positive about how Aboriginal people, not only in the bush but in urban areas right across the map, are making extraordinary progress with very little support.

'She had a grasp of the importance of community-building long before most people in government, in universities or in bureaucracies. She went to the evidence globally to see where the gaps had been closed with other indigenous peoples, like the native American Indians and the Saami of parts of Scandinavia. And she'd sit in the dirt in a village, listening, always listening, to what people needed, and wanted to be able to move forward. She learnt a lot in the silences between words and, as a result, knows people's names and stories, which builds great trust.'

With Olga's help, the Foundation published a series of reports on Indigenous health, making public alarming facts, such as Aboriginal children in the Northern Territory being twenty times more likely than white children to be diagnosed in hospital as suffering from malnutrition. As a result, she urged more attention to be paid to the health of mothers and babies in Indigenous communities. With infant mortality in these areas twice as high as for Australians overall, she saw that many Aboriginal kids started with a health disadvantage right from the moment of birth. Twice as many had low birth weight as other Australian babies – an important indicator of chronic health problems to come later in life, and a possible cause of serious illnesses, such as kidney failure, diabetes and heart disease.

Although Fred Hollows had originally set up his charity primarily to improve eye health in Outback Australia and overseas, Olga managed to steer them towards doing other important health work in partnership with Aboriginal communities. 'From my perspective, it's older people who get cataracts and, in the parts of the country that most needed help, the median age of death is thirty-eight years,' she says. 'So people die before they have a chance of going blind.

'In that context, I saw the early intervention and prevention work as critically important. I looked at some of the health data, and found that people in the Tennant Creek area where I grew up had some of the highest rates of end-stage renal disease in the world. When I was there, we might have been as poor as bloody hell, but no-one suffered kidney failure. So how had we gone from being kidney disease–free to having the worst rates in the world?'

The answers, when they came, were no real surprise. Poor nutrition during pregnancy led to babies being born with damaged or unhealthy kidneys. Then they were exposed to repeated bouts of bacterial strep A infections because of poor environmental health, with runny noses, eyes and ears. That was all further compounded by poor nutrition, so that children ended up wasted and stunted during childhood, and became teenagers with early signs of sickness.

Under Olga's guidance as Indigenous Programs Manager, the Foundation formed a solid partnership with the Jawoyn community near Katherine, which had asked for help to combat malnutrition, and appointed the first community-based nutritionist in the Territory. It also supported a Jawoyn initiative to provide healthy breakfasts and lunches for schoolchildren, paid for, on their suggestion, by deductions from Centrelink family allowances. It turned out to be a huge success. 'Early intervention can make a lifetime of difference,' she says. 'Fred's work was largely responsible for putting the state of Aboriginal health on the national agenda, and I wanted to keep it there.'

The store at Beswick continued to go well, too, providing more and more healthy food options, and the Foundation helped three more communities progressively regain control of their stores, and transform them. Their success was acclaimed as the blueprint for overhauling stores in Outback communities across Australia.

Education was another area Olga singled out for attention. She pushed for adult educators to go into communities to re-engage people in learning, and worked on programs to improve schooling and school attendance rates. She was shocked when a community told her that fifty kids from the tiny 150-person township of Manyalluk were no longer able to go to school 40 kilometres away at Barunga because their school bus had broken down, and they had no other way of getting there. It appeared the school had merely noted that fifty children were no longer attending, but had done little to help.

The community said they wanted their own school at

Manyalluk for their children, to prevent anything like this ever happening again. The only trouble was, in order to be eligible for a local community school, they had to have a demonstrable record of kids participating in learning activities. Between the Foundation, the community and a number of other providers, they were able to organise regular half-day sessions – until the government finally agreed to build a new school there.

Olga eventually left the Foundation in 2000, went to Sydney to work for the New South Wales Aboriginal Land Council, then in 2001 returned to Darwin to work in the Northern Territory Chief Minister Claire Martin's office as Principal Policy Advisor in the Office of Indigenous Policy. In that role, her proudest achievement was getting the Clontarf Foundation Academies, the series of programs in Western Australia designed to keep boys at school by encouraging them to play football, set up in the Northern Territory and introduced at schools in Yirara, Anzac Hill, Palmerston, Sanderson and Casuarina.

'But after two and a half years, I found working in bureaucracy was not for me,' she says. 'Writing policy papers and submissions is all very well, but the reality is that it's very difficult to change the government's position on things. I'm used to being a doer.'

The landscape in Aboriginal affairs in the Northern Territory shifted seismically in 2007, and in a way that few people could ever have predicted. In response to the *Little Children are Sacred* report about sexual abuse of Aboriginal children, the Howard Government announced a national emergency in remote Aboriginal communities.

The subsequent government 'Intervention' involved sending the police and army into isolated communities to combat child abuse, imposing blanket alcohol bans, winding back Aboriginal land rights under the 1976 Aboriginal Land Rights (Northern Territory) Act, health checks for Aboriginal children and the quarantining of welfare payments in seventy-three communities. The authors of the *Little Children are Sacred* report, and many Aboriginal people, strongly condemned the action. They argued that it totally trampled over the ability of many communities to take their own initiatives; was completely contrary to experts' advice that measures should only be taken after consultation, and in partnership, with local communities, welfare organisations and women's groups; and was bureaucratic, racist and extremely damaging to those people it was seeking to protect. Olga, who'd been doing some work as deputy director of the Northern Land Council, was right there at the forefront, branding the move 'Madness!'

True to form, she was never content with just talking. A softly spoken but purposeful woman, with a gentle manner and a ready laugh, she did what she'd always done in the past: she put herself, and any others around her, directly to work. 'We were all upset – as she was too – but she was also so calm and constructive about the next steps,' says good friend Irene Fisher, the former CEO of the Sunrise Health Service, which covers 112 000 square kilometres of the Northern Territory east of Katherine and was put at the frontline in dealing with the health aspects of the Intervention. 'She formed us into voluntary committees and put us to work, writing papers and discussion documents. She's always so dedicated, and so tireless. She's the most hardworking person I've ever met and never shies from the hard slog, yet is so forgiving of people who don't understand and is very, very generous with people who are either stupid or naive. I admire her tremendously.'

As a result of Olga's work, an alternative proposal for urgent action based on consultation and partnership was written, and backed, by no fewer than forty Indigenous organisations, and sent to all government ministers, the Labor Opposition and the prime minister. She received not one single reply. 'It was such a primitive approach to the problems, with so much bureaucracy in the place of services provided at a local level,' says Olga. 'We needed investment in communities and resources, instead of fees being paid to endless consultants. It was an opportunity completely squandered, and which has created so much damage in grinding good, proactive communities back down into the dust.'

There were some alternative approaches out there, however. One came from the Australian Red Cross under its CEO, Robert Tickner, a former federal Labor Minister for Aboriginal and Torres Strait Islander Affairs. He decided the organisation should start treating issues of Indigenous disadvantage as a priority. With such a huge challenge ahead, he needed someone special to head up that wing. Olga was approached, with her vast experience with the Fred Hollows Foundation, the Northern Territory government, the land councils and many community advocacy groups, and she agreed to become his Head of Indigenous Strategy.

'We were so lucky to get Olga on board with us,' says Michael Raper who, as the Director of Services and International Operations, leads the delivery of Red Cross programs both in Australia and internationally. 'She is absolutely brilliant. It's a very difficult area to work in and, without Olga's credibility, connections, knowledge and strategic abilities, we know we would find it virtually impossible to plan and connect and operate in Aboriginal communities. Olga also brings experience and a real passion for building meaningful partnerships and creating programs that will work.' He also says she's dedicated to capacity building in communities – developing the capability and skills of Indigenous people to achieve their goals and solve their problems.

Olga's own philosophies sit very comfortably with those of the Australian Red Cross: to improve the lives of vulnerable people in Australia and internationally by mobilising the power of humanity. 'No other organisation today has this much potential,' she says. 'How we harness that potential is the challenge. The Red Cross's fundamental principles of humanity, impartiality, neutrality, independence, voluntary service, unity and universality is what makes it different to every other organisation, and are what attracted me.

'And its main aims to prevent or reduce human suffering wherever it is found, with programs about food security, families' wellbeing, and youth, social and emotional wellbeing, are extremely important in the Indigenous arena as well as everywhere else. It's about early intervention and capacity-building in order to break the cycle of disadvantage.'

Olga's always believed in Indigenous people being allowed to play a role in their own destinies, instead of simply being treated as passive onlookers who shouldn't be trusted with anything to do with their own lives. That way, she firmly believes, lies disaster. 'Taking control of their land, resources and every aspect of their lives can only lead to even more entrenched disadvantage and power imbalance,' she says. 'The starting point has to be the fundamental recognition of Aboriginal rights and negotiations on the basis of equality. For a meaningful, long-lasting sense of wellbeing, they need to be permitted to be active subjects in their own lives, instead of objects for government and bureaucracy to manipulate; governments need to be "enablers" rather than "disablers". If there persists this idea that "the blacks can't be trusted", how *can* we ever hope to have mutual cooperation?

'We're also saying, when Aboriginal affairs or any major legislation is proposed that affects us, "Give us a place at that table!" They don't need to be elected positions; it could be an existing mandated role, such as the Social Justice Commissioner for Aboriginal and Torres Strait Islanders.'

Jeff McMullen sees her as a perfect match for the Red Cross. 'Robert Tickner now has one of the most valuable people in community-building in his organisation,' he says. 'She's one of a kind. Her core belief is that she wants us to be a nation of equals, and she pushes on, and won't let anything get in her way.'

Olga, now fifty-five and living with new partner Geoff Kealy, fifty-six – a man she first met in her teens while at school in Townsville – inherited some of that desire for justice from her dad, a staunch trade unionist, and her mum, the elder who also went to university late in life to get her degree. 'She's got a great ability to drive things, and she has a very analytical mind as well to go with that sense of justice and personal integrity,' says Peg. 'She was never stupid enough to go into politics, although she had plenty of offers. She prefers to do the hard yards quietly, modestly, and out of the limelight. But all the key decision-makers have the greatest respect for her. She's someone I'd really admire even if she wasn't my daughter!'

Olga's own middle daughter Alexis, twenty-one, currently at the Australian National University, feels just as proud. 'She's very passionate about, and devoted to, her work, especially when it comes to matters affecting Indigenous people, and has always instilled in her children a strong work ethic,' she says. 'In a way I can't really explain, Mum is a sort of leader in our family; a strong matriarchal figure, who seems always to hold it together when everything (and everyone) falls apart. She is the one people turn to for help, advice, resolving conflict. Her wisdom, fair hand and selflessness make her a natural leader, although she's incredibly modest.'

Yet there is still a lot of work to be done. Sadly, it came as little surprise to Olga when a major United Nations report revealed, in January 2010, that Australia's Aboriginal people had the worst life expectancy rates of any Indigenous population in the world. Of the ninety countries examined, Indigenous people in Australia and Nepal fared the worst on the globe, dying twenty years earlier than their non-Indigenous counterparts. In addition, said the UN's *State of the World's Indigenous Peoples* report, they face much more violence, discrimination, unemployment, poverty, ill health, maternal and infant mortality, malnutrition and inadequate housing, and have much less access to a good education.

Such statistics can prove enormously depressing, but Olga refuses to become downhearted. 'Sure, it's tough at times, and you can get disheartened and burnt out,' she says. 'But there are lots of remarkable people out there making major contributions, and a lot of non-Aboriginal people who are in there for the long haul and doing amazing things. There's plenty happening at a community level and that's what I find inspiring and uplifting. That's what keeps you going.'

16

A True Rose of the Desert

SUE LE LIEVRE, *Looma, the Kimberley, Western Australia*

She was just leaving the clinic after a hard day's work when a woman's scream rent the hot evening air. Immediately, she felt her senses tremble to attention. All she'd wanted was a cool shower and an early night, but the raw edge of desperation in the sound made her blood freeze.

'Who's there?' she called out into the blackness. 'What's the matter?'

A wail came back immediately. 'My baby! My baby!' There was the sound of a strangled sob. 'He's not breathing properly. Help me!'

Remote area nurse Sue Le Lievre didn't hesitate for a second. 'Come into the clinic!' she shouted as she strode back, unlocked the door and snapped on the lights, all in one swift movement. 'Bring him here.'

A woman emerged from the darkness, cradling the tiny, limp body of a child in her arms. In the harsh light of the clinic, Sue could see the woman's face was stained with tears, her brow creased in worry and her eyes filled with pleading.

Almost on automatic pilot, Sue took the baby from her, laid him gently on the table and started her examination. He was only about four months old, but was obviously very sick. His breathing was fast and shallow, his nostrils were slightly flared, his chest was drawn in and all his muscles were engaged in the effort of trying to breathe – all symptoms of acute respiratory distress.

Immediately she put an oxygen mask over the child's face and switched on the flow, then prepared an adrenaline neb and watched as the adrenaline slowly began trickling into his airway. She contacted the paediatric doctor on duty at Derby Hospital and described the situation over the phone. 'Continue the adrenaline nebs until I get there,' he said, 'I'll be there as soon as I can.'

For the next two hours, Sue tended and monitored the child, alternating the adrenaline with oxygen and saline. The child's mother sat nervously holding her baby, stroking his head. A couple of times, she asked Sue if she could go outside and smoke to try to calm her nerves. Sue wouldn't hear of it. 'I was concerned that if the baby realised she wasn't there, he might use up his energy crying and that wasn't on,' she says. 'So although it sounds harsh, I made her stay there with the baby. It was a very long two-hour wait!'

The doctor and nurse eventually arrived with the ambulance, examined the baby, and mother and child were transferred straight to hospital. The child was diagnosed with bronchiolitis and remained on oxygen for the next forty-eight hours.

As Sue locked up the clinic for the second time that night, she felt relieved, knowing the baby was now in a proper hospital. And as she climbed into her four-wheel drive Troopy in the remote Outback deep in the Kimberley of Western Australia, she noticed how exhausted she suddenly felt.

When you're the only person standing between life and death in such an isolated spot, it could sometimes be a huge weight on your shoulders. But when things turned out well, it certainly made you feel it was all worthwhile.

Over the years, Sue has become used to describing where she works as one of the most beautiful places in Australia. The rugged earth is rich and red, and the foliage glows as green under the clear blue skies as anywhere else in the tropical north, with torrential rain in a good wet season leaving it stunningly beautiful in the winter.

Looma, the remote community that's home to her clinic, is in the north-east of Western Australia, about 100 kilometres away from Derby and 2300 kilometres north of Perth, with a population that ranges between 290 and 400. Every day, she drives the 15 kilometres from her house in the even tinier township of Camballin, sharing the dusty, corrugated road with cattle, kangaroos, goannas, snakes and the odd tourist.

She's on call twenty-four hours a day, seven days a week, to deal with every emergency, from a baby struggling to draw breath to someone who's just broken a leg in a fall, from chest pains to car crash injuries sustained on some of the most treacherous roads in Australia. There are asthma attacks, snakebites, diabetes . . . every kind of affliction that's ever beset anyone, in the Aboriginal community, any of the stations in the area or among tourists passing by.

For emergency inter-hospital transfers, she drives 37 kilometres along a gravel road to the point where it finally meets the bitumen, to rendezvous with the ambulance dispatched from Derby Hospital. For everything else, she copes with the able assistance of two health workers who now live in the community.

'I think when the emergencies come in, you get yourself into a routine and you slip into gear straightaway,' says Sue, smiling. 'Sometimes I can get a bit anxious, but that's healthy and you have to be prepared for anything. I wouldn't like to do it as a young nurse, without my previous experience in midwifery, theatre and the neonatal units.'

There was the day, for instance, when a four-year-old girl was brought into Sue's clinic unconscious. Her family was distraught. She'd been crying all night and had finally fallen asleep – and now she wouldn't wake up. With one look at her, Sue knew the little girl was in serious trouble. She hooked her up to a monitor and tested her blood sugar level, only to find it was dangerously low. She slipped a gastric tube down her throat and dripped in some glucose solution, and inserted a cannula into a vein to give her intravenous glucose, as ordered by the paediatrician on call.

All the while she was working, the family was looking on anxiously. 'Is she going to be all right, sister?' they asked. 'What's wrong with her? How could this have happened?' Sue wasn't sure, but knew the glucose would be doing its work. She just thanked God the family had rushed her to the clinic when they did, as she calmly and efficiently went about tending to the unconscious child. 'Keep them warm, sweet and pink – that's what our paediatricians told us during our clinical lectures, so that's what we do,' she says. 'It's a convenient little formula when dealing with sick kids.'

After twenty minutes, right on cue, Sue saw a flicker of movement course through her patient's body and, just as suddenly, her eyes fluttered open, she woke up, sat up and started talking. Her family stood stunned, open-mouthed, at the sudden transformation. 'It was like a major miracle had taken place,' laughs Sue. 'I had to smile to myself as I'd seen something similar happen before with hypoglycaemic diabetics, and the recovery can be extremely dramatic. I, of course, was delighted!'

It turned out the girl had tried some of her grandfather's pills that had been lying on the table: medication for both hypertension and diabetes. With the airstrip not in good enough condition for the flying doctors to land there, an ambulance was sent from Derby Hospital and the child was admitted for her progress to be monitored. 'But she was fine in the end,' says Sue.

'You do have some real heart-stopping moments in this profession and, because you're working so far away from other services, you know that what you do can be critical to someone's health. There are so many more life and death situations in that kind of place. But then I find it very rewarding. Every time, for instance, I see that baby who was once so acutely ill with bronchiolitis now running around as an energetic and healthy five year old, I remember that night and feel as though I achieved something special. I *love* that feeling!'

*

Suzanne Lee was born in Melbourne, but went to live in the bush just outside Perth with her parents when she was four months old. Her dad, William, a returned serviceman, had been saving for years for land, and eventually he managed to buy a two-hectare block at Welshpool, which, post–World War II, was still pretty much untouched scrub. The three of them, soon to be followed by three more daughters, Cheryl, Rosemary and Honi, settled in an old shack that had been erected years before at the end of one of the bush tracks, made of hessian sacks painted over with calcimine paint to make it waterproof.

It was a pretty tough beginning, but the kids, knowing nothing else, revelled in the freedom of a bush childhood, unencumbered by possessions. In the winter the little wood stove lived inside the hut, close by the beds; in the summer it sat outside. Water came from a tap a kilometre's walk away and a regular chore for each child was carrying bucketfuls to the shack for washing and cooking. Later their dad, who worked with rubber for a living, making tyres for vehicles on his return from the war, built his family a log cabin nearby, with hoses connected to the mains for water to reach the new outside bathroom and toilet. 'We thought we were in a palace!' says Sue. 'It was wonderful.'

She grew into a soft, caring little girl who, if ever she saw a sick animal or one of her family or friends complained of feeling unwell, instantly tried to help. She was terribly protective of her three younger sisters, and anyone else she thought wasn't able to look after themselves. Yet she was also very capable – their mum Jean had been determined to bring up all her children to learn to stand on their own two feet. She'd had a very hard life herself, and wanted to make sure each of her kids would be well prepared for whatever lay ahead for them.

Jean had come to Australia from England with her family as a child in 1921 to a farm in Western Australia's south-west, but tragedy was soon to follow. One summer's day, when Jean was eleven years old, her mother Florence was cooking lunch on the old wooden stove in the kitchen and a spark caught her dress alight. She screamed for help but the flames quickly engulfed her. Her husband Harry rushed into the room to put out the fire, but it left her suffering terrible burns. She was taken by buggy to the nearest hospital at Busselton, but died of her injuries the next morning. Harry had friends look after the children for a while, then sent Jean and her sister to an orphanage in Perth and their five brothers to another further north.

Many years later, Jean received a letter from her father. He'd apparently moved to Adelaide, had changed his name – no-one could fathom why – and started another family. She, however, with her siblings scattered and having been raised as an orphan, never forgave him.

'I think that's why Mum was always adamant that we learn to be independent early on,' says Sue. 'It had all been very tough on her. Her whole family was scattered. To us, she was pretty much a no-nonsense lady, slightly Victorian in her ways, while Dad was very hardworking, but a quiet man who never talked much, and rarely spoke about his days in the war. So we were brought up to appreciate anything that came along in life, and with a strong work ethic that was instilled into us from a very young age. It was always all hands on deck. We were very good, as kids, at entertaining ourselves, and we enjoyed everything. It felt idyllic.'

Sue started out at a little bush school at Wattle Grove and

then went on to attend Governor Sterling High school in Midland, a three-hour round trip each day. After school and at weekends, she'd play with all the Aboriginal kids who lived in a children's home her parents ran. They'd go swimming every day, make their own canoes out of sheets of old tin dabbed with tar to play on the river, slide down the mud hills on trays of flattened corrugated tin, play footy and catch mussels and cook them up on a camp fire by the water. 'It was a paradise for kids and on the way home we would hitch a ride with Pop McDonald, who used to plough up the home's vegie garden with his two horses and keep us well supplied with all the vegetables we could eat,' she says.

The only dark cloud in Sue's childhood was when a good friend, then aged about ten, contracted meningitis and died soon after. It was Sue's first brush with death and it was a painful memory that stayed with her. Today, she looks back and sees it as the defining event that made her decide, when she grew up, to become a nurse.

At seventeen, while she was waiting to be old enough to enter nursing training, it seemed young love would interrupt all of Sue's plans. She fell for a boy who'd been working with his dad in the iron-ore mines in the Koolan and Cockatoo islands off the Kimberley coast, 130 kilometres north of Derby, and the pair became engaged. He invited her to go up to see him for a holiday. On the way, she stopped off in Derby. It became the second, and far more enduring, time she was to fall in love.

One of the three biggest towns in the Kimberley, alongside Broome and Kununurra, and the oldest pioneer town, Derby sits on the tidal mud flats on the edge of the King Sound. When the tide is low, the water only just covers the swampy mud. When it's high, it rises up to 11.8 metres – the biggest tidal range of any Australian port. It's a colourful old place, with a lively history intimately entwined with the pastoral and mining industries, and a population of 2500 to 3000 drawn from every nationality and language group. In those days, mobs of cattle from the various stations would camp at Myall's Bore just out of Derby, waiting for the boats to come in for loading. The cattle were then driven along the marsh and down to the yards at the jetty to be loaded onto the boats. It used to be a big night out for the whole town to socialise and enjoy the cool evening air.

To Sue, it was a complete revelation. 'My eyes just opened up the moment I set foot there,' she says. 'I just thought this was an absolutely fantastic world to end up in. There were all these won-derful people and such a mixture of races: Chinese, Asians from everywhere else, Aboriginal people, Caucasians, everyone, and they all lived together quite nicely. There, I met some wonderful people. I fell completely in love with Derby.'

She ended up staying with a couple whose hospitality in the town was famous. It was more or less open house to all their friends . . . and their friends' friends. In their big old tropical house with tall louvred windows that would open to allow in the fresh breezes and close when the rains came, there was always a big, friendly crowd of people, including stockmen, fencers and dog-gers – men paid by the government to trap and kill dingoes and wild dogs – either sleeping inside or in swags on the veranda or in the backyard, under the shade of a giant boab tree. 'The hospitality and the welcome, that's how people seemed to be around there,' says Sue. 'Sometimes the guys out on the stations would bring in some meat, but generally, it was just people getting together, telling stories and taking pleasure in each other's company.

'For me, it was a realisation that this other world existed. I was taken aback by the people, their friendliness and the way everyone smiled all the time. I'd borrow a horse and go riding out on the marsh, talk to people and explore Derby. After a little while, I told my fiancé that I was so sorry, he was very nice, but I wasn't ready to get married and be tied down. I could now see other things in my life. Seventeen was far too young to be getting married!'

It was also too young for her to start her nursing training, so Sue stayed on in Derby for a year, then got a job as a governess at a station 80 kilometres out of Wyndham in the north-west of the state, near Kununurra, where the King River meets Cambridge Gulf in some of the most magnificently craggy scenery in Australia. The original owner was an old pioneer, a bachelor, who ran cattle and had experimented unsuccessfully with growing peanuts, and who'd built the homestead himself from second-hand tin carted out by camels, the floors made from compacted ants' beds. He'd struck an agreement with the new owners that he could stay on till he died. Sue had come to teach the new family's two school-age children and help with their baby, and in her time off she'd chat to the old Scotsman and the Aboriginal people who'd become his only family. During the wet season, when they'd get cut off for seven or eight weeks, she'd join them when they rode out to kill a bullock and fill their saddlebags with the meat to keep everyone fed.

When she'd finished her year there, she went to another station near the former gold-rush town of Meekatharra in the mid-west, teaching another couple of children while she waited the final six months before she could start studying at the Western Australian School of Nursing in Perth. 'I found out that at these places, you have to be interested in reading,' she says with a laugh. 'There's often no social life at all. But I was quite happy. I studied maths, anatomy and physiology by correspondence to get ready for nursing, and read as many of the books as I could from a list the school had given me of the best books of the day.'

Eventually, in 1963, she was able to begin her nursing training, first at the school, then at the hospital in Kalgoorlie, Australia's largest inland city, 580 kilometres east of Perth, and finally at the Royal Perth Hospital, where she took a theatre management and technique course, and circulated through all of the clinics. It was a wonderful grounding in nearly every aspect of medicine and nursing, as well as marvellous experience in how to manage difficult people, particularly some of the surgeons.

As soon as she could, Sue returned to Derby to work at the hospital there. She loved being back in the town and, at twenty-seven, she met and married a local, Gordon Le Lievre. Sadly, it didn't last twelve months, their marriage breaking up as she was pregnant with their child. 'Unfortunately the relationship didn't prove to have the required commitment and my likeable rogue disappeared down the road driving his trucks, totally freed from the responsibilities of parenthood,' says Sue. When their son was born, she named him Kimberley, after the region she'd grown to love so much, and which had brought her so much pleasure and, finally, pain.

*

With the help of Gordon's parents, Sue bought a large old five-bedroom house in Derby and started work again at the Derby Regional Hospital. She worked her way around all the wards before being put in charge of theatre. It was yet another great learning experience. The surgeon there was Kimberley legend Dr Lawson Holman, who'd done world-famous work on Hansen's disease, or leprosy, which had eventually resulted in better treatment of the illness and the closure of the prison-like leprosarium to which many sick Aboriginal people had been banished. He'd also been a great innovator in health services and had come up with the idea of nurses going out into Aboriginal communities to provide preventative medical care.

His thinking and ideas so inspired Sue that she, too, moved into community work, where she had her first taste of nursing outside a hospital. It was a time of many exciting firsts: being on call for the flying doctor nurses when they got too tired to fly, and taking the inaugural trip up the infamous Gibb River Road, a 660 kilometre dirt track through the wild heart of the Kimberley from Derby to Kununurra. Along the way, she visited the stations scattered all the way up to Drysdale River Station, introducing herself to everyone who lived there, helping the mothers and new babies, and asking them what else was needed. It was the beginning of many of the new programs that were to be introduced into the Western Australian Outback by remote area nurses: immunisation; screening; antenatal care; health-care services for disease prevention; and registration of anyone with a chronic illness, charting their progress and seeing what other services they might need.

Many of the white station-owners would ask if the nurse would visit them, too, or if their services were for the Aboriginal community only. 'My answer, every time, was that we wouldn't knock anyone back – it didn't matter if they were white, black, green or blue,' says Sue. 'So everyone ended up coming to us.'

In the meantime, Sue had met bush poet Johnny James, a real character around the Kimberley. They started seeing each other and, one day, he asked her if she would like to go further into the Outback with him to help set up a station and start a new family. It wasn't the most romantic proposal she'd ever had, but since she liked him, was never shy of hard work and also adored being out in the bush, she was happy to give it a go. The couple began almost from scratch.

Everyone said Sue and Johnny would never find water on the 630000 hectares of rugged, raw land on the edge of the Great Sandy Desert 70 kilometres south of Derby, but they did. Their water supply was a well, choked with tree branches and the rubbish of ages, not to mention the dozen or so snakes that had set up home inside. The fire they lit burned for three days solid, and it took another week to cart the debris to the surface and establish a source of water again. They then worked long days and often long nights too, putting down boreholes around the rest of the property, with trap yards, tanks and troughs to follow over the years. 'We'd just fall asleep and camp by the bores and work until we got them established,' says Sue.

The little postwar Yakka Munga homestead in the middle of the scrubland didn't offer too much in the way of comfort. With cracked 30 centimetre–thick walls fashioned from ants' beds mixed with donkey fat and spinifex, and timber beams roughly hewn by axes, when you looked up in the kitchen you could see the stars shining at night through the holes in the tin roof. Most meals were eaten outside under a tree inhabited by a large python that one of their helpers insisted could never be touched, as she belonged to his totem.

Eventually, after six months of bone-crunching hard labour, they put their first mob of cattle up for sale. By then, Sue had given birth to a daughter, Aleta, but that didn't stop her working. She'd drive out with the six-week-old baby strapped into the front seat to do her bit. But when the cheque for the cattle didn't arrive, they phoned the bank to find out why. What they were told crushed them: agribusiness giant Elders had a caveat over the property from its previous owner – something neither of them had ever known. 'John and I just looked at each other, stunned,' says Sue. 'We couldn't believe it. All that hard work . . . But we just had to get on with it. We decided to pull the belt in another notch or two, sold cattle for meat around the place and went bull catching to earn more money.'

They were some of the toughest days Sue had ever known. When she and Johnny did their own bull catching, Johnny would drive a bull buggy – an old four-wheel drive with roll bars and padded along the front with tyres – follow the bull and nudge the beast when it was off balance, so it would fall. Then he'd drive the bullbar slightly over the animal so it couldn't get up, and tie its legs together so it could be carefully manoeuvred into a truck driving alongside. The bulls were yarded until the couple had caught their quota for the meatworks. 'Sitting on those bulls for the first time and removing those front and back leg straps as it was pulled into the truck was a hair-raising experience,' says Sue. 'As soon as that bull hit his legs inside that truck, John and I would have that ramp up and closed so he couldn't jump out. It was hot, heavy and extremely dangerous work.'

It was no less relaxing, though, when Johnny won a few contracts for catching bulls elsewhere, and had to go away for three or four months at a time. Then she, Kimberley, Aleta and their new son Darren would have to stay behind and look after the station themselves, making sure the bores were running, doing some fencing, checking cattle and horses, fighting bushfires, and working at the local hospital on and off to supplement their income.

Once, she noticed a breeder bull wandering into the paddock in front of the homestead and couldn't work out what he was doing there. She went out to check the fences and found a bunch of miners knocking them down. She quickly got on the two-way radio to the Pastoralists and Graziers Association of Western Australia and, with their help, came to an agreement with them to reinstall the fences and put the stud cattle safely back.

Sue had worked as hard as she could, but it wasn't enough to save the relationship. Johnny's temper, fuelled by his drinking, had been growing worse over the years and he sometimes became violent towards her. Unwilling to see their children exposed to that, she decided to leave him. But when the smallest children, then aged six and seven, went back to the station for a visit, he announced he'd decided to keep them there and wouldn't let them return to her. Sue, usually so gentle and mild-mannered, wasn't about to lose her children and persuaded a helicopter pilot in town to fly her to the station. They landed early one morning, carried the sleepy children into the helicopter and whisked them away. 'I couldn't believe it; it was like a movie,' says Aleta today. 'Dad had threatened that we'd never go back to her. We were quite scared of him, but we couldn't imagine our lives without her. She was pretty incredible.'

Her mum regretted that things had turned out the way they had, but never thought twice about going in to rescue her kids. 'I hated leaving the station and John, too, but I wasn't going to put up with that,' Sue says. 'We gave it a good try. But I did think: How could this happen to me? I always thought if I got married, it would be forever. But sometimes life just doesn't work out the way you plan.' In 2003, Johnny, aged fifty-six, was killed in a helicopter crash while mustering cattle around one of his bores.

Derby, Sue's favourite place in the world, happily welcomed her and her family back with open arms. Her first husband, Gordon, reappeared in her life, too – fifteen years after he'd vanished – to ask their son Kimberley if he'd like to join him contract mustering. Sue gave them her blessing, delighted they'd be able to have some father–son time, and she's been friends with her ex ever since. But by then missing hospital work, she returned to Derby Hospital and became the Clinical Nurse Specialist for the emergency department and operating rooms. This rounded out beautifully the previous experience she'd had working at the King Edward Memorial Hospital for Women in their neonatal intensive care unit. In the years to follow, however, hospital work changed a great deal, with much more attention paid to managing systems, processes and budgets. Frustrated with what seemed to be a shift away from the clinical focus, in 2000 she decided to return to community health. A new challenge was neatly presented with a newspaper ad for a remote area nurse to work at Looma.

The position appealed to her instantly. What could be better, after all, than being right back in the heart of her beloved Kimberley? Looma was also an extremely proactive, strong community of between 250 and 600 people – depending on what was happening at the time – and the locals had their own meetings to plan for the future of the township, its buildings and water supply, setting up a vegetable garden, and had turned it into an alcohol-free zone. They'd acquired a few stations nearby, too, and had employed a white manager to run one of them. As another bonus, Sue had got to know some of them during her years working in Derby, so they were also happy and relaxed at the prospect of her becoming their sole nurse practitioner.

'The people there generally have a great sense of humour, a lovely sense of humour, and I found we had a great rapport,' says Sue. 'I worked with an excellent Aboriginal health worker there, a mature, experienced and very well-respected woman, who was a huge help when dealing with such a wide variety of issues. Most of the work was focused on preventative health programs, but there were also a large number of people with chronic diseases and on multiple medications. We set up our own recall system on a self-styled software program to ensure these people were periodically screened for various blood tests, and seen along with the results by the visiting GPs. As an appropriately educated and experienced nurse practitioner I was able to order pathology tests, X-rays and specialist referrals. We also had limited prescribing rights. I think nurse practitioners will be able to address some of the inadequacies of the health system, and provide more immediate access to quality and emergency care in remote areas, and, with their advanced qualifications and willingness to go to the nether regions of Australia, this will only enhance the contributions made by nurses in previous years.'

*

In 2005, Sue was named the winner of the *Australian Women's Weekly* and Clinique Legends of the Land competition for her 'deep commitment to the Outback and her selfless desire to help others in need'. She still refuses to believe she's anyone special, however. 'My work is a gift because I love what I do,' she says. 'I've always been very lucky in my life.'

It's more that the rest of Australia is lucky to have her, says close friend Pepita Pregelj, who once worked with her. 'She's a wonderful woman, very kind and giving, and so hardworking. She was always a fabulous mentor for me, and I'm now nursing, and I really look up to her. A lot of what she did stemmed from her great love of the Kimberley, its life, its Outback and its people. She's been through plenty of hardships, but she's always been very interested in everything, and great fun. She was just born to be a nurse!'

Her family, too, are great fans. 'She had a pretty hard run at times, but she put her focus and her drive into her nursing and she's given a lot,' says Aleta, now studying for a teaching degree in Darwin. 'We're very proud of her. At the cattle station, she was the backbone of it all and could work as hard as any man – as long as there was a reason for it. But her nursing was her passion, and she's a great nurse. I would describe her as a desert rose. A desert rose seems to thrive in the harshest of environments and blossoms even in adversity. But her modesty sometimes infuriates me!'

Aleta's older brother Kimberley is driving trucks and is based at Geraldton, by the coast 420 kilometres north of Perth. He's given Sue three grandchildren, Kaisey, Kirra and Toby. Her younger brother Darren has set up his own business as an automotive electrician in Derby.

As for Sue, now sixty-seven, she's currently taking a bit of a break while she decides on her next move. Nursing, however, has always been her life's work and passion. 'I think I'm the luckiest woman alive,' she says. 'I loved my nursing, loved working with many of the people I met along the way, and of course I love the land. I have been very fortunate.

'I've always had jobs that are challenging and give me huge satisfaction. And the people of the Outback are warm and easy and once you tune in to the land, it grabs you and it's spiritual. It's a wonderful life – I feel lucky to have experienced so much of that spirit of the Outback. It's so strong and enduring and inclusive.'

ACKNOWLEDGEMENTS

First of all, my greatest thanks go to the many, many thousands of people who read my previous book, *Women of the Outback*, and recommended it to their friends. As a result it ended up travelling far beyond the Outback, and even Australia, with emails coming from readers who'd been moved by its stories of courage and fortitude from as far afield as Scotland and South Africa. Because of its success, this book was conceived.

This time we decided to extend the celebration of all the greatest qualities of Outback people to include both men and women. This book is therefore a tribute not only to the incredible people described on its pages – to each of whom I owe a tremendous debt of gratitude for opening up their lives to a stranger – but to everyone who confronts and overcomes the challenges of Outback life for themselves and those around them who need a helping hand.

Thanks, therefore, to publisher Andrea McNamara, who was keen on this project from the word Go and provided so much encouragement and support, as well as in-house editor Julia Carlomagno, who was incredibly helpful with both words and pictures. Also thanks to copyeditor Brooke Clark, for patiently going through the pages and suggesting changes, which always clarified and improved whatever I was trying to say.

I'd also like to thank Australia's Governor-General Quentin Bryce, who so generously provided a foreword for the book. A woman from the Outback herself, she became known from the very start of her term in office as a great champion both of, and for, those living in rural and remote Australia.

From a personal point of view, I'm grateful, as always, to my agent Selwa Anthony, who first set me on this journey of discovery through the Outback and was there for me all the way, through encounters with dust, dirt, drought, flood, sunburn, redback spiders and snakes – albeit always from a careful distance.

To my partner Jimmy Thomson, I owe a huge debt. He was always there to encourage me through the worst of times, celebrate with me through the best of times, and read my drafts every time in between. I couldn't have done it without him.

I'd also like to thank my mum, Edna Williams, who saved my life frequently by typing up a number of transcripts and amused me no end with her take on Outback life. Thanks to dad Bill Williams as well, who had to cope with her frequent absences from their evenings as she laboured over a hot computer in their study.

Along the way, I'm also very grateful to Rex – Regional Express Airlines – Australia's largest independent regional airline, who kindly donated air tickets for some of my travel to the Outback;

to the indefatiguable Megan Rowe who helped me out in so many ways during one of my trips north and made some of the downtime a thousand times more fun than it might otherwise have been; to her wonderful mum Mary who was also so kind; to the immensely talented David Hahn for the use of two of his beautiful photos; and to Rose Lester and Sonia Mazzone for all their help with their darling Mrs Brown.

Finally, I'd like to express my appreciation once more to the subjects of this book who give so much of their time and energy to help keep the Outback and its people going – usually at great cost to their own lives, and often with little recognition or thanks. This book is a way of saying one big thank you from both the Outback and the rest of Australia. We'd all be the poorer without you.

WOMEN OF THE OUTBACK

Sue Williams

Drought, flood, harrowing isolation and horrific accidents . . . the Australian outback is no place for a lady. But the women of the Outback are a different breed: tough, resilient and endlessly resourceful. They're both the backbone and the heart of Australia, keeping their farms going, their families together and their communities alive - and often against overwhelming odds.

Maree was left with three small daughters when her husband and young son were killed in a light plane crash. Molly lived alone in a 1920s homestead in the middle of the Simpson Desert for twenty years without even a phone. Alice admits she couldn't tell a cow from a bull when she first went to live in the Outback.

This book tells the inspiring stories of fourteen remarkable women, from high-achievers to everyday heroes. Their tales are often heart-rending and regularly touched by tragedy, but are always life-affirming. They portray Outback Australian women as they really are - and as we all wish we might be.

'every word cried out to be read . . . [a] remarkable book'
BOOKSELLER & PUBLISHER

'humbling and awe-inspiring'
WOMAN'S DAY

THE BUSHRANGERS

Evan McHugh

From the first convict runaways to the spectacular show-down that ended Ned Kelly's career, Evan McHugh delivers a swashbuckling tale of daring exploits and a cast of roguish characters who blazed their way into Australian history.

These are incredible stories of the men (and women) who achieved fame not just by what they did, but by the way they did it, many of them lifting themselves from down-trodden underdogs to self-made heroes. There are heroic figures like Cash and Company, the prince of bushrangers Matthew Brady, Bold Jack Donohue, brave Ben Hall, Captain Thunderbolt and of course, Ned Kelly. But there are also villains like Pearce the Cannibal, Jeffries the Monster and 'Mad Dog' Morgan.

Bushrangers is as fast paced as a stolen thoroughbred and as arresting as a squad of troopers. Through extensive first-hand accounts and gripping detail about Australia's lawless past, bestselling author Evan McHugh brings a fresh perspective to a turbulent era of crime, defiance and emerging Australian identity.

THE DROVERS:

Stories behind the heroes of our stock routes

Evan McHugh

*'For the drover's life has pleasures
that the townsfolk never know.'*

From the High Country to the Outback, there are extraordinary stories of the men and women who have travelled across Australia behind mobs of cattle, sheep and horses. These quiet achievers, of every race and creed, forged an Australian legend.

Evan McHugh brings alive the hapless convicts attempting to round up the First Fleet's escaped cattle on foot; overlanders blazing through trackless wilderness to supply the vast stations carved from the bush; stockmen who risked blizzards to bring cattle to alpine pastures; and drovers who crossed the continent behind the largest mobs of cattle the world has ever seen.

These stories overflow with colourful characters: cattle-duffers like Harry Redford, renowned boss drovers like Nat Buchanan and strong women like Edna Zigenbine and Red Jack, who could measure up to any man. They lived a life most of us only dream about and came to love the beauty of Australia's most famous and infamous stock routes, including the Birdsville, Murranji and Strzelecki tracks, and the Canning stock route.

McHugh's meticulous research and vivid eye for detail is the closest you'll get to saddling up your moke and poking a mob of cattle off camp.